PENGUIN TRAVEL LIBRARY

ON FIJI ISLANDS

Ronald Wright was born in England and received his M.A. in 1973 from Cambridge University, where he read archaeology and anthropology. He has excavated in Latin America and Africa, and farmed and driven trucks in Canada. Since 1980 he has made his living as a free-lance writer and broadcaster, presenting documentaries for the Canadian Broadcasting Corporation and American Public Radio. His first book, *Cut Stones and Crossroads: A Journey in the Two Worlds of Peru*, was published to wide acclaim in 1984 and is also available in the Penguin Travel Library. Mr. Wright lives in Toronto with his wife, Janice.

ON
FIJI
ISLANDS

▲▲▲

Ronald Wright

PENGUIN BOOKS

PENGUIN BOOKS
Viking Penguin Inc., 40 West 23rd Street,
New York, New York 10010, U.S.A.
Penguin Books Ltd, Harmondsworth,
Middlesex, England
Penguin Books Australia Ltd, Ringwood,
Victoria, Australia
Penguin Books Canada Limited, 2801 John Street,
Markham, Ontario, Canada L3R 1B4
Penguin Books (N.Z.) Ltd, 182–190 Wairau Road,
Auckland 10, New Zealand

First published in the United States of America by
Viking Penguin Inc. 1986
Published in Penguin Books 1987

LIBRARY OF CONGRESS CATALOGING IN PUBLICATION DATA
Wright, Ronald.
On Fiji Islands.
(Penguin travel library)
Bibliography: p.
Includes index.
1. Fiji—Description and travel.   2. Wright,
Ronald—Journeys—Fiji.   I. Title.   II. Series.
[DU600.W8   1987]   996'.11   86-25567
ISBN 0 14 00.9551 9

Printed in the United States of America by
R. R. Donnelley & Sons Company, Harrisonburg, Virginia
Set in Janson
Map on pp. vi–vii by Paul Pugliese

This book is for
J. ROD VICKERS

NAURU

BANABA
(Ocean Island)

SOLOMON ISLANDS

PAPUA
NEW GUINEA

FIJI

Area
shown
in detail

NEW
CALEDONIA

Brisbane

AUSTRALIA

P   A   C   I   F   I   C

Sydney

NEW
ZEALAND

Melbourne

Fiji Islands

EQUATOR

SAMOA
ISLANDS

TONGA

TAHITI

OCEAN

VANUA LEVU

RABI

YASAWA GROUP

Savusavu

TAVEUNI

miles
0   40
0   40
kilometers

VITI LEVU

KORO

LAU GROUP

Tavua

OVALAU   WAKAYA

Lautoka

Nadrau

Levuka

Nubutautau

Nadi

Korolevu

Nausori

VIWA

BAU

Sigatoka

Suva

LAKEBA

BEQA

MOALA

KADAVU

Acknowledgments

Many people helped me during the research and writing of this book. Fiji's inhabitants extended their remarkable courtesy and hospitality, and Alberta Culture gave generous financial support without which the journey might never have been made. Any list of individuals will be fraught with omissions, but I should like in particular to thank here the following for many forms of hospitality and kindness. In Fiji: Jemesa Bonowai, Ratu Sir George Cakobau, Fergus Clunie, Paul Geraghty, Michael Howard, Ratu Lemeki Natadra, Tevita Nawadra, Nii Plange, Josaia Ratumaitavuki, Marshall Sahlins, Aseri Vueti, Rabi Island Chairman, Manager, and Council of Leaders, the Superintendent and Ministers of Rabi Methodist Church, the Principal, staff, and pupils of Rabi Secondary School. In Britain and Canada: Janice Boddy, Sir Ronald and Lady Garvey, William McKellin, Bella Pomer, Ralph Premdas, Rod Vickers, Penny Williams, my parents. At Viking Penguin: Jennifer Snodgrass, William Strachan, Charles Verrill.

I alone am responsible for the content of the book and the way in which others and their views have been presented.

R.W.

Contents

A Note on Fijian Spelling and Pronunciation

The written form of the Fijian language is usually the Bauan variant, which occupies a position in the islands similar to that of High German in Switzerland. Two systems exist for writing it: the so-called phonetic, scarcely used nowadays except in maps and foreign publications, and the Fijian alphabet devised in the 1830s by the missionary and linguist David Cargill. Cargill's system is based on the Roman alphabet, but redundant characters are omitted and a few have been given values either partly or wholly different from what one might expect. These exceptions are as follows:

> *b* represents *mb*, as in "member"
> *d* represents *nd*, as in "sandy"
> *g* represents *ng*, as in "singer"
> *q* represents *ng(g)*, as in "hunger"
> *c* represents *th*, as in "then"

Vowels are pronounced with values similar to those of Spanish or Italian, and *r* is rolled much like the Spanish *rr*. In words having a long vowel (a vowel of lengthened duration), that vowel is always stressed. Neither writing system represents this distinction, even though it may change completely the meaning of a word. For example:

kaka,   "stutter"

kakā,   "parrot"

In general, the stressed syllable is the penultimate.

Though the Fijian alphabet with its unexpected values for certain letters may appear strange to the uninitiated, its logic and economy will soon win over anyone willing to spend the little time needed to learn it. For comparison, here are some names written in both systems:

Bau	Mbau
Beqa	Mbengga
Cakobau	Thakombau
Cicia	Thithia
Gavidi	Ngavindi
Nadi	Nandi
Qaraniqio	Nggaraninggio
Sigatoka	Singatoka

Incidentally, the choice of single letters to represent consonant clusters was made for good linguistic reasons—not because the missionaries had run out of type pieces, as a hoary old myth would have it.

ON
FIJI
ISLANDS

PROLOGUE

In the Fiji Museum there is a curious wooden artifact with a carved handle and four sharp prongs. Beneath it is the short but eloquent inscription: FORK USED IN EATING REVEREND BAKER.

The display also contains dishes used for serving the Wesleyan's cooked flesh, and informs the reader that Mr. Baker was the only missionary eaten in Fiji, and that he passed away (if that's the right expression) in 1867.

Foreigners linger at this exhibit. Societies that do not eat people are fascinated by those that do (or did). Many old books about Fiji have the word "cannibal" on the title page; the islands were once known as the "Cannibal Isles." It's an interesting word: derived from "Carib," the name of an island people almost wholly exterminated by the non-cannibals who came to civilize them.

1
▲▲▲
NADI

No culture shock this time, Derek promised on the plane. "Everyone's clean and nobody wears guns." The shock had been severe when we'd visited Peru two years ago. Severe even for me, and I had been there enough times to know what to expect. But that arrival at Lima in a grey 5 A.M. dawn, the sour smell of the airport (half fuel, half drains), the armed guards in shabby uniforms, the small boys fighting for our luggage—all that had been too much. Then had come a cab ride through vast shantytowns and empty lots strewn with slowly burning rubbish in which people were scavenging; and Derek had said that his worst stereotypes of the Third World were coming to life around him.

Fiji, apparently, was different. The concrete architecture and lush vegetation lit by the headlights of the Nadi Hotel minibus reminded me of West Africa; but they belonged to an Africa that was refined, where immigration officials were mannerly and relaxed, where the airport bank was open in the middle of the night, where hotel limousines not only existed but appeared on time. These impressions, gleaned at 3 A.M., were strengthened next morning. The air smelled of blossoms and moistened earth; the hotel maids, who looked and dressed rather like Africans, were singing in the corridors. Most surprising of all, the neatness and tranquillity extended to the town outside the front door, and the countryside at the back. The hotel did not seem to be an island built for foreigners in a sea of squalor.

I had heard conflicting stories about places like Fiji, Bali, and Tahiti. To some observers they were what they seemed—innocent, content, and with an inner strength that kept them that way. Others dismissed such a view as an illusion, a myth either created for tourists or about to be destroyed by them.

Derek, who had spent more than a year in Fiji on an archaeological project, was of the first school. I had been intrigued by his descriptions. Fiji sounded like an anomaly—a place that had survived colonization with its native population and culture not simply intact, but successfully adapted to the modern age. Eighty-three percent of the land still belonged to indigenous Fijians: remarkable when compared to New Zealand, where the Maoris own about ten percent, and Hawaii, where the tiny native remnant own virtually nothing; even more remarkable when one discovers that native Fijians form not quite half of Fiji's population. I had spent enough time in the former colonies of Europe—in Africa and Latin America, especially Peru—to form a pessimistic view of the consequences of European expansion. For the original inhabitants it had almost always meant dispossession, exploitation, and social decay. In North America, where I live, it is easy to forget the dimensions of the tragedy, so completely has one population been consumed by another. In Hawaii, only slightly smaller than Fiji and with many cultural similarities, the same appalling transformation occurred. But here in Fiji it seemed that something unusual had happened; or rather that something usual had failed to happen. I wanted to find out why and how.

♦

After breakfast Derek went out to buy a newspaper; I began writing up my journal. The flight from Vancouver had begun with a stewardess's memorable phrase: "The lifejacket has a mouthpiece for oral inflation." You fly across the world's emptiest hemisphere, keeping pace with the night. Five hours to Honolulu—nothing but blackness below; then the glare of an overlit American city, an orange sore on the dark skin of the Pacific. Six hours more darkness to Nadi, and a day of one's life left in safekeeping with the international date-line.

This longueur had been interrupted when dinner arrived: a ham slab with some tired alfalfa sprouts resembling a tuft of dog hair. Derek glanced up from his science fiction story and remarked: "Imagine what a hassle it would be if we were herbivores and they had to toss a bale of hay in front of each of us."

At this the stranger in the aisle seat became helpless with laughter and spilled a martini in his lap, the first of several such accidents. He introduced himself:

"Wendell Gorky. *Doctor* Wendell Gorky actually, of academia, not medicine." He began to talk with the sudden intimacy of the habitual drinker. "From Kansas, which, you should know, is pronounced by natives like myself as *Kayenzas*. Go on, say it."

"Kayenzas."

"Kayenzas."

"No! *Kay*-enzas."

"A linguist I presume?" said Derek. But Gorky continued unabashed, identifying himself as an ethnobotanist, confessing an obsession with aphrodisiacs and a terror of insects.

"That's why I work in the South Pacific. Not many bugs, you see."

By the time the Fiji landing cards were distributed, Gorky was asleep.

RACE—INDICATE ONE ONLY
OF THE FOLLOWING:

Fijian

Indian

European

Chinese

Rotuman

Other Pacific Islands

Part-European

Others

"They mean it genetically," Derek said. "All whites are called Europeans here."

The same is true of the other categories. "Fijian" is not an adjective like "Canadian," applicable to all citizens of the country. It refers only to those of indigenous descent. The *Fiji Handbook* makes the point:

> *Taukei* (owners) is the word in the Fijian language which the Fijians use when referring to themselves, so that Taukei and Fijian are, to them, synonymous. The ownership of the land is one subject which can generate great heat in Fiji. . . . The non-Fijian who describes himself as a Fijian is, in the minds of many Fijians, laying claim to the land.

When the plane touched down the ethnobotanist awoke, cupped his ears in his hands, and began to complain in a fractious voice about the engine noise. The three of us looked, I suppose, like the monkeys on the log—Hear-No-Evil, See-No-Evil, Speak-No-Evil—Gorky, tiny and hunched; Derek, rotund and bald, half hidden behind opaque glasses and the smoke of endless hand-rolled cigarettes; and myself, with lips stiffly pursed, not wanting to talk to Gorky: D. H. Lawrence's "white monkeys" entering a land of the dark races.

Gorky rose for his hat, almost reached the overhead bin, then collapsed like a deckchair.

"I say, are you all right?"

"Fine as frog's hair!"

He rose a second time, managed to reach the hat—a bush hat with the brim buttoned up at one side, intended no doubt to match his stained safari suit—then appeared to be seized by it and pulled across the aisle, where he measured his length on some empty seats.

Derek and I escaped; soon afterwards we saw our neighbour "deplaned," as they say, in a wheelchair, and bundled into a van belonging to the Nadi Travelodge.

◆

Derek came back to the breakfast table with a *Fiji Times* and a long-haired young Indian.

"Hi! I'm Krishna," the Indian said. "Hire my taxi all morning? I show you sugar plantations, Fijian village and cultural centre, duty-free camera shops in Lautoka, and good curry restaurant. Only twenty-five dollar." He beamed. I could tell that Derek was already persuaded.

"Okay? Okay?" Krishna said.

"Okay," said Derek.

"Twenty," I said.

"Okay," said Krishna.

Krishna's taxi was a Toyota Crown, powered by diesel and protected by a Hindu icon of his namesake next to the cigarette lighter. Most people on the Nadi streets and along the roadside were Indians—shopkeepers, cabbies, sari-swaddled women, farmers dangling machetes—descendants of indentured workers brought to Fiji before the First World War. Krishna was wearing what amounts to a uniform among the younger Indian men: widely flared bellbottoms, tight and low on the hip, a shark's tooth on a silver chain around his neck, an enormous gold watch draped loosely like a dancing girl's bracelet on his slender wrist, and a Hawaiian shirt with the word "Fiji" in red letters lurking amid orange vegetation.

The Lautoka road passed several new hotels—concrete shoeboxes surrounded by thatched bowers symbolic of the South Seas. Not far beyond these was the "cultural centre," built in the same rustic style—a collection of tourist stalls beside the road. Krishna stayed in his taxi; we went inside. The place had an air of doubtful authenticity, a suspicion confirmed by wooden masks displayed for sale on the walls. The ancient Fijians didn't make wooden masks—these were artifacts of the Nairobi airport tradition, the Third World's revenge for glass beads and gaspipe muskets.

Derek bought two barkcloth placemats from the bushy-haired Fijian saleswoman. We were then approached by her son, a boy of about fourteen:

"Good morning, sirs. If you like I can show you the village."

"What do you charge?" Derek asked.

"Whatever you think is right."

We followed him into a small Fijian community that occupied some flat land between the road and the Pacific. The houses were modern, freshly painted, modestly prosperous. Unlike the tourist stalls and hotel bars, they were built of cement blocks and clapboard, with metal roofing. Many were shaded by mango and breadfruit trees; hibiscus, bougainvillaea, and frangipani bushes grew around them. As a child reading sea stories I had imagined the breadfruit as an apple tree hung with loaves. I saw now that it has large leaves the shape of swans' feet, and its fruit resemble giant avocadoes with reticulated skin. There were no fences or formal streets, the village houses were arranged in a roughly circular pattern around a central green, called a *rara*, and separated from each other by stretches of well-trimmed grass. The inhabitants appeared to be out for the day or resting indoors. It was quiet; I could hear waves on the beach, wind in the trees, a distant radio, and an occasional passing car. There was no clutter or untidiness. The only things that seemed out of place were the carcass of an old Bedford lorry and beside it an elliptical stone, about three feet long, with a cup hollowed in the top.

"In the old days," the boy said, "we used those for pounding roots." He walked on ahead. Derek said:

"It was probably a sacrificial stone where they killed their prisoners—and I think he knows it."

Around the *rara*, an expanse of lawn about a hundred yards across, stood the most important buildings: the Methodist church, the chief's *bure*, and the houses of clan heads. The church could have passed without comment in rural Canada—white clapboard walls, a steep metal roof, and Gothic windows with panes of coloured glass. More interesting was the *bure*, or ceremonial meeting house, which rested on a low earth platform and was being rethatched; its wall posts and woven bamboo framework were temporarily exposed. When finished, Derek remarked, the *bure* would look like an elegant haystack with doors. This building, a focus of the community, was clearly authentic—built in the traditional Fijian style for Fijians, not tourists. In front of it stood a flagpole and a small thatched shelter, open to one side.

"That we built for Queen Elizabeth when she came here," the boy said proudly. "You know Queen Elizabeth?"

"Not personally."

"She visited here because our village, Viseisei, is the oldest in Fiji. Viseisei means"—he searched for the right word—"to scatter, to spread out. Our ancestors scattered from here after they reached Fiji in the great canoe, *Kaunitoni*. This whole district is called Vuda, which in Fijian language means 'original.' "

"Ah, yes," Derek said when we got back to the taxi, "the *Kaunitoni* migration myth. It's a modern fabrication. Don't believe a word of it."

♦

During the last century, missionaries, officials, and antiquarians collected many Fijian oral histories and legends while the traditions were still fresh. No early account mentioned a mass migration from across the sea, or the great canoe *Kaunitoni*. Most *yavusa* (kin groups or "tribes") claimed descent from a rock, cave, totemic animal, or mythic hero. The Fijians believed they had lived in Fiji from time immemorial, since Degei, their supreme god, created the world.

Fijians of the early contact period (c. 1800–1850) naturally thought Fiji was the largest and most important country in a world made mostly of water. They were unpleasantly surprised, when first shown European maps, to see their islands so small, and other lands so large. They suspected the foreigners of deception in these matters. Thomas Williams, the missionary and pioneer ethnographer, wrote in 1858:

> The Fijian is very proud of his country. Geographical truths are unwelcome alike to his ears and his eyes. He looks with pleasure on a globe, as a representation of the world, until directed to contrast Fiji with Asia or America, when his joy ceases, and he acknowledges, with a forced smile, "Our land is not larger than the dung of a fly;" but, on rejoining his comrades, he pronounces the globe a "lying ball."

By about 1890, a generation of Fijians had been educated in mission schools; they had come to accept that they lived in a small and remote part of a vast world. And Degei, their god, had been ousted by Jehovah, and demoted to the status of a heathen devil.

A vacuum was waiting to be filled, and there were those ready to fill it. In the late nineteenth century a theory known as diffusionism was in vogue among some archaeologists and ethnologists. Diffusionists argued that civilization could have been invented only once, and human culture had spread over the world from a single source: usually Egypt. Two adherents of these views, Carey and Fison, were teaching at the time in Fiji mission schools. They noted the negroid appearance of the Fijians, and thought they could trace links between the languages of Fiji and Tanganyika (now Tanzania). Carey went so far as to compare Fijian customs with those of ancient Thebes, and concluded that the Fijians' ancestors had been brought from black Africa to Egypt, whence they escaped to roam the oceans until landing in the South Pacific. These ideas were set down in a book that became a text in many schools.

Before long, half-baked versions of the African connection were circulating among the natives. In 1892 the Fijian-language newspaper *Na Mata* held a competition to select and publish the "definitive" origin legend. By 1893 the myth had acquired the canoe *Kaunitoni* and its occupants. However, most Fiji Europeans were not familiar with Carey and Fison's book or with *Na Mata*. Anthropologists began collecting the *Kaunitoni* story from informants without being aware of its parentage; it became established among scholars as firmly as among Fijians. In later years the tale received further respectability by being carried in the *Methodist Mission Monthly* and on a series of radio broadcasts.

The timeliness of the *Kaunitoni* story explains its success. It was a modern myth that gave all Fijians a common origin and a place in the new, larger world when their own beliefs were in shreds. The resemblance of the migration to that of the Jews must have been compelling to Christian converts. Indeed, the Fijians were restrained in their handling of such material, when compared to the Rastafarians or British Israelites.

◆

Krishna's taxi sped flamboyantly, in the manner of Third World taxis, towards Lautoka, the second city of Fiji.

"I like the dry side," Derek said, more than once, but for me this part of Viti Levu (Great Fiji, the main island) was a disappointment. I had imagined soaring hills and wanton vegetation; but the western or leeward side lies in a rain-shadow. This year there was a drought, preceded by a hurricane; the land had a used-up look: sere hills, small fields of stunted sugar cane, pale greens and browns, and in one dry valley a shantytown of corrugated iron shacks on hard red earth.

"Poor people," Krishna said.

"Fijians?"

"Indians. Indians without land. Fijian doesn't live like Indian. Fijians live all together in village, all help each other. Indian lives anywhere, always struggling with neighbours and relatives. Indian is very individual man. If he succeed, get rich. If he fail, end up in shantytown."

Whenever no vegetation or rise in topography blocks it, the Pacific comes in view to the west: a great slab of silver indistinct in the haze of smoke and dust. To the east, low mountains rise slowly like the weary hills of Africa. The large islands of Fiji are not vertical crags thrown up by the volcanic action that raised Hawaii and Tahiti; they are mainly remnants of an ancient land mass, and their age shows in rounded contours and gentle slopes. In Fijian the dry side is called the *talasiga*, the "sunburnt country"—bald from centuries of slash-and-burn farming and brush fires. Exhausted land is colonized by worthless spear grass, but here and there the forestry service has made small plantings of Caribbean pine. These trees look out of place in the company of scattered palms and the great poincianas and monkeypods that shade the road.

"See that mountain there? We call that the Sleeping Woman. When you see it from the top of Tabletop Mountain, over there"—Krishna pointed—"it look like pregnant lady."

Drifts of smoke rising from the slopes were soon lost in the general blur, and lower down dense palls hung over cane fields burned for harvesting.

"I thought you said they didn't burn cane here?" Derek challenged an earlier assertion of Krishna's.

"Some do but they shouldn't. Burnt cane is easier to cut, but it must be crushed quickly or it no good."

Many of the Indian bungalows were large, surrounded by shrubs, with a car in the drive. Others were less grand, but all looked neat; even the shantytown was orderly and substantial when compared, say, to the slums of Lima. It occurred to me that the entire population of the Fiji Islands is one tenth of Lima's. There was no comparison, yet I could not help making comparisons. Some houses were flying small red pennants from bamboo poles. In Peru this sign tells that home-brewed beer is for sale. I asked if it meant the same thing here. Krishna was offended:

"When people have a prayer meeting they put a red flag there. House must be very clean and correct. It serious business."

The narrow tracks of a sugar railway now ran beside the road. A train appeared with a vulgar blast on its electric horn: a boxy yellow engine pulling a dozen flat-bed cars piled high and wide with blackened cane. The railway, the shiny Toyota and its Hindu icon, the women in saris with pots on their heads, the holy zebu cattle wandering insolently over fields and gardens—all had a disorienting effect. I felt I had no measure of the place. Was this the Third World or the First? The Old World or the New?

And Lautoka: a crisp modern town of twenty thousand; white concrete shops displaying cameras and videos; names like Maneklal Duty Free Camera Emporium, Vishnu Patel Jewellers ("nose and ear piercing a speciality"); and down the middle of the main street, as if to remind everyone what this town is about, a sugar railway beside a row of royal palms. On the waterfront, a graceful park. There, some bushy-haired Fijians on a bench beneath a poinciana call out *"Bula!"* and Derek, to show his command of the language, answers them more formally, *"Ni sa bula"* ("Health to you"). And to fix the word in my mind he points out the trilingual sign of a chemist, in English, Hindi script, and Fijian: *Vale Ni Wai Ni Bula*, House of the Waters of Health.

◆

Later that afternoon, back at the Nadi Hotel, we sat in the garden and played chess. Out of the sun, the air was indeed "soft," as Derek had said. Clothes, from a practical point of view, were not needed, yet there was enough of a breeze that one felt no discomfort in shirt and jeans. We ordered draft Fiji Bitter—a good beer made locally by an Australian firm—and drank in drowsy silence. The only sounds were the quarrelling cheeps of mynah birds (which came to Fiji with the Indians), a dog's bark, and fussing from the chickens that lived behind the hotel kitchen. Yes, the air was soft, suffused with whiffs of woodsmoke, incense, curry, and Derek's strong tobacco.

It grew dark; the waiter who brought the beer became invisible except for his white shorts. After dusk some small creatures (birds?) began moving in fits and starts across the lawn. I got up to see what they were. They were frogs—strange frogs that did not jump but ran like sparrows.

Derek had arranged for Krishna to return after dinner and take us to the Nadi Travelodge, about four miles out of town, where there was to be a *meke*, a performance of Fijian songs and dance.

In North America the Travelodge is a chain of motels whose sign is a sleepy bear in a nightshirt. There was no sleepy bear in neon at the Nadi establishment. The place was opulent (especially by contrast with our modest hotel); it had hardwood floors, thatched walkways, and the waiters wore uniforms—green *sulus* (Fijian kilts) fastened with orange cummerbunds, and, above these, aloha shirts (often called *bula* shirts in Fiji) depicting palm trees and setting suns.

The *meke* had begun. Four rows of Fijian men and women— about thirty people in all—sat on the lawn between the bar and the swimming pool. Floodlights lit their costumes: raffia skirts for the men, coloured raffia skirts and floral print bikini tops for the women. All wore wreaths of frangipani petals in their hair, and their black bodies glistened with coconut oil—perhaps the only authentic item in the entire rig. (In ancient times women and men respectively wore short tassel skirts, barkcloth breechclouts, and little else.) But these pseudo-Polynesian trappings did not detract from the burly Melanesian physiques; the natives made the whites look as pallid and shrivelled as recently emerged occupants of a fallout shelter.

We took seats near the bar. The singing was an arrangement of harmony parts with two lead voices followed closely by a choral block. Three kinds of percussion instruments, all traditional, accompanied the singers: long, fat bamboo tubes pounded in unison on the ground; small sticks struck together; and wooden gong-drums, resembling short dugout canoes (but not tapered at the ends) whose "gunwales" were beaten with wooden drumsticks in a rapid syncopated rhythm. The drumming sounded alien and impressive, but one could hear influence of Western music in the diatonic melodies.

In pre-contact times *mekes* were vehicles for oral histories, epics, and legends. The early missionaries tried to purge them of "heathen" content by replacing the old words with Bible stories translated into Fijian. Gradually the *meke* became influenced by Christian hymns and, in recent years, by international pop music. But ancient singing styles do survive in the *meke ni yaqona*, songs performed only when *yaqona* (kava), the ceremonial drink of Fiji, is publicly presented to a high chief. These are sung in elaborate polyphony, with up to eight individual vocal lines, and a limited melodic range of no more than a fifth.

After some slow and rather syrupy songs there came a performance of spear-brandishing by the men. "Warriors" leaped towards the unsuspecting audience, who screamed, then laughed as the dancers' fierce expressions dissolved into grins. The spears were long sticks adorned with coloured streamers, mere toys compared to those of Thomas Williams's day: "They are deadly weapons," he wrote, "generally of heavy wood, and from ten to fifteen feet long. One variety is significantly called '*The priest is too late*.' "

Later on the tourists were invited to take part in a dance. The tipsier ones were ready enough. We recognized a familiar shrunken figure bobbing among the others like a chimpanzee at a ball. Gorky saw us. He hobbled to our table, then beckoned frantically to a bearded white man at the bar.

"Gentlemen, welcome to Fiji!" he said, draining his glass. "Let me introduce you to an Australian friend. This man's name is Jerry. Jerry, meet—"

"Derek."

"Ronald."

"G'day," Jerry said. "Those spearchuckers looked like they meant business. Big chaps these Fijians. I reckon they were well fed in the old days. Did you hear about the cannibal who *passed* his brother in the jungle?"

The master of ceremonies announced the last song. A Fijian woman got up in front of the microphone and gave a running commentary in English against the background of the lilting, soulful chant:

"Isa Lei is a Fijian farewell song, which has many, many meanings. It expresses happiness, joy, and sorrow; beauty, and lingering memories of happy events, hope, and love.

"What does Isa Lei means? Isa Lei means 'so sorry.' Isa Lei means 'so sad to know that you are departing from our dear islands.' Isa Lei says that you are going. Isa Lei means 'be kind, be truth,' and longs for the time when again we shall be meeting you."

"I could live in this country," Derek said. "I'd like to live somewhere where the only ice you see is in your drink." A country-and-western band—these musicians were also Fijian—struck up tunelessly in the bar. "There were lots of Yanks here in the war," he added. Gorky overheard.

"Yanks, huh? You Frostbacks watch your language." He ordered something called a "Nadi sunset special." It seemed to be a blend of rum, grenadine, and coconut milk, and arrived with a hibiscus bloom floating on the surface. Gorky transferred the flower to his ear, where it sprouted forlornly from his brushcut.

"Now this is what I call a global village experience," he said.

◆

"You guys want girls?" asked Krishna as we approached the Nadi Hotel.

"Not tonight."

"Only twenty dollar."

"That's a lot of money round here," Derek said.

"Ten for the girl, ten for me."

"Isn't that rather a large commission?"

"I'm their agent. Everybody need an agent. Let me know if you change your mind, anytime. Everyone in Nadi Town know Krishna."

It was past midnight when we got back to the room. Derek opened the small fridge (an excellent feature, this) and poured two big scotches.

"Most of the hookers are Indian; I used to see them all the time in Suva. The Fijians do it for fun, the Indians for money. It's the story of this country. Most of the really poor are Indians, and so are most of the rich—apart from a handful of Europeans and Chinese. A Fijian woman down on her luck can always go back to her village. An Indian has to sell her labour or herself."

♦

Fiji has been called the "little India of the Pacific." In the western province of Ba, which includes Nadi, Lautoka, and much of the country's sugar land, Indians outnumber Fijians almost three to one; for Fiji as a whole the ratio is close to fifty-fifty.

There was a time when demographers predicted that Indians would displace Melanesians in much the same way that the white man supplanted the "Indians" of North America. In the early years of contact the Fijian population fell drastically from the effects of foreign diseases, wars, and rapid culture change. If the natives had been exploited as cheap labour at the same time, they would probably have declined like those of Hawaii or Brazil. But the first British governor, Sir Arthur Gordon (1875–1880), for reasons both pragmatic and idealistic, arrested the social disintegration of the Fijians by allowing them to keep their lands, villages, and as many traditions as could be tolerated.

However, Gordon also had to meet the demands of white settlers for land and labour on which to build a plantation economy, and he did this by leasing vacant Fijian land in trust for its native owners, and by encouraging the immigration of "coolie" labour from over-crowded India.

The ancestors of most Fiji Indians arrived as indentured labourers between 1879 and 1916, when the system was abolished. The social inequalities of India made many people susceptible to recruiters' promises of high wages and a land of opportunity. Since Hindus believed that travel across the ocean brought irrevocable loss of caste, recruiters often told them that Fiji was just over the horizon from Calcutta; besides, they would have the option of returning home in five years at their own expense, or in ten years courtesy of the Fiji government.

What awaited the migrants is described in this account by a man who came in 1911:

When we arrived in Fiji we were herded into a punt like pigs and taken to Nukulau [the quarantine island] where we stayed for a fortnight. We were given rice that was full of worms. We were kept and fed like animals. Later we were separated into groups for various employers to choose who they wanted. . . . We then went to Nakaulevu where we saw the lines.

The "lines" were the coolie barracks—long shed-like buildings separated into sixteen compartments. Each "room" was seven feet by ten; it held three single men, or a married couple and their children. (Towards the end of the indenture system the rooms were enlarged by law to ten feet by twelve.) The compartment walls of the coolie line extended only six feet or so from the floor, with chicken wire reaching the remaining distance to the roof. Privacy was minimal. Because of this, and because far more men than women were recruited, sexual abuse of women was common; and there was additional violence—often involving cane knives (as machetes are called in Fiji)—from the tensions this caused. The Indians had a word for life in the lines; it was *narak:* hell.

But Fiji itself wasn't hell, and indenture did not last forever. Few opted for repatriation when their time was up; some obtained plots of land and hired indentured labour themselves. Other "free" Indians, mostly Punjabis and Gujeratis, came to Fiji on their own initiative and set up stores and businesses.

When the government of India abolished indenture in 1916, Fiji was home to sixty thousand of its former subjects; at that time the native population was close to its nadir of eighty-three thousand, reached after the world influenza epidemic of 1919.

◆

We took the bus from Nadi to Suva, the capital, at the other end of the island. The vehicle had a windscreen and a roof, but no glass in the side windows, merely a row of canvas blinds that could be lowered against rain. A sign above the driver's turbanned head: COACHWORK BY LAL INDUSTRIES, SUVA. As in many developing countries, the power train and chassis were imported, but the rest was local enterprise. In this case the lack of glass was more an indication of climate than of poverty: if there were windows they would be open most of the time anyway. The only disadvantage became apparent when we hit some dusty sections where the Queen's Road, Fiji's major highway, was unpaved.

A country where highways still have names: the Queen's Road runs around the southern perimeter of Viti Levu; the King's Road, slightly longer and less developed, around the north. It reminded me of childhood in England, when people still spoke of the Great North Road for the cartographer's A1, and Watling Street (a Roman Road renamed by the Saxons) for the A5. The Sikh driver drove purposefully and gave precise indications of how long we would rest at each stop; the bus had no trouble keeping to its relaxed schedule of four and a half hours for the 120-mile trip.

The hills east of Nadi had the look of a rumpled bed: bald, overgrazed, with sugar cane on the lower slopes and occasional tufts of wild vegetation like punk haircuts on the crests. Twice we passed large concrete mosques, their Moorish arches and twin towers evidence of the small but active Muslim minority, about one in seven of Fiji Indians.

After half an hour the road descended from low hills to reveal an idyllic bay with blue water, yellow sand, and a grove of coconuts whose trunks were orange from the lichen growing on their leeward sides. Among the palms were modern buildings with ancient outlines—the truncated pyramidal shapes of *bures* roofed with wooden shingles. This was the Fijian Resort, one of the self-contained tourist havens that bead the south coast. Next to it was a real Fijian village, the source of ethnic entertainments for the hotel guests. There is a symbiosis of beach, coconuts, native village, and resort; the pattern repeats itself at every scenic spot along the shore. Good beaches are rare on Viti Levu because much of the coast is ringed by shallow reefs and mangrove swamps. The ancient Fijians chose the best sites for their villages, the bays sheltered their canoes, and the sandy soil was good for coconuts. After contact, the nuts (processed as copra) became a good source of income, but not as good as waiting on tables and singing *mekes* in the hotels built on leased Fijian land.

At Sigatoka the driver shouted "Fifteen minutes" and parked next to an older bus with its name, *Spirit of Simon*, painted in red on the side. The town stands at the mouth of Fiji's second-largest river, and prospers from market gardening in the valley. Derek pointed out a bamboo raft laden with lettuce and bananas. "They call those 'one-way liners' because they only go downstream."

Here Fijians outnumber Indians. I looked in the crowd but did not see a half-caste. The two races seem to mix only for business and travel. They have kept mutually aloof since the early days of contact, when the Indians despised the Fijians as *jungli*, "forest men" or "savages," and the Fijians, ever conscious of rank, looked down on the Indians because they were landless and appeared to be slaves of the British. It didn't help matters that the British called the Indians "coolies": *koli* is the Fijian word for dog.

"In the old days," Derek said, "the Fijians used to sacrifice people when they built a temple. A chap had to stay down the post holes when the dirt was filled in. When I was here before, I heard a rumour that the custom didn't quite die out until the 1940s—some Fijians volunteered an Indian for the job. They were most upset that he did it with bad grace. The poor bugger tried to climb out of the hole and they had to whack him on the head with a shovel. It was hushed up, of course."

Relations between the races were not always bad. The naturally hospitable Fijians helped enough runaway Indians to worry the British during the cane workers' strikes of 1920 and '21. And despite official efforts to encourage separation of the two groups, some cultural exchanges did take place. The Indians adopted the custom of kava drinking, and the Hindus even added a Fijian god to their pantheon, believing that Degei, the Fijian creator-serpent, was none other than Kaliya, the snake banished by Lord Krishna to a remote island. By making offerings to Degei, the migrants gained a spiritual foothold in their new home. The Fijians, for their part, took a liking to curry: it made the new meats introduced from Europe more interesting.

♦

Near Sigatoka, dunes become visible between the road and the sea—great mounds and crescents of yellow sand borne by the wind from sandbanks at the river's mouth. Until stabilized recently by the planting of tenacious grasses, these dunes moved year by year, century by century, in peripatetic dominion of the littoral.

Some of the earliest archaeological sites in Fiji have been found here and on Yanuca Island, seven miles to the west. An ancient pottery style known as Lapita was found with charcoal that yielded radiocarbon dates beginning at about 1200 B.C. and continuing through most of the millennium before Christ.

Lapita is a coarse but well-made ware of large jugs, bowls, and dishes, decorated with geometrical borders and impressions. Its distribution may have important implications for the earliest voyages of man in the southwestern Pacific. The art of making pottery was later forgotten in much of Polynesia, but resemblances between the Lapita decorative style and artistic motifs in other media found at the time of European contact have led prehistorians to suggest that the makers of Lapita pottery were the ancestors of the Polynesians, who eventually spread through the Pacific within a great triangle uniting New Zealand, Easter Island, and Hawaii.

All this, though plausible, is bold extrapolation from rather meagre evidence. It is far from clear what might have been the relationship between the "Polynesians" and the "Melanesians" who also populated Fiji. Fiji is often said to straddle these two cultural and racial spheres, but modern linguistic research and the abandoning of crude ideas about race have caused this old dichotomy, except in a geographical sense, to be questioned. (Micronesia, the region of many small islands to the north of Melanesia, has little relevance for the prehistory of Fiji.) For one thing, it has been found that the so-called Melanesian and Polynesian languages, once thought to be quite distinct, belong to the same Austronesian family—a vast group that includes languages of Malaya, Java, the Philippines, Fiji, and Hawaii. Outlying members are found in Madagascar and South China—tempting material for latter-day diffusionists but notoriously unreliable.

The racial picture is equally complex. Fijians are taller and burlier than most other "Melanesians," and though they have frizzy hair of the "afro" type, their skin colour ranges from a deep blue-black to brown. People tend to be darker in the western Pacific, lighter in the east, but this racial spectrum is fraught with anomalies. Many "Polynesians" are closer in appearance to Fijians than to the imaginary Polynesian of the travel poster. The ancient Pacific peoples were superb navigators; they travelled their ocean in convoluted patterns over thousands of years. And there were peripheral players—Chinese, Philippine, Indonesian, possibly even Peruvian—who became important at certain times and places.

As for the people of Fiji, though the *Kaunitoni* myth is spurious, the first Fijians *did* arrive in canoes. But it happened so long ago that they forgot; and when the first white men asked them whence they came, they said only that they were *kai Viti*, "people of Fiji," since the world began.

◆

Beyond Sigatoka the hills gradually assume more cover as the bus crosses from the "dry side" to the wet. Near the road grow tulip trees with dark, glossy leaves and shining canopies of scarlet blossoms. Vines creep along the ground like snakes, climb the trees, and malevolently drape themselves on bushes as if scheming to drag the other vegetation down. The hills, too, grow taller and greener. At Yavu, in a coconut grove, there is a village with many buildings of traditional thatch. Above, the hills rear suddenly, symmetrically, like Maya pyramids, and their shapes echo in nature the steep gables of the houses. Looking up, you see the even silhouettes of man-made terraces—an ancient fortified town—and the hills look more than ever like the jungle-covered fanes of Guatemala.

Around the corner: a resort, honestly named the Fantasy. Farther on, another, the Naviti Beach: white people in baggy white shorts, green sun visors on faces bent over golf clubs; and near the entrance a sign: CAR PARK FOR FIREWALKING ARENA.

The bus stopped for ten minutes at the Hyatt Regency. I disembarked and bought a pineapple juice (from a tin!) which cost too much. By now I was drowsy; the warm air blowing freely through the windowless bus brought smells of flowers, damp earth, and copra-drying fires, that seemed to blend and thicken as the day lengthened and the colours became enriched.

The country flattened out into low-lying rice paddies hatched with banks and ditches. On isolated knolls that rose from the wet land like bubbles on the surface of a mire stood farmhouses half hidden among palms. The ocean was close, bordered by mangroves. We could see the island of Beqa, a tumulus on the horizon, where the firewalkers (of whom more in a later chapter) live.

Beyond Navua the land is too wet to be reclaimed. Zebu cattle graze in the shadows of surprising trees: banyans like low green rainclouds spread wide above their cataracts of aerial roots; and pandanus—leggy trees holding spare green mops aloft on trunks that grow from legs like menorahs inverted in the earth—each one a giant mantis stalking the landscape between a sky now golden and the silver exhalation of the swamp.

The mountains form a rampart on the far side of the narrow plain. Again they present fantastic shapes, not pyramids here but fecund, rounded forms, and among them a rocky phallus crowned with dark jungle and arrayed in cloud: the volcanic plug called Joske's Thumb.

The road climbs over a spit of high ground separating the lowlands of Pacific Harbour from Suva Bay. Here there are more houses: shacks of poor Indians and Fijians; comfortable weekend cottages of Fiji's well-to-do. In a soccer field by the road a Fijian brass band, dressed in a motley of *sulus*, shorts, and white and coloured shirts, was playing fervently on glinting instruments.

The bus descended quickly to the outlying suburb of Lami. Across the bay, above the tin roofs, palms, and mangroves, stood Suva—three or four skyscrapers rising whitely from the green.

2
▲▲▲
SUVA

An old yellow two-storey building across from the city market; letters along the balcony: HOTEL METROPOLE. The only door I could see gave entrance to a stand-up beer hall with a wet floor, some full-size billiard tables, and a multitude of tough-looking Fijians holding cues with the graceful menace of men who still fish with spears.

"Around the corner and up the stairs," Derek said briskly.

At the top of a steep flight was a landing and a panelled glass wall pierced by a small embrasure like the cashier's wicket in an old bank. RING FOR SERVICE, said one sign; ALL ACCOUNTS ARE TO BE PAID ON CHECK-IN, said another. Derek rang. An elderly Indian appeared, recognizing him immediately.

"Welcome back sah."

"Hello, Hari."

Hari produced a registration card.

"Put down seven days," Derek said expansively.

"Are we really going to be here that long?" I whispered.

"Probably."

Hari took us down a long passage with dusty yellow and grey walls. The carpet was red only at the edges, worn in the middle like a shortcut across a lawn.

"Bathroom here sah." Hari pointed at a mahogany door to a room already identified by an ammoniacal smell.

"Room six sah. Your old room." Hari ushered us in obsequiously. There was an odour of must and insect killer. Above the beds were gibbet-like frames that seemed to have been put up for the benefit of suicides—supports for absent mosquito nets. The other furnishings were from a Pinter play: a ripped armchair, a dresser with a cracked glass top, and in one corner a washbasin so scoured that patches of cast iron showed through the enamel.

Derek turned on the overhead fan, sat down on the bed nearest the window, and sighed contentedly.

"Number six. Lots of memories. Christine and I had this room when she came to visit me."

"You brought her here?"

"Everybody who came to visit stayed at the Metropole. It became something of a tradition."

I was relieved when Derek suggested we go out onto the balcony at the front of the building for a beer. I needed a drink. I'd stayed in much worse hotels, but not by choice. Before leaving the room I opened a dresser drawer; two large cockroaches ran out.

"Cockroaches are a fact of life here," Derek said.

No doubt.

The balcony I recognized from Derek's reminiscences on many a Canadian winter night. When it was thirty or forty below zero outside, we would open a bottle of brandy, watch his Fiji slides, and talk quietly of warm tropical evenings. But here in Suva it was still rush hour, and we had to shout above the roar of Leyland buses. One of the things I always forget about the Third World is the noise.

From the wharf at the end of the street reared the superstructure of a cruise liner, its monumental whiteness dominating the ramshackle market and waterfront. Across from the Metropole rose another eminence—the office block and department store of the Burns Philp South Sea Company, built in such period art deco that the stucco "1930" on the façade was hardly necessary. The main entrance was on the corner, beneath a tower capped by a steep tiled roof suggestive in outline of Fijian architecture.

We ordered a second round from Hari and watched the Suva traffic subside. Below us passed young Indians in bell-bottoms and *bula* shirts; Fijian matrons in ankle-length dresses, big combs stuck in their hair; with their husbands, bureaucrats perhaps, wearing ties, dark *sulus*, and carrying briefcases. Occasional tourists, pale as mushrooms, ambled to and from the ship.

Derek had relaxed with the beer.

"The good old Metropole! You've got to admit the place has character."

"I'm afraid I'm reaching the age when I'd rather look at character than live in it," I said, and he laughed.

◆

Derek was in a silent mood at breakfast, staring at the *Fiji Times*, coffeecup in one hand, perpetually smouldering cigarette in the other. It was some minutes before he spoke:

"I'll see you later. I'm going to the museum to look up Fergus and Senitiki."

I took the hint. Derek is best avoided when taciturn. I told him I'd look for a better hotel.

Stepping out into the sunshine brought a feeling of liberation. Suva, unprepossessing the day before, was now an unexpected delight. Away from the market area the streets were spotless, the paint fresh, the different outfits of Indians and Fijians a kinetic display of colour.

I crossed the footbridge over Nubukalou Creek—a tidal mooring for small boats—scowled at the Kentucky Fried Chicken franchise on the corner, and proceeded past the post office, glancing from time to time at *Suva: A History and Guide*, by the linguist Albert Schütz. A capital city of only seventy thousand—a human size. There were quaint touches of the British tropics, Leyland buses for instance, driving on the left, with their sooty exhausts, archaic local coachwork, and strange destinations: NAUSORI / / RAIWAI / / RAIWAQA. Yet there was none of the decay too often found in former outposts of the British Empire. Suva was evidently no Banjul or Belize.

Western civilization hangs on much of the post-colonial world like an ill-fitting suit of clothes, a hand-me-down, uninvited, un-comfortable, and uncared for, worn with resentment because its wearers have come to feel naked without it. So often the European legacy is maimed cultures and dying villages, threadbare economies and torn constitutions. But here one felt immediately that the for-eign clothes were worn with style and with subtle alterations to improve the fit.

At the centre of Suva is a tiny wedge-shaped park called the Triangle, with a great *ivi*, or native chestnut tree, at its apex. Wooden benches encircle the massive bole, and these were filled by substantial Fijian gentlemen, possessed of the same venerable calm as their setting, reading the *Fiji Times*. An office tower's morn-ing shadow had not quite withdrawn from nearby palms; birdsong invaded each lull in the traffic roar.

Victoria Parade, the closest Suva comes to possessing a corniche, has on its seaward side several old buildings of architectural merit. The Aquarium (formerly the Town Hall) is a fine example of the late-Victorian pavilion style. Slender iron columns support a bal-cony walled with panels of cast-iron filigree. Most of the early structures have these wide, roofed balconies and verandas—they allow air to circulate while keeping the sun from the walls. By contrast, Suva City Library, built in 1908 with the help of a grant from Andrew Carnegie, is an American neo-classical megalith that looks too ponderous for climate and surroundings.

Although Suva was designed as a new capital, replacing ram-shackle Levuka (on the island of Ovalau) as the seat of government in 1882, a conspiracy of creeks, swamps, and haphazard surveying saved it from the loathsome predictability of a grid. I turned inland and was soon in a maze of quiet residential streets. Flowers sur-rounding the blue and pink wooden bungalows were so luxuriant that they looked as if they awaited only a week's neglect to rot a house and feed upon it. At the end of a street the town vanished, replaced by a shallow ravine filled with banana trees, coconuts, and papayas. I turned right and walked downhill, emerging some min-utes later in Albert Park, a large, rather dismal rectangle of bare turf. All its trees were cut down so that Kingsford Smith could land here on the first flight across the Pacific in 1928; they were never replanted. Instead there are some rugby goal posts and an ugly grandstand which obscures what would otherwise be a fine prospect of the Government Buildings—Fiji's Parliament and ministries.

But such buildings! They seem to have sprung from a collaboration of Lutyens and Albert Speer. Fifty years of tropical rains have weathered the austere concrete finish—meant to look like ashlar stone—into great streaks of light and dark grey and patches of moss. The only colour is a small golden dome, perched like half an orange on top of a clock tower that might have been stolen from an automobile factory of the 1930s. In concession to the climate the architect recessed the windows so deeply in the walls that they seem to be glassless; and on the side facing Victoria Parade the structural walls are altogether hidden in the gloom of frowning balconies and empty towers. The buildings have the air of a lost city rescued from the jungle—an art deco Angkor Wat.

Schütz's guide makes no comment on the architecture but does relate an anecdote. It seems that Fiji's Parliament occupies land that was formerly a seedy neighbourhood of bars and brothels. A sailor, confronted after a long voyage by the imposing structures on the site of his favourite haunt, exclaimed: "My word, Annie has done well."

◆

Derek pressed a bell on the palm tree:

"I have to admit this was a good idea after all."

We were sitting at a garden umbrella table beside the swimming pool of the Grand Pacific Hotel, gazing out over that tiny alveolus of the Pacific Ocean known as Suva Bay. After my walk to the Government Buildings yesterday, I had crossed Victoria Parade for a drink in this establishment famed as the Raffles of Fiji. It looked exclusive from the outside—a façade of Doric columns painted brilliant white, a semi-circular drive shaded by royal palms, and a *porte-cochère* of Romanesque ironwork flanked by a magnificent Fiji fan palm like a peacock's tail in full spread.

Inside there was a sleepy, half-deserted air, a feeling of space and emptiness conveyed by the arched ceiling of the cathedral-like lounge, the skylights, white paint, and overhead fans suspended from long stems. In 1916, when the hotel was only two years old, Somerset Maugham noted: "It is cool and empty. . . . The servants are Hindus, silent and vaguely hostile. . . . The food is very bad, but the rooms are pleasant, fresh and cool." Time had evidently passed the Grand Pacific by, and so have most of the tourists since the opening of the Suva Travelodge next door. I found "budget rooms" (originally servants' accommodations, I assume) available for little more than we were paying at the Metropole. They lacked windows but did have louvred doors, a private shower, fan, and fridge. This last item made it easy to persuade Derek to move.

He was now so caught up in the colonial atmosphere that he was drinking gin and tonic—something I didn't know he liked. The sun was hot, but there was a breeze; we could hear the shallow water of the reef lapping at the edge of the hotel garden.

Across the bay clouds hovered over Joske's Thumb, which the locals say looks like a man trying to claw his way out of hell. Paul Joske was a German who came to Fiji with the Polynesia Company in 1870. Between 1873 and '75 he operated an unsuccessful sugar mill where Parliament now stands. The mountain was originally called the Devil's Thumb, but after a scandal involving incest and Joske's suicide, the German took Satan's place in the hills.

"That's a Korean fishing boat," Derek said, pointing to a line of surf and the rusty hulk of a boat high out of the water just below the horizon. "The captain drove it up on the reef one night last time I was in Fiji. Full power, drunk as a skunk."

Our drinks were brought not by a vaguely hostile Hindu but by an uncharacteristically androgynous Fijian wearing a white *sulu*, green cummerbund, orange shirt, and a hibiscus flower in his hair. The beer and gins were fine, but lunch had confirmed Maugham's opinion: the food was still very bad. For supper we walked the half mile north along Victoria Parade into central Suva.

We were attracted to the Star of India restaurant by a chicken painted on the window with the words SEE ME EVERYWHERE, EAT ME HERE! We entered through a bamboo curtain, and it took a minute to adjust to the dim glow seeping from paintings of Indian village life done on back-lit plastic panels around the walls. I had a Tandoori chicken, tasty but undercooked. Derek had a chicken curry.

"I should have remembered not to order this," he said. "I forgot about Fiji butchering—they just lay the chicken out on a slab and hack it to bits with a cane knife. You get slivers of bone in everything. There's really no need to do it that way."

Seated at the next table were two Australians who had apparently made the same mistake. I overheard:

"Wot's this then?"

"Chicken tikka."

"Call this chicken? This ain't chicken. Wrong colour for chicken—it's a seagull or somethin.' Just give me a good stike anytime, and I'm roight."

The plates cleared away, Derek ordered us each a Drambuie, rolled a cigarette, and looked more content than at any time since our arrival.

"You know, I think this is going to be just fine. I was afraid at first that you weren't going to like it, compared with Peru."

I told him he needn't have worried on my account, but I had noticed his mood and wondered if he was finding Fiji unequal to his memories. I myself have a tendency to idealize places when away from them; it can lead to disappointment.

"No," Derek said, "I liked it the first time and I'm sure I'll like it now. I never worry about things like that."

It must be nice, I thought, never to worry. Derek was obviously settling into his normal frame of mind—a placid insouciance that fell just short of serenity because of a decadent element of surrender about it. He looked like a well-fed, slightly dissolute friar from the *Canterbury Tales*. His bald head fringed by thin black hair made the comparison irresistible; but the tobacco-stained teeth and mustache effectively dispelled any aura of sanctity.

We left the restaurant and turned in the general direction of the hotel. The streets were quiet: a few knots of people, an occasional taxi. The pavement was wet from a recent shower, and a sea breeze swung the painted shop signs (so preferable to neon) above us: MUKHERJEE CARPETS; BRIJLAL VIDEO AND HI-FI; JINABHAL DUTY FREE.

Down the street a lone sign flashing in gold: LUCKY EDDIE'S

DISCO . . . LUCKY EDDIE'S DISCO. Loud rock music was wafting from a door guarded by three Fijians in tight T-shirts.

We bought tickets at a booth shaped like a privy with a low, barred window—all you could see of its occupant were his hands. A long staircase led up to the source of the noise. The walls were black and so was the ceiling, festooned with fishing nets in which sagged bits of coral and cork floats. It took me back twenty years.

The racial composition of Lucky Eddie's clientele seemed typical of the islands as a whole: Indian men with their shy girlfriends, a few whites, Fijian men and women, mostly single, perhaps on the make. We found a booth with a window that gave some relief from the smoky air.

By ten o'clock the place was full and the music—from a bank of speakers on a small stage—loud. Standing drinkers crowded against the booths; I wondered if we were expected to share. The thought had scarcely left me when I felt a heavy hand on my shoulder. I composed a smile and looked up. A Fijian woman answered with an intense but poorly focussed grin and plumped herself down beside me.

"My Swiss boyfriend send me some cash today," she revealed. "It make me sad thinking 'bout him, but happy too. So I told myself, 'Rosi, you're going to have a good time tonight.'

"I've got it all right here in my bra."

She patted her resilient bosom.

"Now you don't think I'm a bad woman. Oh no. Ask my friend. She tell you. *Sally! Sally!* Come sit down here."

After several yells a shy, embarrassed Sally sat down beside Derek. Rosi did all the talking.

"We got money. We're not like these other girls here expec' you to buy us drinks. I got it all right here in my bra!"

A large hand descended onto my knee and lingered there. She moved closer and pressed her bosom, presumably opulent in more than just the usual sense, against my arm. So this is what it's like to be sexually harassed, I thought. I didn't want to appear unfriendly, but the aspect of Rosi was alarming. Fijian women share the robust build of the men, and Rosi was heavier than most.

"I've been to Switzerland, yes I have," she continued. "Ask her!

I can speak German. *Wo kommen Sie? Ich bin von Fiji Inseln!*" She brought her mouth to my ear and shouted, "*Wo kommen Sie?* See, I speak German."

This was followed by a wet and equally noisy kiss in the ear. The hand moved to my thigh:

"Come on, buy us some beer."

◆

Thurston Botanical Gardens: luxuriance, a feeling that a brigade of gardeners could barely keep them tamed, to keep this bush from that, those grasses from the freshly weeded borders, that tree from claiming all the sky.

Venerable *ivi* and *baka* (banyans) and a few low mounds and mossy stones remain to show that this was once the ancient Fijian village of Suva; appropriately enough, the Fiji Museum (our destination this morning) stands at one edge of the gardens, and Government House, the Governor-General's residence, borders them to the south.

Dew dripping from pergolas; fallen frangipani petals lighting the path; a pond filled with lotus flowers opening pink and mauve in the sun; and in the water, huge goldfish grown fat on lesser fry. In a thicket there's a bandstand with an absurdly large clock tower and a dedication:

ERECTED BY HENRY MARKS AND COMPANY LIMITED
IN MEMORY OF
THEIR LATE DIRECTOR
G. J. MARKS,
FIRST MAYOR OF SUVA,
WHO WAS DROWNED IN THE
ST. LAWRENCE RIVER, CANADA
THROUGH THE SINKING
OF THE SS EMPRESS OF IRELAND,
23 MAY 1914

Imagine: a man survives prickly heat, bad food, inferior whisky, canoe voyages through shark-swum reefs, then drowns in the Nordic austerity of the St. Lawrence.

The museum was only a dozen yards away, but we could scarcely see it through the trees.

"Don't be put off if Fergus seems unfriendly at first," Derek warned. "It's just the way he is. He's actually a remarkable chap."

Derek had worked with Fergus Clunie, the Museum Director, during his archaeological project. He had told me several stories about the "remarkable chap" and I was anxious, in both senses, to meet the man. Clunie was third-generation Fiji European. His grandfather had come out from Scotland to grow sugar—a planter of the old school, apparently, who settled trouble in the "lines" with his fists. Fergus's father had been a doctor upcountry, where he sometimes found himself competing with other kinds of medicine. He had a little African figurine that kept on disappearing; then, days later, he would find it neatly wrapped in leaves and placed in a bamboo cylinder over his porch or under his threshold.

"Apparently that was the Fijian equivalent of a doll with pins in it," Derek continued. "Anyway, Fergus's dad would eventually find it, shout out 'What! This bloody thing again!' or something like that, kick it around in front of the servants to show he wasn't afraid, and then put the figurine back on the mantelpiece and throw away the wrappings."

We entered the museum and walked upstairs to the offices. Fergus and Senitiki, one of the Fijian curators and an old friend of Derek's, were having their morning tea break. Without a word large mugs of the same brew, already thickened with milk and sugar, were brought for us by Sela, the librarian. Sela was a quiet man, crippled by polio, but like most Fijians he was athletic; he had even competed in the Olympics for the handicapped at Montreal. Fergus Clunie himself was one of those who have a presence beyond their years. He couldn't have been much older than myself, late thirties perhaps, but his clipped and forceful manner brought to mind what I knew of his formidable ancestors. This impression of age was strengthened by a beard, balding crown, and heavy brows. He did, as Derek had warned, virtually ignore me, but I could see that this— like his frequent use of swearwords—was the defence of a shy and sensitive man.

"We're off to Nadrau in a couple of days," Derek told him. "Then

we plan to walk out of the highlands down the Sigatoka valley—
if I survive. Two years behind a desk . . ." he patted his paunch.
Nadrau—situated more or less in the middle of Viti Levu—had
been Derek's base during his archaeological project in Fiji, when
he conducted an extensive survey in the area now flooded by the
Monasavu hydroelectric dam. His work had involved a lot of ar-
duous exploring in heavily wooded country, and the excavation of
ancient fortress and village sites found there.

"When I left Fiji I was the fittest I've ever been in my life. Too
bad I didn't keep it up."

"Good hike'll sweat all that lard off you, boy," Fergus said. "Keep
a look out for ancient terracing when you're up there. Should show
up if the country's been burnt. Farming terraces for *dalo* [taro] is
what I'm after. Ask around. There's still some old buggers know
all sorts of stuff. Amazing what some of 'em know—stuff you'd
think they'd have forgotten. No use talking to our generation. World
War Two was as bad, to my way of thinking, as Christianity.
Brought in the outside world, see. Then education came in. And
that blasted cassava they grow now—bloody stuff grows anywhere,
all seasons. The whole social fabric surrounding yam and *dalo* cultivation fell apart. But ask around; some of the old buggers can
surprise you."

Fergus sipped thoughtfully at his mug of tea. Nobody spoke.
He continued:

"This chap came round yesterday with a rusty old American
machete from the war. Wanted to give it to us. 'I can't pay you
anything for it,' I told 'im. 'That's all right; please take it,' chap
says. Turns out he found it along with some human bones, so he
buried the bones and took it home. Wife said, 'Put a new handle
on it and it'll make a good kitchen knife.' But that night the skull
came visiting him, hanging over his bedside, teeth gnashing and
all."

Fergus chuckled. I tried to place his accent. Sub–New Zealand?
No, south London lower-middle by way of Sydney—Fiji's own
dialect of English. There was no trace of Scottish.

"Chap had a problem. Can't just throw it away because that

would upset the ghosts even more. Got to pass it on somewhere, and he reckoned the museum was the place."

"Did you take it?" I asked.

"Course I took it. Part of our job. We're really the last *bure kalou*—the last spirit house—in Fiji.

"Had another chap come here not long ago, a necromancer I know from Vanua Levu. Asked if he could leave his *tanoa* [ceremonial kava bowl] here for four days and nights. Course, soon as I heard four I knew something was up. Four's a magic number, see, same as ten—don't know why but it is. Chap was hoping to collect about fifty spirits in the *tanoa* and take it back all fortified." Clunie glanced at his watch. "Be a good source of revenue, wouldn't it? Ten dollars a night. Wouldn't do our name much good if it got out, though.

"Well, time for work. You know your way around, Derek. Show 'im the war clubs."

◆

The museum collections reveal the course of the remarkable hundred years in which the Fijians passed from cannibalism to Methodism, from the age of stone to that of steam. The outside world came late to Fiji. No significant contact was made until the dawn of the nineteenth century.

The "discovery" of the islands—for what that ethnocentric notion is worth—is credited to Abel Tasman, who sighted Taveuni and some outlying members of the Lau group in 1643 while on his way to Java. The next recorded visit by a European was not until 1774, when Cook made a similar sighting. The first white man to gain any idea of the extent of Fiji was Captain William Bligh of *Bounty* fame. In 1789 the mutineers put him and several loyal officers to sea in an open launch. Bligh knew that his only chance was to make for the Dutch colony at Java, some 3600 miles to the west. The route took him right between Fiji's two main islands, but having heard in Tonga of the Fijians' reputation for cannibalism, he made no attempt to land. When almost out of the group, Bligh's craft was chased by two canoes from the Yasawas, but even though his party was desperately short of supplies Bligh was unwilling to find out whether the natives' interest was friendly or dietary.

In 1800, or soon thereafter, an American schooner named the *Argo* was wrecked on a reef near Lakeba Island in the Lau group. The strange artifacts salvaged by the natives were soon lost, and most survivors of the crew were killed and eaten, but there was an invisible cargo that the white men brought in their veins, bowels, and breath.

A plague known as *na lila balavu*, the "wasting sickness" or "long disease," decimated the people of islands near the wreck, then spread with booty and captured survivors to the major centres. On tiny but powerful Bau it killed Banuve, the Vunivalu, or Warlord, who in death was renamed Bale i Vavalagi, "Victim of the Foreigners." Portents appeared in the sky. On the day that Naulivou, the new Warlord, was installed, "there was a total eclipse of the sun, the heavens were like blood, the stars came out, and the birds went to roost at mid-day"; a "hairy star with three tails" blazed overhead. To the Fijians these things were baleful harbingers of change.

The effects of contact between European civilization and an isolated people were unsuspected in Fiji but familiar to much of the world since the age of discovery began. Smallpox had descended on the Aztecs just as Cortés besieged Mexico City, and Moctezuma had been immobilized by terrifying omens and visions. A similar pestilence had spread tribe by tribe from Panama to Peru, where it ravaged the Inca Empire and killed the ruler on the eve of the Spaniards' arrival. Then, too, the plague and subsequent conquest were associated with comets, earthquakes, and eclipses—symbols of cosmic chaos.

Because the peoples of the New World and Oceania had been isolated from the rest of mankind for so long, the onslaught of unknown pathogens was catastrophic, and the course of infection was far more severe for non-immune natives than for habituated Europeans. In Fiji the agonies of the sick were so appalling that victims were often strangled to release them from pain, as a *meke* of the period recalls:

The great sickness sits aloft,
Their voices sound hoarsely,
They fall and lie helpless and pitiable,
Our god Degei is put to shame,
Our own sicknesses have been thrust aside,
The strangling-cord is a noble thing,
They fall prone; they fall with the sap still in them.

Many die, a few live on . . .
Hark to the creak of the strangling-cords,
The spirits flow away like running water . . .

Another plague hit Fiji two years after the first. It was probably dysentery, brought by *El Plumier*, the third foreign ship to linger in Fijian waters. She arrived off Vanua Levu in the course of an eventful voyage involving near shipwreck on the reefs, lengthy repairs, a mutiny, and the rescue of one Oliver Slater, an *Argo* survivor who had "lived among the savages for two and twenty months." Slater's rescue exposed Fiji to yet another white contagion—the lust for profit. He had seen the sandalwood thickets at Bua Bay on the west end of Vanua Levu, and knew that the wood could be obtained for a song, then sold for about £80 a ton in China, where it was prized for making incense and ceremonial figurines. In Fiji and Tonga the wood was used only as the aromatic ingredient in coconut oil for the body, and local demand was not especially high.

Slater came back with an old schooner which he filled with fifteen tons of sandalwood in return for a few broken cutlasses. He had to transfer the precious cargo to a larger ship in Australia. The word got out. It may sound odd to speak of a "wood rush," but that is exactly what happened. Ship after ship set sail for the "Cannibal Isles"; the profits made were enormous. One loaded 250 tons of sandalwood—worth £20,000 in China—for trade goods costing £50. Predictably, every accessible stand of the wood was cut out within ten years; and in that decade (1805–1815) Fijians and foreigners formed some idea of what they could expect from one another.

The sandalwood era was the age of the "beachcombers"—white

brigands who chose to live among the Fijians as gunmen and interpreters in exchange for power and women. Fiji at that time was composed of about a dozen major chiefdoms constantly engaged in shifting conflicts and alliances. The ablest chiefs soon saw the possibilities of European firearms and tactics; for as long as muskets, powder, and ball were to be had, they made use of their foreign protégés to expand and consolidate their conquests.

Most successful of all was the chiefdom of Bau—a twenty-acre island off the east coast of Viti Levu, whose influence on the rest of Fiji was out of all proportion to its size, both before and after European contact. By establishing shrewd relations with beachcombers, traders, missionaries, and early settlers, Bau maintained its position as the foremost Fijian chiefdom throughout most of the nineteenth century. Under its able ruler Cakobau, Vunivalu from 1853 until 1883, Bau transformed itself from cannibal conquest-state to constitutional monarchy, and finally into a Crown Colony of Britain, within a single generation.

There were times when the currents of change seemed too strong to ride—when Ma'afu the Tongan virtually colonized eastern Fiji; or when the European planters sought to use the Kingdom of Bau as a puppet regime to cloak their exploitation of its native subjects—but in the long run Cakobau proved equal to these challenges. When he and the other high chiefs handed what was by then the Kingdom of Fiji to Queen Victoria's representative in 1874, they managed to enlist the protection of the Crown against pressures that could otherwise have ruined them.

♦

Resting at the bottom of a display case filled with various belongings of King Cakobau is his throwing club. It has a bulbous business end shaped like a fluted squash and a handle some eighteen inches long; the smooth black wood is finely inlaid with ivory stars and crescent moons.

"Fergus let me hold that once," Derek said. "It's perfectly balanced. It felt as though it leaped into my hand and was itching to leap out again and kill."

Fijian weapons and warfare are among Fergus Clunie's chief interests; he has written an authoritative study on the subject. Several cabinets in the museum are devoted to an extraordinary diversity of ornate wooden instruments of death. Bludgeons, shillelaghs, bats, cudgels, knobkerries, and battle axes: the English language cannot compete with Fijian in the range of terms for naming each type. Nor does the generic "club" do justice to these masterworks in ebony-like *vesi* wood, carved, polished, and adorned like Arab flintlocks. These are not the crude weapons of the cartoon caveman.

Until the decline of warfare in the second half of the last century, no Fijian male went about unarmed. War parties from rival chiefdoms constantly raided without warning. Often these skirmishes were little more than a rough sport, like mediaeval English soccer games, in which one or two people would be killed; but there were also much more serious wars, and frequent treachery within a state. Alliances were quickly formed and just as quickly broken. With Orwellian rapidity, yesterday's foe became today's friend—but seldom a friend who could be fully trusted.

Some scholars have tried to blame the worst excesses of Fijian warfare—amply documented in early accounts—on the introduction of European weapons. It is true that pitched battles between Fijians armed only with clubs and spears produced relatively few casualties, mainly because the warriors were so adept at dodging, but whenever a rout occurred or a fortified town was breached the carnage was probably just as bad before 1800 as after. There were no inhibitions against killing women, children, and defenceless old men—enemy blood was enemy blood. A man who failed to kill in battle could redeem his reputation by clubbing a non-combatant to death. A young warrior's greatest fear was to die before having killed. In *Fijian Weapons & Warfare* Fergus Clunie writes: "A coward or *datuvu* whose club was still unstained with blood at the time of his death was doomed to pound human excrement with his dishonoured weapon in Bulu, the afterworld, onward into eternity."

The pre-contact pedigree of cannibalism has also been questioned. In a book elegantly called *The Man-Eating Myth: Anthropology and Anthropophagy*, W. Arens takes the extreme view that there have never been cannibals anywhere on earth (except for "survival cannibals" such as air-crash victims). People-eating tribes, he claims, existed only in the imaginations of their enemies and of Europeans seeking to blacken the reputation of "savages" to justify colonizing them. In many cases he may be right; but he completely ignores the Fiji evidence. Numerous independent sources confirm that the ancient Fijians had an elaborate system of beliefs, rituals, special utensils, and favourite recipes for large-scale cannibalism. This could have resulted only from long development. None of the Fijians questioned by early Europeans ever tried to deny or hide the fact of cannibalism; on the contrary, they expected the whites to tolerate it as *vakavanua*, the "way of the land."

Victims were most often cooked in earth ovens *(lovo)* made of hot stones among which the meat and vegetables were buried. A wild "spinach"—botanical name *Solanum anthropophagorum*—was deemed essential to avoid the constipating properties of human flesh; and yes, the latter was sometimes figuratively called *vuaka balavu*, "long pig."

The reasons behind Fijian cannibalism were no doubt as complex as the rituals surrounding it. Human flesh was both a sacrifice to the gods and a satisfaction of appetite. It was prized for its flavour and supposed aphrodisiac qualities. (Victory feasts were often followed by sex orgies in which the Fijians' customary modesty was abandoned.) Paradoxically, cannibalism could be a way of insulting one's enemy or honouring him. To be cooked in the ovens was considered a noble end, the reward of the brave:

Sa vei ko Qaqa?	Where is the courageous?
Sa yara ki rara.	Gone to be dragged [into the town to be cooked].
Sa vei ko Dadatuvu?	Where is the coward?
Sa la'ki tukutuku.	Gone to report.

Arens doth protest too much. Almost every nation on earth has committed atrocities in others' judgement, if not in its own. It is we who say that roasting dead people in an oven is savage behaviour, whereas roasting live ones with napalm is not.

♦

Another face of ancient Fijian culture is represented by two sailing
canoes that fill the main hall of the museum. The smaller craft is
a dugout with a log outrigger; its weathered appearance shows that
it was once in use. But the larger vessel is pristine, its twin hulls
a deep black, decorated at the prows with pearl-white cowrie shells
symbolic of nobility. At more than thirty feet long it is in fact a
scale model, about one third full size, of a *drua*, the class of great
catamarans built in Fiji until the late nineteenth century. This
replica was made some years ago by one of the last master boat-
builders, an old man from the Lau group, where fine woodworking
is still done. Only traditional techniques and materials were used.

The *drua* had two hulls of unequal size, over which was laid a
deck equipped with a collapsible house. The mast, stepped in the
middle of the deck, carried a lateen sail of pandanus mat. Steering
was done by trailing oars of *vesi* wood up to twenty feet in length.
The largest canoe seen by Thomas Williams (c. 1850) had the following dimensions: length of main hull, 118 feet; deck, 50 feet by
24; mast, 68 feet high with 90-foot yards. She was named *Rusa i
Vanua*, or "Perished Inland," for fear that she would be impossible
to launch. Such a craft "would safely convey a hundred persons,
and several tons of goods, over a thousand miles of ocean." In the
last years before the *Pax Britannica* some Fijian war canoes were
mounted with light cannon.

The outrigger, or lesser hull, was always kept to windward. Good
sailors applied just enough sail to keep it skimming the surface.
They could tack into the wind by reversing the entire sail assembly,
so that the bow of the canoe on one tack became its stern on the
next. The early anthropologist Basil Thomson described this as:
"the most precise and beautiful manoeuvre known to seamanship."

Any canoe of more than forty feet in length could not be hollowed
from a single tree. A hull was made of several large planks, built
up from a keel in two or three sections. The pieces were cut and
curved to fit perfectly, then joined by means of bindings sewn
through mating flanges pierced with holes. Ribs were not used;
even the largest composite hulls imitated the dugout form. From
the outside the joins were almost undetectable.

Before 1800, this work was done with polished stone chisels, abrasive shells, and saws of animal teeth. The finest craft took years to build and were not considered finished without sacrifice. The first launching was over human rollers, while decks and spars were splashed with blood.

"When are you boys leaving for Nadrau?" Fergus had reappeared while I was admiring a *tanoa* four feet in diameter, carved from a single block of wood.

"Two or three days," Derek said. "Senitiki said he'd come with us on Sunday to try and find Aseri at his village. I'm hoping Aseri will come along and be our *mata ni vanua*. Apparently he's not doing much since you fired him."

"A good lad that, but don't let him drive anything." (Aseri's misfortunes with the museum Land-Rover had cost him his job.)

Fergus grinned. "Looking forward to all that country food?"

"I can still taste it," said Derek. "Cassava and tinned fish." He shuddered.

"You heard about the tinned mackerel scare, did you? People started dying from that damned Jap mackerel. Instead of the government taking it all off the market and burying it, what they should've done, Japs came over and said, 'Oh, ha, velly solly. We'll take it all back and destroy it. No plobrem.' Course, they prob'ly turned round and sold it somewhere else. Full-page adverts in the newspapers: such and such a brand is all right. Course, merchants trying to cash in. All comes out of the same bloody factory anyway. Just different labels, different shapes of tin. I wouldn't touch any of it if I were you."

◆

Senitiki joined us for breakfast at the Grand Pacific. Maugham might have recognized the quality of the fare. My slice of pineapple, evidently the first of the day, was dry on one side like an old sandwich.

We rented a car for the drive to Mokani, Aseri's village. The rental office was an old caravan in a car park opposite the Hare Krishna Take-Away ("For a Higher Level of Taste").

North from Suva the King's Road winds through the poor neighbourhoods of Raiwai and Raiwaqa: blocks of flats half hidden in washing ("Another Project by Your Housing Authority"), then a busy open road between the capital and its small airport at Nausori. A skull and crossbones on a billboard reminds you of mortality: FIJI ROAD SAFETY COUNCIL WARNING—DEATH STRETCH AHEAD.

At the end of a muddy track, Mokani. Small children ran beside the car, shouting, "*Kai valagi, kai valagi*" (foreigners, white people). In a field some young men were playing soccer.

"There's Aseri," Derek said.

"We'll go to the house first," Senitiki suggested in the quietly authoritative voice of the Fijians. "Someone will send to bring him."

Mokani: houses of clapboard with tin roofs, though some have walls of split bamboo woven in chevron patterns. Splashes of colour show between the dark-green shade of mango and breadfruit and the light green of the tended lawn. The wooden houses are painted red, blue, ochre, bright as a Mexican high street, but even these seem muted beside the opalescent crimsons, pinks, purples, and yellows of the flowers surrounding them.

We removed our sandals, entered stooping, and without standing upright sat down on the floor where indicated by Aseri's parents, people in their sixties, of much dignity and little English. Having sat, we quietly made the ritual handclaps that signify respect for the household and its ancestors—in ancient times the dead were buried beneath the floor. (Derek had told me what to do and added, "Don't be surprised if Aseri's mother sniffs your hand. It's a traditional greeting." As it turned out, she didn't.)

Aseri arrived, out of breath, and took his seat as deferentially as the rest of us. Handshakes and greetings were exchanged.

"Derek! How long can it be since you leave Fiji?" Aseri said.

He was a big man in his mid-twenties, dark muscles swelling from a white singlet. He'd seen something of the world with the Fiji UN forces in Sri Lanka and Lebanon, and wore the tidy mustache of one who has been in the army.

Derek produced a packet of powdered *yaqona* root bought yesterday in Suva market. (*Yaqona* is the Fijian word for *Piper methysticum*, a plant of the pepper family, and the drink made from its roots. It is called *kava* in most Polynesian languages and "kava" or "grog" in Fiji English. The drink has great ceremonial significance, ranging, according to context, from social lubricant almost to a sacrament.) He passed it to Senitiki and asked him to make the *sevusevu*, or introductory presentation. Senitiki, smaller than Aseri, shy and serious with a wrinkled brow, rose from a crosslegged position to his knees. Holding the small newspaper package in both hands, he made a short speech in which I recognized Derek's name and mine. The Fijians have this wonderfully convenient custom: no principal person has to enact a ceremony himself. It is done on his behalf by a spokesman. If you happen to arrive alone, a member of the household automatically fills this role. The custom derives from the practice of chiefs, who seldom act or speak formally except through their heralds, the *mata ni vanua* (literally "face of the chiefdom" or "eye of the land").

After his speech Senitiki respectfully slid the *yaqona* across the mat to Aseri's father. The old man picked it up, inhaled its fragrance, and made a brief welcoming address, ending with the words *Woi, mana, mana dina*, in which the other Fijians joined. The phrase resounded like a prayer or chant, as well it might, for the words mean "Lo, power, power indeed" and refer to the spiritual force that resides in all things, especially the *yaqona* plant. Father then passed the packet to son. Aseri got up and lifted the family *tanoa* from its peg on the wall. His mother brought three drinking cups made from halved coconut shells and a plastic bucket full of water.

Aseri poured some water into the *tanoa*. He put a quantity of the *yaqona* powder inside a muslin cloth, wrapped it up carefully, and immersed it in the bowl. Kneading slowly and deliberately he infused the soluble essence of the root, adding water from time to time until the desired mix was achieved.

"Aseri always makes strong grog," Derek said.

Everyone grinned, as if in anticipation of some potent home brew. When drunk in earnest, kava has a relaxing, mildly narcotic effect, compared by some to that of an opiate.

We were joined by Noa, a friend of Aseri's who had guessed that kava drinking was afoot. Noa sat to Aseri's left and assumed the role of server. When the mix was ready Aseri squeezed the muslin hard, then grasped the wet ball in both hands and twice rotated it solemnly above the rim of the *tanoa*. Mixer and server gave three slow but vigorous claps in unison. The grog was made.

Derek quietly reminded me what to do: "Clap once when the cup is offered to you, take it in both hands, then drink."

"All at once?"

"All of it."

Derek was served first, then Senitiki, as his "herald." Between each drinker the coconut cup was refilled from another kept beside the *tanoa*. The brew looked like muddy water; it had a pleasant woody taste, and coated the mouth with a fleeting numbness as it went down. After drinking and handing back the cup I remembered to clap quietly three or four times in appreciation. Someone approvingly said "*Maca*" ("It is dry").

After the first, formal round the gathering relaxed.

"Derek," Aseri asked, "is this the first time Ronald taste grog?"

"No. We drank it a few times in my flat in Edmonton."

"How much grog you took back to Canada last time?"

"Quite a few pounds." This was translated for the older generation; laughter followed.

In the twenty minutes or so between each round people smoked, chatted, read the newspaper, or simply stretched their legs from the formal crosslegged position—a great relief for the two "Europeans." Aseri brought out some reports of archaeological digs he had worked on since getting his first experience with Derek.

"When I was working on Rotuma," he told us, "we had this strange fellow come and visit. He said he was an expert on plants. He got on the wrong plane and went to Nadi, not Rotuma. Then he fix that but when he arrived he had no luggage. He blamed Air Pacific. All he had was one small briefcase. Well, he opened that, and what do you think was in it?" Aseri paused. "Four bottle of Johnnie Walker!"

"That sounds like the chap we met. Said his name was Wendell Gorky."

"That was his name. *Doctor* Gorky. He tell us just to call him Doctor."

Much of the conversation was in Fijian. Derek seemed to catch a little of it, but I, of course, was at sea. How different from Peru, where people were ashamed of the native "dialect," as they called it, where to address someone in the Inca tongue was often taken as an insinuation that you thought him a despicable *indio*. Here no special effort was made to speak English for our benefit, but this wasn't thoughtlessness on the part of Aseri and his family. Rather it gave the feeling that we two *kai valagi* were accepted, at home. There was none of the inferiority complex towards former colonial masters that you find in most parts of the Third World. Nobody wanted to impress us with his English; and that said much.

Village sounds outside the house: chickens, children, a distant radio playing the sugary harmonies of Fijian pop; once or twice the mysterious syncopated sounding of a wooden drum, crisp and urgent, like a call to war. And exactly on the hour, a chime from Senitiki's watch.

The house was in the modern style—a one-room rectangular wooden building, painted blue inside and out. But the use of space was the same as in the old days. Several layers of pandanus mat covered the floor, and the sleeping area was separated from the rest by a large *masi*, or barkcloth, hung from the main crossbeam. Pictures along this beam reflected the fundamental Fijian values of kinship, faith, and loyalty: family portraits, a calendar of Christ the Good Shepherd, an old tinted picture of King Edward VII, photographs of the Queen and Prince Philip, a wedding shot of Charles and Diana. The house had no tables or chairs—Fijian domestic life is lived on the floor. Two cabinets against the wall contained dishes and glassware, but all cooking was done in a separate kitchen hut outside.

Suddenly it rained. A tropical rain that came without wind or warning, that tumbled unannounced in gallons. The noise on the metal roof made talk impossible; the bright views of the village, seen through the open doors, were now darkened and half hidden behind curtains of water and a cloud of spray rising from the ground. There was no change in temperature, and in ten minutes the sun was out again, glinting on the puddles. The soft air brought the scent of woodsmoke and wet earth. It was quiet in the house. The new, moist silence was like a fresh canvas, and for a while only the songs of birds were painted on it.

"Derek, tell us a story," Aseri said.

Derek rearranged his legs and reached for his tobacco. He rolled a cigarette, thinking. When it was lit he spoke:

"When I was in Nadrau last time we were sitting in the house of the Tui [Chief] drinking *yaqona* like this one night—were you there that time, Aseri, when the Tui Nadrau mentioned the *tevoro?* Anyway, as I'm sure Aseri remembers, our work involved a lot of walking around in the bush and examining anything unusual that might be from ancient times. That night the Tui Nadrau warned me about a certain stone in the woods nearby. He said, 'There's a *tevoro*, a devil, who lives in that place. If anyone goes near the stone or touches it, his hair falls out.' So I said to the Tui, 'I have nothing to fear from that *tevoro*—it's too late for him to punish me.' "

Aseri looked up at Derek, glanced at Noa, who was equally bald.

"I think Derek and Noa must go to the same barber shop," he said.

3
▲▲▲
NADRAU

Three tall bottles of Fiji Bitter settled the dust of a day spent mostly on the King's Road. Supper had not lived up to the Tavua Hotel's claim, THE PLACE TO STAY AND EAT THE BEST, painted in childish letters on a billboard by the road; but the beer tasted good. Derek was rolling his acrid Drum tobacco, Aseri smoking Rothmans from one of the packs we had brought for *sevusevu* gifts. There was no one else in the lounge. Bare lightbulbs clinically illuminated layer upon layer of shiny cream paint on the tongue-and-groove plank walls. The black ceiling fans, with all but a few blades missing, looked like mutilated flies.

It had been a long day, begun in a taxi belonging to the ominously named Fletcher Christian Tours; later, soon after nightfall, the lights of our bus had failed. But they were repaired quickly enough by a committee of passing Indian lorry drivers shouting at each other in a Hindi sprinkled with words like "fuse," "short," and "blow." A strange scene: the darkened bus, stars and jungle shadows, waving flashlight beams; and the sounds of the bush—insects and frogs—competing against the battery-powered tape players of young Indians playing different tunes.

In the afternoon there was an unpleasant incident when the bus driver apparently swindled a Fijian boy who was selling freshwater prawns wrapped in a plantain leaf, their whiskery heads protruding like a sad bouquet. The driver argued over the price, seized the prawns, and drove off angrily, tossing a few coins through the open door. A woman at the back shouted something abusive; Derek asked Aseri if we should protest.

"It's all right," Aseri had calmly replied, with a subtle grin. "A few days ago some boys sold a packet of prawns with only the heads in and the weight made up by stones."

♦

We waited next morning at Tavua market for transport up to the highlands of Nadrau. Reports conflicted: a truck had just left; there would be a bus in the afternoon; the only way was by taxi; and so on.

"Can I be of assistance?" An elderly Fijian approached, wearing a black *sulu* and holding a red and green umbrella against the sun. "There will be a truck coming down from Nadrau at one o'clock, I think, and it will go back there soon after. Follow me, please."

He took us to an empty market stall made of packing-case boards and sheltered by a sheet of corrugated iron.

"We can sit here and drink a bowl of *yaqona* while we wait. My name is Ratu Aca; I am a brother of the late Tui Nadrau. Did you know he died last year?"

"Yes," Derek said. "I was very sorry to hear that. I knew Ratu Napolioni quite well. He was a very fine gentleman." He paused for a moment. "Has a new chief been chosen yet?"

"I believe Ratu Lemeki, his son, will be Tui. But you know these things take time. He has been chosen by his clan, but not everyone has formally agreed yet. In Fijian custom everybody must agree before he can be—what is the word—installed."

Ratu Aca gestured imperiously to some Indian kava sellers at the next stall, calling for a bowl.

"Indians don't drink grog in Fijian way," he said to us quietly. "We show respect to *yaqona*; it used to be holy among us—that is why we make the handclap. But Indian just . . . like this." He pantomimed reaching for a *yaqona* cup and knocking it back like vodka.

His remarks were not overheard by the Indian who now brought over some mixed *yaqona* in an enamel basin. Ratu Aca handed the man some coins, then turned to us.

"I make small *sevusevu* to you."

Here in the market, with the enamel basin, it was not done formally. Derek merely thanked in English, clapped once, and took the proffered *bilo*, or coconut-shell cup.

With the kava, the coastal heat, and the serene company of Ratu Aca, the hours of waiting slipped by in delightful languor. We reciprocated the *sevusevu*, and when it came time for a third basinful Ratu Aca said:

"Let's play game. It will pass the time, and we can decide who buys the next round. You must guess my age."

He wrote a number on a scrap of paper and gave it folded to Aseri.

"If you guess right, I have to buy the grog; if you are all wrong, you must buy."

We studied the Ratu (a Fijian title roughly equivalent to "lord"; ladies of high rank are similarly called Adi). He looked a bit like Jomo Kenyatta but without the beard. The eyes were bloodshot—a side effect of grog?—but otherwise he seemed extremely hale. Mid-fifties, probably, but better to underestimate for politeness' sake.

"Forty-nine," I guessed.

"Forty-six," said Aseri.

"Fifty-two," said Derek.

"You buy!" chuckled Ratu Aca. "Open the paper. I am sixty-two years old." He was pleased, as the old always are, that we had judged him so young.

"I feel very fit, although I get a bit stiff nowadays. The doctor tell me rheumatism—too wet in the hills—so I stay down here most of the time. When we went to Bau for Queen Elizabeth's visit it was hard for me. The Bau people are very formal—you know Bau is the royal island. We sat for hours in the Fijian way and not once did they let us stretch our legs. Here we take life more easy.

"Excuse me for some minutes. I will go and make enquiries about your transport."

After Ratu Aca left, Aseri suggested that we should look for a whale's tooth to present to the Tui-elect in condolence for the old Tui's death. He and Derek went off on this quest, leaving me in possession of the market stall and our luggage. The drought was severe in Tavua; there was little activity around me. The kava sellers seemed to drink far more than they sold. Opposite, under an awning of flour sacks, a pretty Indian girl of about nine sat patiently on a Fiji Bitter case, watching over half a dozen small papayas. She had not sold one all morning.

"I think we got the only whale's tooth in town," Derek announced when he and Aseri returned. "There seems to be a shortage of them right now. Luckily a Chinaman had this for sale." He showed me an ivory tooth about four inches long, the shape of a rhinoceros horn.

The *tabua*, or tooth of the sperm whale, has a symbolic value in Fiji that transcends any monetary worth. It is a ceremonial object presented at important occasions such as weddings, funerals, when asking a man for his daughter in marriage—for making any solemn request or statement of goodwill. The tooth is hung from a coconut sinnet cord attached by small holes drilled at its point and root. Fine old *tabua* are highly polished, often oiled and stained with turmeric (a native plant of special importance).

Tabua are metaphysical wealth, repositories of *mana*. They have no fixed cash value and there is no firm scale of how large a *tabua* or how many are required for an occasion. Among Fijians they tend to circulate rapidly: a tooth received one month may be given away the next. A few, however, find their way to country stores as pledges or payments on debts, and these are occasionally sold. As with old jewellery in our society, price depends on local demand.

Most Fijian customs—kava drinking for example—are typical of Polynesian or Melanesian culture in general, but the treasuring of *tabua* is unique to Fiji. Whales' teeth cannot have been easy to come by in ancient times; it seems that before European ships began calling at the islands most *tabua* were made from shell, wood, or polished stone. Some must have been obtained from beached whales— it is hard otherwise to explain the high value immediately placed on the teeth offered by foreign sailors. In the early days, one fine tooth would pay for a whole cargo of sandalwood. Later, several were required; and some captains stole a jump on their competitors by presenting enormous *tabua* carved from elephant and walrus tusks.

The name most likely derives from the word *tabu* (pronounced *tambu* in Fijian, of course). Besides its familiar meaning of "forbidden," *tabu* can be "sacred," "holy," or "reserved for a chief."

"There will be no truck today," Ratu Aca told us. "But I have found you a taxi. Twenty-five dollars is the fare. Don't pay any more. Indians are very smart—see tourist men like you, say 'Taxi to Nadrau fifty dollar.' No! Say '*only* fifty dollar.' " He laughed softly, shaking his head. "Indian very smart. If something costs six dollars, they tell you ten, then sell it to you for eight and tell you this is special price."

I had thought that the Ratu was himself waiting to go to Nadrau, but this was not the case. He had spent the morning with us merely out of hospitality, and the only way we could repay him was to take his picture and promise to send him a copy. We exchanged addresses.

"Many, many Canadians come here," Ratu Aca said.

And as if to confirm his remark an Indian walked by wearing a T-shirt with the separatist slogan REPUBLIC OF WESTERN CANADA.

◆

The gravel road to Nadrau crosses the dry, overfarmed Tavua lowlands. In this drought the land looked trampled and exhausted, not an inch untrodden by a human foot: the look of India brought to Fiji.

The road snakes up into grassy hills gashed by ravines, and as the coastal plain drops away the ocean appears, silver beneath a silver sky, hazy with the smoke of field fires. The slanting afternoon light reveals the terraces of ancient forts built on the summits of steep hills. Beside the road grow poinciana, pines, wild banana, and the *balabala* tree fern—a living relic of the Mesozoic. Pines become more common as the taxi climbs, until their planted ranks replace the plundered hardwoods.

The road flattens out at Nadarivatu, where there's an old British hill station, now the headquarters of the Forestry Department. It was founded by Adolph Brewster, son of the infamous Joske, of the Thumb. Brewster lived in the Viti Levu highlands from 1884 to 1909; later he published a lively account of his experiences, *The Hill Tribes of Fiji*, which I had brought along.

"Nadarivatu," Aseri told us, "means in Fijian language the Stone Bowl, because the Sigatoka River rises near here in a place that look like a bowl."

Brewster, however, records an older explanation that links the name to the myth of Tuleita, the Spirits' Way, the path taken by the shades on their journey to the holy mountains and the after-world.

[The Tuleita] passed right through Nandarivatu, which means in English "The Dish of Stone." The name is taken from a flat slab of volcanic rock which lies embedded there, with its surface just level with the soil, a few steps from the side of the Way. On it are two small indentations like in appearance to the wooden platters on which food is served, which are called *ndari*. They belonged to a mischievous spirit, the *Taukei* or Lord of Nandarivatu, who awaited those painfully travelling to the next world. As they drew near they found the bracken on either side of the path drawn across it and twisted together, which caused them to stray and turn towards the place of the dishes, one of which contained nice ripe bananas and the other inexpressible nastiness. Then their irate guardian roared forth in a terrible voice, "Are your ears pierced?"

Those who could answer yes were allowed to refresh themselves with the bananas; those whose ears were whole had to eat of the "nastiness" before being allowed to continue. Brewster never did find out the significance of ear piercing, but many old-timers of his day had huge distended lobes in which they kept bamboo tubes for carrying tobacco, penknives, and the like.

I read the story aloud; Aseri glanced at Derek's earring and remarked, "I think he is safe from this *tevoro*, too."

Above Nadarivatu rises flat-topped Tomaniivi, its darkness in the afternoon light relieved by brilliant splashes of crimson and orange from wild myrtle on the slopes. Brewster, mistakenly thinking he was the first *kai valagi* to climb it, renamed the 4500-foot peak Mount Victoria; both names are in use today. The mountain is the highest in Fiji but not the holiest; that honour falls on a ridge abutting it, called the Nakauvadra ("The Pandanus Tree") range. At the top of Nakauvadra stands a natural dolmen of three large boulders. This is the entrance to the abode of Degei, the creator-serpent whose vast coils extend into the body of Viti Levu, causing earthquakes whenever he stirs in his primaeval sleep. Brewster visited the spot in 1886 and found it strewn with decaying offerings of weapons and *tabua*. The active cult had virtually ceased, but the name of the old god would be invoked for several decades yet by latter-day Fijian prophets.

About an hour beyond Nadarivatu the road emerges from the trees and runs along the edge of a high plateau with magnificent views of grassy hills, crags, and dark ravines. When we stopped on the height above Nadrau the clouds parted and pools of sunlight fell on the landscape. Below, on a ledge between two ridges, stood the thatched pyramids of the village, interspersed with a few bright roofs of tin.

◆

Ratu Lemeki and several female relatives formed a line outside his house, which stands at the corner of the green. Aseri, as our *mata ni vanua*, had already let him know that we had arrived, and he had sent for us. The group uttered a short greeting chant, almost an ululation—a special honour this—and then shook our hands in the Western way. As we went inside Derek discreetly reminded me of Fijian manners: "Shoes off at the doorstep, enter stooped, and always keep your head lower than the chief's. If you have to walk past anyone, say '*Tulou, tulou*'—excuse me. It's easy to remember—if you're too high you say 'too low.' "

Three men were already seated around a half-consumed *tanoa* of grog. Ratu Lemeki showed us where to sit, so that the occupants of the room made a parabola, with the *tanoa* at its focal point and the chief opposite, at the middle of its open side. The women sat

behind the men, between the server and the door. Aseri rose to his
knees and made a speech after which he leaned forward and put a
bundle of *waka* (dried whole *yaqona* roots we had brought for *sevusevu*) within reach of Ratu Lemeki's herald. The herald picked
them up, sniffed them appreciatively, and placed them beside the
chief, who lightly touched the gift to show it was accepted. Our
hosts gave three loud handclaps and chanted in unison, "*Woi mana,
mana dina.*" The herald answered with a speech of thanks and
dedicated the *tanoa*'s contents to the guests. While this *yaqona* was
being drunk, the *chang, chang, chang* of a steel mortar outside announced the prospect of *tanoas* to come.

After a round of the new *yaqona* Aseri again got up on his knees
and assumed the humble yet dignified pose of one about to make
a presentation. In his left hand he held the whale's tooth, in his
right the outstretched *magimagi*, or sinnet cord. He made a long
speech, unintelligible to me except for mention of Ratu Napolioni,
the late Tui Nadrau. At intervals the chief and his herald uttered
"*Vinaka, vinaka*" ("Thank you; it is good"). When he finished speaking Aseri held out the *tabua* for a moment, and upon the nod of
Ratu Lemeki it was received by the *mata ni vanua*, who sniffed it
deeply and passed it to the chief, who did the same. A speech of
acceptance and a further round of *yaqona* followed. Then Ratu
Lemeki quietly told his herald to take down one of three whales'
teeth hanging from the roofbeam. We were about to be given the
considerable honour of a *tabua* from a chief. The ceremony took a
form similar to the first, but as foreigners we were not expected to
do anything besides keep a respectful silence.

With formalities accomplished, the group relaxed.

"God moves in mysterious ways," Ratu Lemeki said. "If my
truck wasn't in the garage for repairs I could have collected you at
Tavua, but then if my truck was running I would have gone to a
meeting at Monasavu and missed you. As it is, my wife and children
are in Suva. They will be sorry not to see you, but it means I have
a spare bed for you to stay in.

"I must say, Derek, that there is more of you than when you
left us."

Half an hour later the *tanoa* was pushed against the wall, and the women began to sweep the mat floor and lay out a "table" cloth for dinner. Fijian women tend to assume what we would consider traditional roles—domestic duties, teaching and nursing—but their status has risen greatly since ancient times, when all but the highest born were virtual chattels of men. "Women, indeed, are regarded as a sort of property," wrote Thomas Williams, "but there is no truth in the assertion that the natives sell their women among themselves. Whatever there has been like this, has been taught them by the white men." (Nor was this all: the Fijian expression for homosexuality translates as "white man's doings.") Napkins, plates, and cutlery were set at each place, and there were finger bowls for those who preferred to eat with the hands. Ratu Lemeki, sitting at the head of the cloth, said a long grace in Fijian. A row of woolly heads replied "*Ameni.*"

Fijians do not linger over their food. About ten minutes were allowed for each course. Soon the big steaming basins of yams, *dalo*, and rice were half empty, as were the bowls of curried bully beef and the platter of fried fish. I was amazed at the quantities of carbohydrate that were eaten. Aseri alone devoured a pile of yams and *dalo* equivalent in size to half a dozen large potatoes.

Afterwards Ratu Lemeki poured everyone a cup of tea; ashtrays were sought and cigarettes lit. Derek complimented our host on the fish—a benefit of the new dam at Monasavu.

"Yes, we call this new fish *maleia*. I think it's a very good fish."

"How do you spell that?" I asked, noting it down.

"It's called *maleia* because they come from Malaya—we never saw them before."

Derek had warned me that all one could expect to eat in the highlands were *dalo* and bully beef, or cassava and tinned mackerel. Meat has always been scarce in the interior. Nowadays people keep cattle as well as the native pigs, but these are slaughtered only for family and community feasts. Villagers will go without fresh meat for months, then sit down and consume a dozen animals in three days. Between feasts, protein is obtained from tinned goods and small game. Birds, bush rats, flying foxes and lesser bats: nothing is *tabu* unless it happens to be the totem of a local clan.

(Brewster relates that the Fijians took a great liking to feral cats escaped from settlers' farms—there had been none in Fiji before contact. When the magistrate of Levuka jail ordered some Fijian prisoners to dispose of his tiresome tom, they asked for, and received, permission to eat the beast for Christmas dinner.)

♦

The house had wooden shutters instead of glass windows, and when we awoke rather late next morning it was still dark inside. Threads of sunlight stretched across the room from tiny chinks in the walls. I got up and immediately tripped over a lawnmower near the bed. So this was the secret of all those well-trimmed *raras*. As I soon discovered, a Fijian village, like a Canadian suburb, hums with the sound of mechanical mowing once a week. In other Third World villages I have known, the job is done by starving goats, which remove all greenery and leave their dung in return. But Fijians keep only cattle and pigs, and they do not encourage them to come near the homes of men. Cutting the village grass is an ancient chore, and bedrooms are the traditional place for storing tools. Mower has superseded scythe, but the cultural pattern endures.

We had retired at 2 A.M., the *tanoa* finally dry. Aseri wrapped himself in a blanket and went to sleep in the living room; Derek and I were given the sleeping platform usually occupied by Ratu Lemeki's children. There were many layers of soft mats and plenty of blankets, but I rolled out my sleeping bag and was glad of it. Nadrau is at almost three thousand feet and the night air is cold.

I cautioned Derek not to snore.

"Don't worry; you'll sleep well after all that grog," he said. The next thing I knew it was nine o'clock in the morning and I'd had one of the most restful nights of my life.

I threw a towel over my shoulder and walked to the outdoor shower stall shared by several houses in this part of the village. The air was still cool, and the water—piped from a mountain stream—icy. The sides of the stall came only to shoulder height; people greeted me as I stood there, shaving, admiring the sun that slanted through the pines and palms around Nadrau and lit up the bursts of hibiscus and bougainvillaea beside the houses. Patches of mist lingered on the slopes above the village, and the crisp-smelling air was filled with birdsong. The birds I couldn't identify, but the garrulous mynah of the coast was absent here.

When I got back to the house Aseri gave me a troubled look.

"Ronald, in Fijian custom you should not carry anything on your head or shoulders in the house or presence of a chief. Your towel. . . ."

To atone for this *faux pas* I became increasingly punctilious in what I took to be Fijian etiquette—stooping lower than before, uttering "*tulou, tulou*" with greater frequency. Derek watched my conduct with rising amusement over breakfast; at last he said:

"Really, loosen up a bit. You don't have to trail your knuckles along the floor like a gorilla."

Breakfast, like all the meals we ate at Nadrau, was brought from a nearby house by a sister and two teenage nieces of Ratu Lemeki. At first they were very retiring, but when we thanked them for the meal one of the girls chatted to us about her plans to become a nurse. She was fully bilingual; her accent had the diphthongs of Fergus, not the flattened vowels of Aseri and the older men, who had learned English as a second language.

"You know," Ratu Lemeki said as he poured a third round of tea, "I used to think that all Europeans spoke English. I thought English was the language of white people everywhere. And then the first time I go to Nadi airport I see very many foreigners with skin like English"—he touched the pale skin of his palm—"but I can't understand one word they are saying. That's when I found out they all have their own dialects—French, German, Italian.

"That was also the first time I ever fly. Oh, it was a bad flight. I went from Nadi to Suva in a small, very small, plane. That night was all clouds, rain, and fog. And you know in a little plane you can see everything the pilot is doing. Well, I looked in the cockpit and saw him twiddling knobs and things, and then I look through his window and I realize he can't see anything out there. And I said to myself, 'We die tonight for sure.' "

Ratu Lemeki took us on a walk to the new waters of the Monasavu dam, which now cover the area that Derek, Aseri, and several Nadrau helpers had explored for archaeological remains. It took more than an hour to reach the plateau where the road ran, as Ratu Lemeki, dressed in red shirt, khaki trousers, and army boots, stopped to introduce us to everyone met on the way. One man accompanied by a pack of dogs was about to go hunting in the forest for wild pig; others were engaged in the heavy task of clearing hillside fields for *dalo*, yams, cassava, and fruit trees.

Fijian agriculture follows the time-honoured slash-and-burn system. The bush, except for valued trees, is cut from a small area and burned when dry. The soil is then turned over with digging sticks or spades, and planted in crops for two or three seasons. Then it is abandoned to the bush for a fallow period of anything between seven and thirty years, depending on fertility. These "plantations"—as Fiji people call their gardens no matter how small— slowly migrate across the landscape, leaving a tangle of secondary growth in their wake. Thus only a small area produces at any one time; but the wisdom of these methods has been proved by the disastrous effects of Western intensive farming in jungles such as the Amazon. The luxuriance of a tropical forest resides in its trees, not in the soil.

From the ridge above Nadrau you can see that the village sits on the very border between the wet and dry halves of Viti Levu. To the west range upon range of treeless hills and *talasiga* slopes block any sight of the sea. Eastwards, the direction in which we were going, the jungle soon claims the land, crowding the trail, shutting one in sinuous leafy avenues with no view except for an occasional glimpse of Tomaniivi rising from the forest. It was impossible to see the man-made lake; the best we could do was follow Ratu Lemeki down muddy paths to the rising water's edge—to ravines which were now still inlets, green with the reflected tones of overhanging, drowning trees. The stillness is what I remember most— that and the smell of leafmould, clay, and strange scents from unseen flowers.

It was late afternoon when we emerged again on the escarpment above Nadrau. Lengthening shadows created a chiaroscuro of meandering knife-edge ridges and bald hills. There was no hint that this was an island, that the Pacific Ocean lay all around; it was as if we stood in the middle of a vast, unpeopled continent. Viti Levu, "Great Fiji": these four thousand square miles had become the world.

The chief stood quietly for a time, then pointed out features of interest: the ridge behind the village, cut by a large ditch and built up with terraces, obviously an ancient fort; and beyond, forming the northwestern horizon, the plateau of Taladrau, according to legend the Nadrau people's original home. He turned in the opposite direction and drew our gaze to a rock outcrop about three miles away, erupting from the green hillside like a lone tooth in a child's jaw:

"That big rock there is the ancestor place of our neighbours, the Navatusila people. It is called Cadrasiga—in Fijian language the Rising Sun."

The landscape of Fiji abounds in such *yavutu*, or mythic origin places—rocks, hilltops, springs—believed to be the dwelling places of the tribal ancestors, or anthropomorphized ancestors themselves. Brewster writes of how the early Wesleyan missionaries made a point of destroying or desecrating such things. But the old traditions did not disappear so easily. Nanuku Creek, which feeds the new dam, is still known as the abode of Tui Roko Marama, a serpent-queen who is the ancestral god of the Nadrau warrior clans.

◆

Fijian social and political structure was (and largely still is) a hierarchy of kin-based groups, beginning with the *i tokatoka*, a patrilineage or extended family made up of brothers' households. A number of these composed a *mataqali*, or patrilineal clan; and several *mataqali* formed the *yavusa*, or "tribe," a kin group descended from a common ancestor-god such as the Tui Roko Marama.

Ideally, a *yavusa* comprised six clans fulfilling complementary roles: *mataqali turaga*, from whose members came the chiefs; *sauturaga*, which provided the chief's executives; *mata ni vanua*, or clan of heralds, ambassadors, and masters of ceremony; *bete*, the priests, whose leader, the *kalou ni yavusa* ("god of the tribe") was an oracle and in some ways an incarnation of the tribal god; *bati*, the warrior clan; and *kai vale* ("house people"), the servants.

In practical terms—because of war, feud, extinction, and migration—the number of *mataqali* in a *yavusa* might vary, and their theoretical functions were not always adhered to. At Bau, for example, the head of the *sauturaga* clan (the "prime minister") deposed the royal chief in a coup d'état about two centuries ago. Since then the ruler of Bau has been called not *tui* but *vunivalu*—the warlord or commander-in-chief.

The *yavusa* was the largest social group based purely on kinship, but a number of these might confederate (not always voluntarily) to form a paramount chiefdom, or *vanua*, whose leader would hold the title *tui*. Even broader alliances, called *matanitu*, were sometimes formed, but they seem to have been unruly and ephemeral in precontact times. When Cakobau took the unprecedented title Tui Viti ("King of Fiji") and tried to impose the first national government, his regime was generally known as the *matanitu*.

The layout of a Fijian village expresses social structure in both space and time. In a village of a single, ideal *yavusa* the houses of the six clan heads would be built around the edge of the green. Dwellings are called *vale;* in addition there are *bure*, or houses of ceremonial function: the chiefly *bure*, where public business is discussed; the *bure kalou*, or spirit house of the tribal god (replaced nowadays by the church); a clubhouse *bure* for men; and possibly a lodging house for visitors and tributaries. Older men of high status sometimes have private *bure* where they relax away from the family and entertain their friends.

The distance of a house from the *rara* is an indication of its owner's status within his clan at the time the village was first planned; and a further measure of his worth is the mound (*yavu*) on which the house stands. Chiefly houses may rest on a *yavu* more than three feet high, faced with river stones, whereas a commoner's house is often no more than a few inches above ground level and surrounded by a token row of pebbles. These differences in size do not determine a man's prestige so much as reflect it. The size and finish of the *yavu* show the amount of labour he could marshal from kith and kin when he built it. In ancient Fiji the largest mounds of all belonged to the tribal temples; in some cases they were stone-faced step pyramids several yards in height.

A traditional Fijian house lasts only some twenty years, but its *yavu* stays in the same family for generations, regardless of whether the site is occupied. A house is usually abandoned and allowed to rot whenever the head of the household dies. The next generation builds on a different site nearby, but the family will return to the original *yavu* when the new house in its turn must be abandoned.

To a Fijian, therefore, the disposition of occupied and deserted house mounds says much about the cycles of life, death, and prestige. The sight of a small house on a large *yavu* is, like a stately home with closed-off wings, a sign that the family has gone down in the world.

(All of the above, it must be said, is an oversimplification of Fijian social structure; but it has become entrenched in academic literature and the landholding laws of Fiji. Anthropologists and Fijians—and there are several who are both—still dispute the validity of this "official" model; the variation from region to region is probably far greater than is generally recognized.)

The falling sun cast long shadows among the orderly collection of haystacks that is Nadrau, and aromatic smoke was rising from the kitchen huts. You could see that the village reflected much of the traditional settlement pattern. The dwelling houses *(vale)* are rectangular in plan and have ridge-poles, but the *bure* are square, with pyramidal roofs. Derek pointed to the largest of the *bure* type:

"That's the house of the village god. The living god, I mean. There isn't a temple anymore, of course, but it's interesting that his is the only dwelling with a pointed roof. I used to play chess with his son when I lived here, but I can't tell you much about him. He has clairvoyant and healing powers. In fact, just before we began our project he predicted that foreigners were about to come and stay in the village. It's a rather sensitive matter—I never felt good about asking questions."

I would have liked to know whether the living god went to church on Sunday like all the other villagers, but I, too, didn't have the nerve to ask. We dropped the subject when we caught up to Ratu Lemeki.

"On the coast," Derek continued, "they use the word *bure* for any thatched building of the Fijian type, but that's just because most of the dwellings are made of modern materials now. You can't blame them—concrete stands up much better to hurricanes."

You could see that the same thing was happening gradually in

Nadrau. Perhaps a third of the houses were of wood or cement block with metal roofs. The *vale levu*, or great house, of the late chief was already gracefully rotting; patches fallen from the thatch revealed the intricate lattice of its frame. At one side of the *rara* was a large stack of concrete blocks—amassed to build a modern chiefly house for Ratu Lemeki when he is installed as Tui.

◆

On our second evening in Nadrau we drank *yaqona* from sundown until after midnight. It induced a numbness in the mouth and throat that reminded me of chewing *coca* leaves; but instead of the surge of energy produced by cocaine, I felt relaxed and euphoric. There was no impairment of speech or limbs; I could walk steadily when rising, as all kava drinkers must, to relieve myself at regular intervals. (At night it was acceptable to urinate discreetly in nearby bushes instead of making the trek to the privy on the hillside. Ratu Lemeki had humorously indicated this the first evening: "I've got some sugar cane in the plantation behind the house which is getting very dry.")

There were six drinking now: ourselves, the chief, his herald (who knew little English), and the mixer, named Eroni, which he said was the Fijian equivalent of Ronald.

Ratu Lemeki's present house was a sturdy wood-frame building left by the Americans after the war. (Thousands of American and Commonwealth troops were stationed at Nadrau and many other parts of Fiji against the risk of a Japanese invasion.) In the soft light of the hurricane lamps the old unpainted lumber acquired almost the texture of wattle and thatch. The floor was soft with layers of springy grass sandwiched between the housemats and the boards beneath. The house was in effect a study in voluntary acculturation—in what Fijian culture has chosen to accept from the West. There were no tables or chairs, but there was furniture in the shape of a wardrobe, two china cabinets, and a large wooden trunk—items the Fijians find much more useful. A wooden partition covered in barkcloth separated the living room from the sleeping and storage area. Along a crossbeam above this division there hung the usual calendars and photographs, together with several *tabua*, and some large white cowrie shells, which only nobility may possess. One photograph showed a Fijian chief of the last century in ceremonial dress. He was swaddled in enormous rolls and tongues of barkcloth *(masi)*; all you could see of the man was a muscular bare arm and a stern countenance glaring from fold on fold of chiefly wealth.

"That's my great-grandfather," Ratu Lemeki said. "The picture was taken about a hundred years ago; the original is in the British Museum, I think. When my father attended the royal visit at Bau, the Queen gave him two copies of the picture as a gift. That man had twenty-six wives."

In the 1860s and '70s Ratu Lemeki's ancestor decided that Nadrau would not try to resist the new order proclaimed by Cakobau and the white men. His Navatusila neighbours had taken the opposite course, sheltering renegade cannibals from all over the island and committing the defiant murder of Reverend Baker. They even sent a choice cut of the missionary to the Tui Nadrau in the hope of making him an accessory after the fact, but he refused to accept it and ordered it thrown away. (Years later, however, a Nadrau man confessed to Brewster that the Reverend's thigh had been intercepted on its way to the garbage dump: "What is the use of lying? If the truth be known I did eat part of Mr. Baker. . . . I and some other small boys got hold of it, and cut it up into small pieces and cooked it . . . with the proper spinach.")

Ratu Lemeki spoke a careful, unelided English in a strong, quiet voice like an educated African's. Fijians who have English as a second language speak it well, but they tend to lose plurals (Fijian does not inflect) and articles, which exist in Fijian but are governed by different rules. Besides revealing the syntax of their own language, mistakes made by Fijians (by all foreigners, for that matter) show up the illogicalities of ours. I speak; you, we, and they speak; but he *speaks?* What earthly use is this one vestigial declension? The Fijian and the Fiji Indian seldom bother with it.

The conversation of the Nadrauans was a remarkable blend of sophistication and naïvety. They were well informed about recent air disasters in Canada and about the career of train robber and folk hero Ronald Biggs. And they listened, delighted, to Derek's bear stories, the stock in trade of any Canadian.

"Bear is like gorilla?" Ratu Lemeki asked. "Stand up and walk like man?"

"Wild pig is the only dangerous beast here," Eroni offered, "except men and devils."

Eroni always spoke in a cheerfully ironic tone that raised a laugh. He was special kin to the Chief; his mother was a close relative of Ratu Lemeki's, which made him *vasu*—a person allowed certain privileges including the role of jester in the Tui's presence. It suited his personality.

Just then the door blew open with a blast of cold air and the glimpse of a starry night.

"Come in, sir," Eroni said. "Come in, Mr. Devil."

This time the laughter was a little forced; I guessed that the presence of devils outside at night was not always a joking matter.

Derek took out his tobacco (he had been smoking Rothmans until now) and began to roll.

"What's this you have there? Drugs?" Eroni demanded. "I will show you Fiji drug." He produced a twist of dark native tobacco, like a tarred rope, from his pocket. He tore a narrow strip of paper from a *Fiji Times* and with impressive skill made a cigarette about eight inches long, thin and tightly packed in a spiral of newsprint.

"Once an Indian in Tavua asked me if I want to buy a marihuana cigarette, so I said 'OK' and he sell it to me. Well, I brought it home and I waited for the courage to try it. I heard it make people crazy, and my wife say I'm crazy enough already. Then one day I went into an empty house. I shut all the doors and start to smoke. . . ." He paused, drawing theatrically on his homemade spliff. "Nothing . . . nothing . . . nothing. I think, what's all this marihuana about? So I open up this cigarette and have a look inside, and I see it is made of one leaf tied with a little bit of thread. And inside there is only three small things like peanut, like little bits of brown peanut. So I throw it away. Later another Indian tell me, 'That bad Indian sold you a *beady*'—some sort of Indian tobacco, not drug at all.

"But that, my friend"—he wrinkled his nose at Derek's Drum—"smell like real drug."

Derek laughed and passed his tobacco to Eroni, accepting the Fiji twist in return. (Things are always passed around the kava circle, never across the front of the *tanoa*.) He took a cautious puff, then handed it to me. I thought I could manage strong tobacco, but this was unbelievably acrid, a hot brown soup that invaded my windpipe and nostrils.

"Fiji drug," said Eroni. "*Tavako.*"

Curious, I thought when I'd recovered, how quickly tobacco caught on with Fijians. When they first saw it in the early 1800s they thought the sailors smoking it might be gods with power over fire. But by the time Brewster was travelling among the hill tribes tobacco was firmly established. I do not smoke regularly, but I found myself agreeing with him that *yaqona* induces a craving to do so.

I lost count of how many times Ratu Lemeki's great *tanoa* was filled and emptied. It was a magnificent piece of woodwork, with six legs and a long *wa tabu*, or "sacred cord" of braided *magimagi* attached to a nubbin between the front legs. This cord, decorated with large cowries, is stretched out toward the chief for formal presentations but kept coiled beneath the bowl in social drinking.

Cigarette smoke and the odour of kerosene lanterns filled the softly lit house; it felt cosy, like a ship's cabin or an English pub. The talk turned again to language.

"In Nadrau," said Ratu Lemeki, "we understand many dialects because we live in the middle of the island. The name *Nadrau* means "The Hundreds," and they say it comes from the time when a hundred languages were spoken around here."

There are now thought to be about thirty main dialects of modern Fijian, with a major linguistic divide between west and east Viti Levu. Many dialects within each sector are mutually intelligible (with practice), but the divide between the two areas may be as great as between German and Dutch, or even Dutch and English.

The Nadrau people gave examples of how their speech differs from the Bauan *lingua franca*, which is taught alongside English in schools. The language of Bau is the only version of Fijian spread by newspapers, radio, and the Church; almost all Fijians are literate in it, even if they have no English. There is some resentment of this enforced uniformity—but the standardization of Bauan has ensured that Fijian survives as a viable language in the modern world.

The process probably began before the European impact. Thomas Williams noted *circa* 1850 that the dialect of Bau was already in use along the coasts. He added: "Mbau [Bau] . . . is at once the Athens and the Rome of Fiji; and it is the language as spoken there, into which the Scriptures have been translated."

In those days the Bauans were not as happy about this as might be imagined: they regarded their language as too sacred and exalted for the lips of foreigners. One wonders what they would think of the many borrowings from English with which Bauan is now sprinkled, although words have been thoroughly naturalized with that talent for absorbing outside elements that is so characteristic of Fijian culture:

bia	beer
bulumakau	cattle, beef ("bull and a cow")
kabani	company
kokoroti	cockroach
kovana	governor
lokamu	jail ("lock 'em up")
vusi	cat ("pussy")
Tevita	David
Varani	France

◆

The days at Nadrau settled into a rhythm of slow mornings, afternoon walks, and evenings around the *tanoa*. The other villagers seemed almost as relaxed—no one stirred from his house much before nine—but this is not to say that they were idle. Gardens had to be dug and weeded, cattle herded, and there were communal tasks like house repair, mowing the acres of grass, and preparing for the next big feast.

In a few weeks there was to be a wedding; men of the husband's *mataqali* were building a large shelter for the party and digging *lovo* (earth ovens) in which to roast the animals.

"At my own wedding," Ratu Lemeki told us, "we killed twenty-seven cows."

Weddings of commoners result usually in the death of only one or two beasts, but there is always a reciprocal give-away between the relatives of bride and groom. In *Under the Ivi Tree*, anthropologist Cyril Belshaw describes a typical occasion, when nine *tabua*, ten four-gallon drums of kerosene, and twelve *masima* were exchanged. (*Masima* are cylindrical blocks of sea salt bound in vine basketry—traditional items of wealth.) Non-Fijians often criticize the apparent "waste" of such gifting; but goods are merely redistributed, not destroyed. In any case, Western weddings are hardly an example of restraint, to say nothing of annual potlatches such as Christmas.

"Ronald, will you say grace for us tonight?" Ratu Lemeki asked, as we sat crosslegged before the last of the ample dinners in his house. (We had decided to begin our hike across the middle of the island the next day.) I was not brought up with the custom of saying grace; the best I could do was recite an old formula remembered from school. By Fijian standards it was much too short.

"For what we are about to receive, may the Lord make us truly thankful. Through Jesus Christ, Our Lord, amen."

"*Ameni, ameni.*"

I felt dishonest in this sham of piety, but could not have refused the request without causing deep offence. I am not formally religious. An irreverent remark of Derek's came to mind: "I think Christianity was good for the Fijians. I'd much rather they were Methodists than cannibals." Fiji seemed a rare exception to the usual pattern: in too many parts of the world Christianity has been little more than the spiritual arm of conquest and exploitation. How many cultures were maimed by dogmatic attacks on their central values? How many tribes have been softened up by missionaries, then exterminated or enslaved? But the Fijians managed to blunt the excesses of Methodism: they became devout followers of Christ, but they kept their *mana* and *yaqona*, their holy places and tribal gods.

◆

After dinner the six-legged *tanoa* was brought to the middle of the room, and its sinnet *wa tabu* with the cowrie shells stretched out towards the chief.

"I'll say my formal goodbye tonight so you can get away first thing in the morning," Ratu Lemeki said. "You should make an early start; otherwise you may not reach the next village by nightfall. Tonight I have a little treat for you—green *yaqona*. If you never tried it fresh before I think you will like it. It is sweeter, and you do not feel so slow the next day."

(It was true that our slow mornings at Nadrau might have had something to do with the soporific properties of kava.)

Present were Eroni; Apimeleki, a man about Aseri's age who had worked for Derek on the project; and the *talatala*, or Methodist minister, a gregarious young man attired in a red floral *sulu* and black leather jacket. Eroni and Apimeleki brought in a block of sandstone and a large kava root, freshly dug up and washed. Eroni stripped to the waist and began the hard work of grinding the root on the stone until he produced a large ball of putty-coloured pulp. This he passed to Apimeleki, the mixer for tonight.

Everyone put out his cigarette and assumed the formal sitting posture. The presentation went something like this:

> Mixer: *Sa buli oti na yaqona.* ("The *yaqona* is formed.")
> Chief's herald: *Dou losea.* ("Wring it.")

Apimeleki placed the *yaqona* in a cloth and gracefully mixed the infusion, raising the muslin ball in his hands and squeezing the mixture through his clenched fingers for Ratu Lemeki to assess the strength.

> Chief: *Sa rauta.* ("It is sufficient.")
> Mixer: *Sa darama na yaqona.* ("The kava is prepared.")

Herald, mixer, and Eroni clapped thrice in unison, chanting *"Woi mana, mana dina."* The herald then rose to his knees to make the speech of dedication:

> Chief's herald: *A i sevu, a i sevu ni yaqona sa koto e na davi me ra bulabula tiko na neimami turaga, me lewai vakavinaka tiko na neimami vanua.* ("An offering of kava in the bowl, that our chiefs may flourish, that the people of our lands may be well governed and prosperous.")

This was followed by similar phrases dedicating the *yaqona* as a farewell gift and expressing Ratu Lemeki's wishes for a safe and pleasant journey. Aseri replied with a speech of thanks for the presentation and the chief's hospitality. When he resumed his cross-legged pose there was another triple clap in unison, after which Ratu Lemeki said *"Talo yaqona"* ("Pour the kava").

The sacred cord was tucked under the *tanoa* after the first, formal round, and conversation began.

"I think we all got another sunburn today," the chief said. "Look at Derek; he is glowing like the sun himself."

Derek's face and unprotected pate were the colour of a boiled lobster. Everyone laughed. Ratu Lemeki added, touching his own dark and rather furrowed forehead:

"Me too. I am black, and I feel it too. Europeans think we do not burn but we do."

Apparently, Ratu Lemeki had been something of a Prince Hal when his father was Tui. Derek had spent more than one beery evening with him at the Tavua Hotel bar in the old days. But now he had an understated dignity that was formal or informal as occasion demanded, that was strong without being self-assertive. The Tui-elect was evidently a man grown to the office he was about to assume.

Eroni brought out his Fiji tobacco and rolled an impressive twist; Derek and I, perhaps from bravado and the craving to smoke induced by *yaqona*, could not resist trying it again. This was a mistake—sunburn catalyzed by *tavako* produced a severe headache. I was not, therefore, feeling my best when Ratu Lemeki called on me to tell a story. Fiji has no television, and its absence has certainly preserved the verbal arts. (I do not like to contemplate what will happen to Fijian village life if the winking light of the world ever intrudes on these kava evenings so central to the social fabric.) But, as one not raised in an oral tradition, I found the prospect of telling a story on demand daunting. Ideas deserted me. At last I remembered reading a short article in the *Fiji Times* on the death of Inca Atau Wallpa—it was in the "Today in History" column and marked the four hundred and fiftieth anniversary of the Peruvian monarch's death. This would do nicely, I thought.

I told the familiar tragedy of the Inca's ransom, of how Atau Wallpa, realizing the white men's hunger for gold, offered to fill a room with it, and two other rooms with silver, in a vain effort to buy his freedom.

"Of course, the Spaniards took the gold and killed the Inca anyway," I continued. "Those things happened exactly four and a half centuries ago, but the native people of Peru"—I avoided the word *Indian* for obvious reasons—"have never forgotten. They are about half the population of Peru today, but they have little land, no power, and are ruled by the descendants of the Spaniards and by people of mixed blood.

"They have a belief, a belief that the Inca emperor—who was almost a god as well as a king—will come back to them one day. They believe that the ancient world still exists as it was, underground—beneath the visible world brought by the Spaniards. And they believe it is possible for these two worlds to turn over, or reverse, so that the time of the Inca will one day be restored.

"In their legends they say that the head of the Inca king—cut off by the Spaniards—is buried somewhere beneath their old capital city. Slowly, all these four hundred and fifty years, the head has been growing a new body. When the Inca's new body is complete, he will emerge triumphant; the worlds will turn over, and the Peruvians will once again be masters in their own country."

I felt the silence immediately. Because of the unusually strong kava, sunburn, and headache, my delivery had been poor—terrible, no doubt, when compared to the oratorical fluency of Fijians. But I expected them to say something, ask questions, or feign interest.

There was nothing. Just a silence, uncomfortable, even shocked. What was wrong? Had they thought I was patronizing them with a fable? Were they perhaps alarmed by the possible analogy between the situation of the indigenous Peruvians and their own worst fears about what might happen to them if the non-native half of Fiji's population took control?

Slowly the lighthearted tone that had prevailed before my tale re-established itself, like tentative chatter at a cocktail party after a glass has crashed to the floor.

4

▲▲▲

THE SPIRITS' WAY

We woke at seven after sleeping the sound, dreamless sleep of *yaqona*. Despite Ratu Lemeki's suggestion that we leave "first thing," he gave us a substantial breakfast of papaya, fried fish, diced yam, and "scones" (a kind of soda-bread).

"Derek, Ronald, *kana vaka levu*, as we say—eat well." Then he turned to me and added, nodding at Derek, "I worry about this one because he eat little last night."

We said goodbye to the Chief's female relatives who had looked after us so well, then followed him through the village to the footpath which leads down to the Sigatoka River and on to the settlements of Nubutautau, Namoli, and Korolevu. Apimeleki had stayed the night (after drinking kava until two) and I was glad of his offer to carry one end of my backpack—it would have been unacceptable to wear it in the presence of the Chief, or indeed when crossing the middle of any village. Like much of Fijian etiquette, the rule derives from the days when men were always armed and it was important to show that anything one carried was not in a threatening position.

Ratu Lemeki led us a hundred yards beyond the outskirts of

Nadrau to where the trail drops out of sight into the ravine of Qaliqali Creek, a tributary of the Sigatoka.

"About halfway to Nubutautau you will come to a spring, but fill your water bottle at the river anyway—it gets very hot on the road."

We shook hands, said farewells and thank-yous. Ratu Lemeki raised both arms above his head in a chiefly gesture of valediction.

As the path dropped the thousand feet to the river it became increasingly muddy and hemmed in by bushes on the slopes of the ravine. At the creek we entered a natural bower of overhanging branches and creepers that shut out the sunlight. A green luminescence enveloped the dark water and the pale rocks over which it flowed; there was a cool smell of leafmould spiced with the scent of orchids. So enchanting was it, and so dark, that I scarcely noticed an elderly Fijian woman bent over a staff, picking her way across the stones like a wandering Oriental sage.

The trail kept to the gloom along the shaded streambank, then turned right and emerged from the trees above the river. The Sigatoka gorge was filled with sun so bright it seemed to bleach the boulders and water-worn bedrock uncovered by the drought-diminished flow. I was able to hop across from stone to stone—the frame and cinch of the backpack held my burden steady. Derek, with a lighter but clumsier load in a shapeless knapsack, cut himself a stick and waded the river, not bothering to roll up his jeans or take his boots off. Aseri, carrying a large overnight bag by looping a handle over each shoulder, did likewise. A few yards upstream I stripped and swam in a warm, deep pool, then sat on a sun-warmed rock and shaved to a chorus of birds. The spot was too beautiful to be left in a hurry, especially since Ratu Lemeki's description of the route indicated that we wouldn't meet up with the river again that day.

The opposite bank had none of the shade that had made the descent so cool. By now it was after ten o'clock. The trail was steep and sun already fierce. After climbing for about twenty minutes it was clear that Derek was in a bad way. Beads of sweat stood out on his crown like dew on a ripe tomato, his shirt was soaked, and his breath came in rasping heaves.

"You guys go on ahead. . . . I'll catch you up at the mango tree up there." He pointed at some distant greenery on the grassy hill.

"I will carry your pack," Aseri said. "Give it here, Derek. I'll take it." Derek protested at first but was not in any condition to resist. Aseri and I divided the load between us. Fortunately there was more bulk than weight: two pandanus mats for ground sheets, some army blankets, and two or three bundles of *waka*.

"I'm sorry. I wasn't like this last time I was here," Derek said, panting.

"That is true," Aseri said. "You should stop smoking."

"It's not the smoking," Derek gasped, "it's two years behind a desk. . . . I knew I was out of shape . . . but not this bad. I'm not sure I'm going to manage this hike."

I told him to take it slowly, twenty steps at a time, with rests.

"If we don't reach the next village by tonight it doesn't matter. I don't mind camping out in the bush. I'm not sure I want to spend the night at Nubutautau anyway. Isn't that where they ate Reverend Baker?" I said this to cheer Derek up, but it made Aseri glum—whether from the reference to cannibalism or the prospect of sleeping out amid *tevoro*s, I wasn't sure.

By noon we regained the height it had taken half an hour to lose. Nadrau was visible across the valley—brown haystacks, here and there a tin roof glinting, and on nearby hillsides little plantations that looked as if dabbed on the landscape by a painter's palette-knife.

The trail to Nubutautau follows ridges clothed only in the spear grass that invades dry soil too often burned. The hills west of the Nadrau Plateau may once have been wooded, but today they are bald except for tufts of cover on inaccessible crags, in moist gullies and ravines. Derek was astonished at how the land he remembered as green (he was last here in a wet season) was now the fawn colour of an autumn prairie. He had revived when the worst of the climb was behind us, and began to point out the regular outlines of terracing on anciently fortified hills. To our right was the crest of Naveitalamoli Ridge, where he had examined a fort built as a refuge for Old Nadrau, which lies beside the Sigatoka a few hundred yards upstream from the crossing. The Nadrau people lived there until the end of the last century, but it was by no means the only old Nadrau. In ancient times Fijian villages moved often—to exploit new farming areas, or because of war and internal disputes.

At about one o'clock we reached a clump of giant bamboo and decided to stop for lunch in its speckled shade. The country lay open to the west; a hot, relentless wind blew from the island's dry side, robbing moisture from everything in its path. Tier after tier of ridges and hills stretched from where we sat to the horizon. Somewhere over there were Nadi and the Pacific, forty or fifty miles away, but you could not be sure where the island ended and the sky began. Scattered clouds cast drifting shadow patterns on the land.

In my pack I discovered three cans of "Camp Pie"—an inferior Australian luncheon meat which, if its label can be believed, "may contain beef, and/or mutton, and/or pork byproducts." There wasn't much else: a few tins of sardines, two packets of pilot biscuits, a bag of rice and, in lieu of dried fruit, a box of Big Sister fruitcake mix. I recognized Derek's shopping style and chided him for it.

"It's all right," Aseri said. "Ratu Lemeki gave us this bag of scones." He passed the bag over; I took a scone, cut it open, and spread it with two sardines.

The trail continued to rise more often than it fell. We expected to find the spring mentioned by Ratu Lemeki around each corner, though it was hard to see how water could exist anywhere on these barren slopes. Eventually patches of vegetation became more frequent. Once or twice we caught sight of the river fifteen hundred feet below, a broken coil of silver wire at the bottom of its wooded gorge.

By mid-afternoon Derek was again feeling the strain. He hadn't smoked a cigarette since breakfast, and that, I thought, was a sure sign he must be near the limit. I too was tired; only Aseri, ten years our junior and with recent army training, kept going effortlessly. At about four we reached a bluff that we were certain must be the last before the descent. Here the path was worn deep into the subsoil by generations of horse traffic. It resembled a dry ditch; the view ahead was obscured. But when the route came in sight again, it continued upwards to another, higher ridge.

"That's it," Derek said. "I'm camping here. Why don't you two go down there"—he pointed to a small valley below us—"and see if there's any water. I'd go myself, only I don't think I can."

The valley was heavily forested, but about a hundred feet below the trail there was a small clearing in which stood a Fijian-style house and a number of fruit trees. The house had a padlock on the door; it looked as if the owner had been gone for several weeks.

"I think he left because there is no water here," said a gloomy Aseri.

Below the farmhouse the land dropped away steeply into a crease in the hills that would contain water if there was any to be had. Aseri and I clambered down a precipitous path half obscured by the carpet of creepers on the ground. After dropping a further hundred feet we entered a sombre grove of large trees growing over the gully of a small—dry—stream. But among the rocks were one or two pools—enough to take a drink and fill our canteen.

I asked Aseri if he thought it would be all right to make camp in the clearing.

"I think we should go on to the village. It will be quite near here."

"We can't, believe me. We've got to camp somewhere round here. What I mean is, will the owner mind if we camp on his farm?"

"Not if we keep away from the house," he answered reluctantly. Obviously he didn't relish the idea of camping at all. But he was outvoted.

Making camp involved rolling out our mats on the springy tangle of vines and long grass, putting the bedding on them, and hoping there would be no rain. We decided not to risk a fire, and dined on sardines and pilot biscuits washed down with water.

"Hunger's the best spice," said Derek, and he was right.

The plantation included banana, guava, pandanus, and breadfruit. (Luckily none was ripe—the temptation would have been irresistible.) Beside the house grew a rangy bush with light-green stems and leaves that looked like a nasturtium's. This was *yaqona;* Aseri guessed it was about three years old and would need to grow to twice this age before ending in the *tanoa.* The clearing occupied a natural terrace cupped by a bend in the ridge. It overlooked a valley whose bottom was invisible, and there were spectacular mountains—surely the last great range between here and the coast—across the western horizon. The sun was now falling behind this jagged wall, casting streams of red and orange across the thinly clouded sky, filling the ravine below with a viscous purple light. Between us and the bloated sun, the small thatched house stood silhouetted on the rim of the abyss.

This land was probably leased from its *mataqali* by a *galala*, an independent Fijian farmer released from his communal obligations by an annual cash payment. The British had made customary services *(lala)* to village and chief a part of Fijian colonial law; but later, under pressure from critics who wanted to give Fijians the chance to become entrepreneurs, the *galala* option was made available on certain conditions. Predictably perhaps, *galala* yeomen did not become the model for native economic development along Western lines; but the option did provide an outlet for individuals who did not fit in well with the intimate reciprocity of village life.

Aseri went down to the pool to refill the canteen. Derek, somewhat recovered, rolled a cigarette. We watched the sunset thicken into twilight. I brought up a subject that had been nagging me all day: what had happened when I told the Inca story last night? Had I somehow caused offence?

"I don't think they were offended," Derek said, "just surprised. How far have you got with Brewster's book? There were some crisis cults around here in his day with rather similar ideas. I think the Inca story may have rung some bells."

◆

Western Viti Levu has been the centre of a good many unorthodox beliefs. Long before Europeans arrived, the area seems to have been influenced by Melanesian cults emanating from Vanuatu (the New Hebrides). The most important of these involved rituals to promote the fertility of yams, pigs, and human beings. Secret rites were held in special rectangular precincts that contained four pyramidal stone altars aligned on the cardinal points. These shrines, called *naga*, were built on level ground beside a river or stream.

According to legend, the *naga* cult was brought from across the western ocean by two gods or heroes: Veisina and Rukuruku. These two names respectively symbolize the male and female principles in nature: *sina* (*cina* in Bauan) is the wild spear grass, regarded as a phallic symbol, and *ruku* carries the meanings of "earth," "female," and "vagina." The special plant of Rukuruku was the candlenut, whose shape suggests the female organs. These oily nuts were mounted on spear-grass stems and burned as torches throughout ancient Fiji—thus the female impaled on the male generated light, heat, and, symbolically, life. According to Brewster-Joske, *naga* worshippers were divided into two societies called Kai Veisina and Kai Rukuruku; each society held its rites in the same *naga* enclosure, but in alternating years. The main ceremony took place at the time of the Polynesian New Year, determined by the reappearance of the Pleiades in late October or early November, which was also when the first fruits of the yam harvest were mature. Large quantities of vegetables, pigs, and kava were consumed, and young men were inducted into manhood. Initiates had to crawl over the prone bodies of men disguised with pig blood and entrails to look as if they had been slain. Then, suddenly, the "dead" men rose up, washed in the river, and partook in the feast—a dramatic symbol of transition.

The "male" (Veisina) and "female" (Rukuruku) societies were both composed of men, and there is confusion in the accounts as to what, if anything, was the role of women. Some reports say that women were tabu in the *naga*, others that they brought food for the men, and yet others that the graduated initiates and young women of the tribe united in a sex orgy at the precinct. These inconsistencies probably result from descriptions of different rituals, or from informants' reluctance to reveal what white men would censure as depravity. Brewster translates the word *naga* as "bed," and suggests that the sacred enclosure was a symbolic marriage bed of the tribe.

As the last refuge of independent heathens who refused to accept

Christianity and the national government, the interior of Viti Levu kept alive the *naga* and other secret cults long after they had been suppressed elsewhere. Throughout the 1860s and early '70s pressure began to build against the "wild" Colo, or peoples of the highlands. Nadrau allied itself with the new order, but Nubutautau became the rallying point for all who opposed the new god, the whites, and Cakobau Rex, the presumptuous Tui Viti.

The eating of Reverend Baker was followed by similar incidents. In 1871 two planters were shot while out duck hunting, and suffered the intended fate of their prey. In 1873 a different highland group massacred the Burns family and their workers on an estate near Ba. This was in revenge for settlers' predations and the fact that Mr. Burns's Solomon Islanders had eaten a young man of the highlanders' group, but the attack spurred white vigilantes and the Cakobau government to mount campaigns against the interior. In September 1873 the stronghold of Nubutautau fell to forces led by Major H. Thurston, brother of John Bates Thurston, Cakobau's chief secretary and later a distinguished British governor. Most of the hill people surrendered and accepted a nominal Christianity. Several hundred were taken prisoner to Levuka and sentenced to periods of slave labour on white plantations.

In the following year Cakobau ceded Fiji and his crown to Queen Victoria. Three months after Cession, he and his two sons visited Australia, where they fell ill with measles. All three survived, but they were allowed to return home while still infectious. The Fijians, like the American Indians, had no natural defences against the disease. Within months at least a quarter of Fiji's population died. To the recently pacified hill tribes this was a clear case of divine punishment for forsaking their old gods and submitting to the foreigners. Most of them renounced the new ways and went into open rebellion against church and state.

In 1876 they were defeated by a British force with native auxiliaries that began its campaign at loyal Nadrau and marched down the Sigatoka valley, collecting almost a thousand prisoners on the way. The first governor, Sir Arthur Gordon, later pardoned the rebels and allowed them to return to their villages, so long as these remained unfortified. But the psychological effects of war, plague, conversion, and defeat combined with underground survivals of the old religion to engender a series of crisis cults, or revitalization movements.

The first of these (and the one with the most coincidental similarities to Peruvian messianism) broke out in 1885. It was called the Tuka, a word meaning "that which stands forever" or "the life everlasting." Followers would become immortal and regain their youthful vigour; a judgement day was fast approaching, and on this day the world would be *tavuki*, or turned upside down; the reversal would make the white men servants of the Fijians, and commoners would change places with chiefs.

Rejection of chiefly authority is a theme of the Tuka that appears in later cults, and in political movements of western Viti Levu today. The pre-contact political structure of the west—especially the highlands—was less hierarchical than that of the eastern coast. Hill chiefs were comparatively humble and subject to consensus. But the colonial government imposed much stronger chieftainship through its system of indirect rule based on the eastern model. In the eyes of the highlanders, therefore, the new privileges of chiefs were part of the Bauan-British colonial axis.

The Tuka movement was started by a man named Dugumoi, a commoner who took for himself the title *Navosavakadua*, "He Who Speaks But Once." This was in fact the Fijian term for the British chief justice, referring to his power of life and death. Dugumoi cobbled together a number of Fijian and foreign elements, as a way to turn the *mana* of the whites to native advantage. Followers were called *sotia* (soldiers) and they were taught elaborate drill by *satini* (sergeants). This was partly an attempt to acquire the military discipline of the invaders, but it also included ritual from traditional gesture dances. (British officers were often amazed by the Fijian affinity for drill.)

Dugumoi had already served a couple of years of exile on the Lau Islands for "sedition," and he claimed the British had tried to drown him by throwing him overboard with an anchor chain around his neck. He had survived because he was immortal. He dispensed this immortality—for a fee—in the form of holy water kept in a bottle. So effective were the water's restorative powers that the many young girls he collected as concubines could renew their virginity merely by drinking it.

His theology was an ingenious blend of the Bible and indigenous beliefs. In Fijian myth Degei, the creator-serpent, had enemies: notably the carpenter god's twin sons, Nacirikaumoli and Nakausabaria. These two had fought Degei and then sailed away to escape his wrath. According to Dugumoi their destination had been the land of the white men, who, unable to pronounce their real names, called them Jehovah and Jesus Christ. Degei thus became identified with Satan, the Old Enemy; but this didn't necessarily mean that Tuka members saw their ancient creator as evil—rather, they interpreted the biblical struggle between Jehovah and the Devil in terms of Fijian mythic conflicts between rival gods.

The time of *tavuki*, the world reversal, was to occur when the twin gods returned to Fiji in the company of all the dead ancestors. The faithful would then be rewarded with shops full of calico and tinned salmon—a side to the Tuka that echoes Melanesian cargo cults. In return for this largesse, an albino pig—no doubt symbolic of the British—was being fattened for sacrifice on the day of retribution.

♦

Twice during the night I dreamt I was sleeping in a car. I woke once when the sky was overcast and low, torn with black patches full of stars. The night was . . . loud; yes, that was the word. The uproar of countless insects and a glimpse of the Southern Cross brought to mind Neruda's phrase, the "barking of the dog stars." At about four I woke again. The moon had risen and seemed to bring with it small puffs of icy air. The foliage of the breadfruit tree above me looked like sooty handprints on the sky.

Dawn brought orange highlights to the distant hilltops. Aseri was up, stamping around to get warm, dressed like a black Palestinian in a balaclava and striped cotton blanket bought in Lebanon.

By seven we were on the road, and had not walked more than

half an hour when we reached a muddy pool beside the path. This was the spring mentioned by Ratu Lemeki, but its water, swarming with tadpoles, was not inviting. Brewster refers to the same spot as one of the landmarks along Tuleita, the Spirits' Way; from his description of the country it is clear that the modern track follows the course of the ancient one, and that the route of the living is largely identical to that of the dead. I wondered if Aseri knew this, and whether it had anything to do with his reluctance to camp out.

Ten minutes beyond the spring we rounded a bluff and entered a thicket of secondary jungle. The path made a tunnel through the bush. At one place where it widened enough to admit the sky we found the remains of a campfire: some stones, burned logs, and charred animal bones.

"Reverend Baker, I presume," Derek said. Aseri was not amused.

The next clearing was much larger; it occupied the crown of the hill and there were bald patches of red earth on its floor. Two *kaka* parrots split the sky with their raucous cries. They were a brilliant, iridescent blue-green on the back and wings, yellow and black on the breast. Aseri said, "There could be wild pig here." But we heard only the liquid, musical notes of more decorous birds and an eerie *woof, woof* from a dove that sounds like the distant barking of a dog. The surrounding jungle was older here and very thick. The black stems and feathery green umbrellas of *balabala* tree ferns stood out from bushes with wine-red leaves and pale yellow vines.

This indigenous tangle abruptly gave way to a stand of Caribbean pine with all the monotypic boredom of a Canadian forest. The smell of resin brought me a twinge of homesickness, but it was very brief.

The trail then made a steep, muddy descent into a forest of giant bamboo more than forty feet high; from this we came out into open country with a fine view to the west. Clouds were throwing their shadow play on a range of hills that dropped down into the Sigatoka valley. The river itself was hidden by a broad bench of level ground covered in windswept grasses; and in the middle of this stood a village of a dozen thatched houses around a square *rara* shaded by mango trees: Nubutautau, home of the infamous Navatusila.

It was hot now and our canteen had been empty since breakfast.

We approached the edge of the settlement, sat in the shade of a mango, and waited to be noticed. A little girl walked by with a piglet straining on a rope before her, like an eager puppy. Aseri quietly asked for water; she smiled and skipped off, returning promptly with two older girls who poured us enamel bowls of cool water from a kettle. An old man with bloodshot eyes stopped to chat to Aseri in Fijian.

I am not sure whether the Nubutautau of 1867 stood in exactly this spot, although the great mango trees could well be more than a century old. The largest group of Navatusila now live by the river in a new village, visible as a twinkle of metal roofs a mile from here, below the bluff. Aseri said there was no point in going there; it was out of the way; we would do better to follow a shortcut across the fields—indicated by the old man—and meet up with the river farther downstream. Besides, the new village was Seventh-Day Adventist: we would not be offered any grog.

It seems ironic that the staunchest defenders of the old religion became members of a sect which forbids *yaqona* and all things Fijian that do not conform with a myope's reading of the Bible. But perhaps it is not so surprising. Apart from the obvious problem (succinctly put by Derek as "It's hard to be a Methodist after eating one"), the facile certainties of Adventism appeal to people with a wounded sense of self and a messianic turn of mind.

We hefted our packs, stepped out into the glare, and started across the savannah. Once or twice I looked back at the little village; it was impossible to imagine that the scene of Baker's murder had been anywhere near here.

◆

Reverend Thomas Baker ran a successful mission on the lower Rewa River (between Suva and Bau) for many years, but yearned for bigger things. In 1864 the Wesleyan Church appointed him Missionary to the Interior, but he did not penetrate the highlands until 1867. He could hardly have chosen a worse time: Cakobau had been crowned King of Bau on May 2 and was striving to extend his writ over as much of Fiji as he could. Christianity, adopted by Cakobau in 1854, was an important prop of the King's shaky regime. In the minds of the independent hill tribes, the new god and Cakobau's ambitions were inextricably linked, and both were equally detestable.

Baker travelled slowly through the mountains. Evidently he managed to alienate a powerful chief en route, for, unknown to the missionary, a fine but sinister *tabua* was following his steps. Tribe after tribe reluctantly refused the *tabua* and passed it on—because the price of its acceptance was Baker's death.

On the 20th of July, Baker and his party of Christianized easterners reached Nubutautau and were received coldly by Nawawabalavu, the chief. Baker apparently presented a whale's tooth of his own, and was given a promise of safe conduct through Navatusila lands. But during the night there arrived the other *tabua*, which had sufficient power to "press down" *(dirika)* the humbler offering of the Wesleyans.

It is not known why the Nubutautau chief decided to do what others had declined. Possibly it was a point of honour, since the village had become the main stronghold of those who resisted the new ways. And perhaps there's some truth to the story that Baker settled matters by gravely insulting his host. According to this tale, the chief took a liking to the missionary's ivory comb, "borrowed" it, and stuck it in the elaborate coiffure that all Fijians of rank sported in the old days. Baker, who should have known better, snatched the comb back. This was more than peevishness: it violated the powerful tabu (still observed) against touching the head—the part of the body most imbued with *mana*, especially in a chief. The story may be apocryphal, but it smacks of a martyr's suicidal arrogance.

In the following year Cakobau, under white pressure, sent a poorly organized punitive force. It was easily routed. For a time the Navatusila exulted in their ferocity (it was they who ate the duck hunters), but after their final defeat in 1876 and reduction to Christianity, a deep feeling of guilt overcame them. They believed themselves cursed for their evil deed. The tribe made a series of elaborate *soro*, or atonement ceremonies, to the Methodist Church, but bad luck continued to befall them. On Christmas Day 1894 the heir to the Navatusila chieftainship drowned in the Sigatoka, and the *bure* in which he was buried later burned to the ground.

The Church added insult to injury in songs taught to mission schoolchildren:

> Oh! dead is Mr. Baker,
> They killed him on the road,
> And they ate him, boots and all.

The Navatusila never denied that they cut down Baker with a battle axe, cooked, and ate him; but they deeply resented the white men's low calumny that they had, in ignorance of footwear, eaten his boots with the feet.

◆

While eastern Fiji and the chiefly establishment settled into a relatively easy coexistence with colonial rule, the west, the interior, and disaffected commoners throughout the islands felt left out, even threatened by the new order. Navosavakadua Dugumoi, founder of the Tuka, was exiled for ten years to remote Rotuma (about 300 miles north of Viti Levu), where he died mysteriously at the time of his release. The British made heavy-handed efforts to root out other survivals of the old religion such as the Luveniwai, a young men's society that involved gaining spiritual power from water sprites. (The shrewd Fijians, recognizing ritual when they saw it, managed to continue much of this cult in the guise of cricket clubs. A related set of beliefs underlies the Beqa Islanders' firewalking ability—now a major tourist attraction.)

The Tuka continued to make sporadic reappearances long after the death of its founder. It surfaced again in 1914, and rites involving the "water of life" were reported as recently as the 1970s. But the Tuka's most significant legacy was the influence it had on a new movement that arose in western Viti Levu and spread throughout Fiji just before the First World War.

The early years of the twentieth century were difficult for many Fijians. The old paternalistic rule of the Gordon to Thurston era (1875–1897) had frozen the sale of native land and allowed Fijians to pay their taxes to the government with produce instead of cash. Neither policy was popular with Fiji whites, who were loud advocates of free enterprise and individual land tenure—ostensibly to promote Fijian advancement along the lines of Adam Smith liberalism but in reality to open up native property to European settlers and middlemen. It was the classic strategy by which indigenous, communal societies have been dispossessed everywhere (notably in the "liberal" republics of the Americas), and it was a wolf easy to clothe in the sheepskin of Progress.

Governor Sir Everard im Thurn (1904–1910) was persuaded to unravel the cocoon sealing the Fijian economy from the outside world. He was not without native allies—frustrated minor nobility, enterprising commoners, and a few unscrupulous chiefs who stood to profit by selling off their *mataqali*'s land. The Taukei, as Fijians call themselves, a word synonymous with "native" and "proprietor," saw their ownership shrinking while a handful of foreign planters and storekeepers grew fat. The land sales were eventually halted, but not before deep anxiety had been aroused.

In this climate a bizarre but timely leader emerged: Apolosi R. Nawai, prophet and entrepreneur. He was born near Nadi, a commoner, physically unimpressive, but a powerful speaker:

> For I alone am the only chief of Fiji: it is the will of God. . . .
> You know who I am, Apolosi R. Nawai. . . . In times past I was
> not known while Bau and Rewa were renowned, but wait and
> you will see. . . . God predestined me to be your chief and to
> bring into being a new scheme by which Fiji would be inde-
> pendent in future and free from Government control. . . .

He claimed to worship Degei and the twins, Nacirikaumoli and Nakausabaria, and to have found a box containing *mana* lost at

Vuda by one of the characters in the *Kaunitoni* myth. But the materialistic side of Nawai's movement was far in advance of Dugumoi's calico and tinned salmon. He founded a co-operative society called the Viti Kabani (Fiji Company), and travelled widely through the islands selling memberships and arousing almost fanatical support.

The authorities, impressed at first by the Company's success at encouraging Fijians to grow cash crops such as bananas, soon became worried by the tone of its leader's speeches. The alarm was shared by the Council of Chiefs, who correctly perceived a threat to their traditional power base. The Viti Kabani, preached Nawai, would eventually take over the entire economy of Fiji: there would be no more European firms, Indian shops, or government taxes. The land alienated before Cession and by im Thurn would be taken back; eventually all foreigners would be expelled from Fiji. The Company organization began to resemble a state within a state; it had district officials, its own meeting halls, and (shades of things to come elsewhere) huge rallies controlled by *ovisa* (officers) wearing red armbands. Apolosi lived in royal style, with shiny cars, silk suits, and a harem said to include one of his own daughters. Vast sums were unaccounted for, but nothing criminal could be proved.

Eventually two whites attended one of his meetings and were prepared to swear afterwards that they had heard Nawai say "*Koi au na meca ni matanitu*" ("I am the enemy of the government"). He was exiled without trial (and without much imagination on the part of the British) to Rotuma in 1917. Inevitably, many of the myths surrounding Dugumoi were assumed by Apolosi Nawai: "I am alive after seven years death," he said on his return in 1924. By then the Viti Kabani was finished, but its founder certainly was not. After a brief spell as a successful restaurateur in Lautoka, he founded a messianic movement called Na Lotu ni Gauna, "The Church of the Era," which attracted a wide following in western Viti Levu. (*Gauna* had been the word used by the Tuka for the era following the reversal of the world.)

Apolosi held meetings, preached, and prophesied. In some statements he attacked the British; in others he claimed that power had been conferred on him by the late Queen Victoria. Consistency never interrupted the mellifluous flow of his rhetoric:

> Only two things will survive, the Church of Jesus Christ in Heaven and the British Empire throughout the world. They are united in Apolosi R. Nawai. . . .
> Cakobau is dead and I am his successor—King of Fiji. [Cakobau, of course, had been dead since 1883.]

He is said to have stood on the site of what is now Nadi International Airport (not developed until the 1950s) and predicted that people would one day come there from the four corners of the earth. Other visions were less prescient. The *gauna* would begin with a cataclysm in 1930; when this failed to come about, Apolosi was unabashed:

> The secret year is 1944 and it is then that the truth for which we have struggled so much will emerge and stand forth as proofs of our worthy lives and the life of the New Era. . . . This is the cessation of earthly time.

What did happen in 1930 was a further deportation to Rotuma, this time for ten years. In 1940 his exile was extended for the duration of the war, and the prophet was moved to New Zealand to keep him well away from the advancing Japanese.

He died, back in Fiji, in 1946, but not before he had given himself the title Tui kei Vuravura, "King of the World."

It is easy to ridicule the absurdities of the crisis cults and the charlatanism of their leaders. But such movements arise in societies under severe stress. Fiji as a whole had a comparatively smooth transition to Christianity and European rule; but the west and interior of Viti Levu suffered the trauma of the colonized: the feeling of having lost control, of having to conform to incomprehensible laws, beliefs, and economics, imposed by arbitrary, powerful foreigners. The Tuka and Viti Kabani tried to restore identity and autonomy by seeking a synthesis of Fijian tradition, the Bible, and the new cash economy.

◆

The Nubutautau savannah ends suddenly in steep cliffs about 150 feet above the river. I looked down into bottle-green pools trapped by smooth basins worn in the bedrock. The waters were utterly clear and still, except for twinkling rapids at each change in level. We scrambled down a treacherous path of loose stones and crumbling rock. One wonders how horses manage such a climb, but they have left proof that they do—dried fragments of their dung still gave off a horsey smell.

At the bottom of the cliffs the path led us into woods that hid the sky; soon we came to a tributary waterfall splashing onto boulders in the forest gloom. It is odd and delightful how few mosquitoes there are in Fiji, and neither were there flies here, because the locals had thoughtfully put a wooden fence around the spot to keep cattle and horses out. We stopped only for a drink, and I regretted not taking a bath when the trail began again to climb. But before long it descended to the first crossing. We forded the river at noon. The Sigatoka had grown since last we met it, below Nadrau. We had to wade through water up to our thighs for a distance of fifty feet. Once across we bathed in a natural pool large enough for Olympic events and so deep the bottom was invisible. Some small boys were fishing with spears, their black bodies darting through the water like porpoises.

The path climbs the opposite bank, then falls again to the river within half an hour. Derek and Aseri kept their boots on, but I crossed in bare feet, with shoes in hand. The Sigatoka meanders constantly between sharply cut cliffs on the erosion side and broad pebble fields on the deposit shore. As the ravine becomes deeper the trail makes no attempt to climb its sides—it merely crosses and recrosses from one shingle bank to the next. On some stretches we had to ford every ten or fifteen minutes. It made for slow progress—the water is cold enough to numb the feet, and the stones of the riverbed are often loose and slippery with silt or weeds. Aseri never faltered, but Derek and I each fell once, soaking our clothes and saving the cameras with difficulty. By half past three we had forded the river a dozen times. I became impatient and in hurrying cut my foot. (It wasn't at all serious, and I was glad not to be in Africa where bilharzia is a worry.)

The trail repaid us for its tiresomeness with spectacular scenery. Instead of the sweeping views of the hill country we were given a series of dramatic vignettes: dark pools below cliffs crowned by a shaggy overhang of roots and vines; natural rockgardens full of thorn-apple and vervain; and barren boulder fields that were graphic interplays of sun and shade. The river sang its wild compositions, now deafening, now faint, according to its mood, with occasional interjections from gaudy parrots flying in pairs.

By four o'clock it was clear that we would have to camp out again. There was no sign of Namoli, the next village; both Derek and I were exhausted. We stopped beside a sandbank covered in vervain bushes whose clusters of tiny red and yellow flowers glowed with the brilliance of Christmas decorations. Now that we were still we noticed other life—a large brown hawk (called *manu levu* by Aseri) who patrolled our wake for lizards and mice, and a pair of Fiji black ducks in a pool ahead. Asleep in the branches of a tree not ten yards from our camp hung a flying fox like a shabby leather jacket. Aseri maintained that the large bat was good eating and offered to kill it, but Derek and I found the idea even less appetizing than Camp Pie.

I cooked rice in our only pot—an old enamel mug I never travel without.

"Good thing you were such a boyscout," Derek commented. "I never thought we'd need any of this camping gear."

Aseri cut large leaves from a wild taro to use for plates. Derek warmed up a tin of luncheon meat, which he referred to affectionately as "tinned dog."

"When I worked on Rotuma," Aseri said, "I ate some dog. The Rotumans eat it all the time; they asked me to try it."

"How was it?"

"It was good."

We spread the bedding below a half-fallen guava tree and nibbled on some of its unripe fruit. The stars were already starting to come out; against the darkening sky I saw the great bat in flight, as big as an eagle. There was something sinister about it—a European superstition, no doubt. It was hard to believe such a creature ate only fruit.

"Ronald," said Aseri in a voice as deep and soft as the twilight, "last night you sleep under a breadfruit tree. Tonight under a guava."

5
▲▲▲
SUVA

"**S**ee any sharks?" asked Fergus Clunie. "Sharks go right up the Sigatoka, y'know. Bloody shark can cross rapids on his belly just like a salmon. Thought I'd tell you when you got back so you wouldn't worry. The locals know when there's one about—can see the big shape moving round in a pool. They would have warned you. You boys want some tea?"

Sela, the librarian, appeared with two mugs. Fergus chuckled to himself and continued:

"Had a big expedition come here from America. Some biologists thought it must be a specially adapted shark to go in fresh water like that. Put together a big project to capture one. Thousands of dollars. Complete waste of time. Just a bloody old shark like any other. Reckon they come in fresh water to kill parasites and things that can't take the shock—that's what they reckon."

We recounted the trip, feeling mildly heroic to have made some twenty fordings through water possibly shark infested—although with the river so much lower than usual this year, the chance of a shark above Korolevu was admittedly slim. The camp beneath the guava tree turned out to be only two hours, and six crossings, from Namoli, a village of patterned wattle walls and children sailing bamboo rafts on the river. From there it had been a mile's walk—

and two more fords—to Korolevu, "Great Village" (not to be con-fused with the Korolevu on the south coast). It lived up to its name: at least a hundred houses and some large two-tiered *yavu* occupied by the graves of chiefs around the *rara*. The town lies at the head of a motor road, and we caught a ride to Sigatoka with a truckload of Sigatoka youths in a hurry to watch a boxing match. The Indian driver took the narrow gravel road at maniacal speed, Fiji pop music blaring from speakers on the back of his cab; but he got us to Sigatoka in time to catch a bus for Suva almost immediately. By six o'clock the three of us had taken a room at the Grand Pacific, showered, and were quaffing Fiji Bitter, the thought of which had become an obsession by the last day of the hike. This was followed by dinner at the New Peking—bowls of wonton (known in Fiji as "short soup"; noodles are called "long soup") and steaks all round.

The afternoon had been disorienting: it was strange to cover a hundred miles in three hours after spending three days on foot to go twenty-five.

I asked Fergus how anyone gets across the river when it's high.

"Locals cross when it's up to their armpits. Got no choice. Horse is best, of course. Carry a pack on each side and away you go. You want a nice lazy horse with no tricks. Trouble is, the buggers sometimes want to go home. Good whack on the head with a stick fixes that—stuns 'em, makes 'em drunk. Horse doesn't like that. Won't fool around after a good whack between the ears."

Aseri did some shopping in Suva, then caught a bus home to Mokani. Derek and I spent an afternoon of beer, chess, and self-congratulation by the pool of the Grand Pacific. A stiff breeze stirred the palm trees. Across the harbour, black and grey rain-clouds loured over what Rupert Brooke called "the most fantasti-cally shaped mountains in the world." The dark, layered sky seemed to be resting on Joske's Thumb. Suva was still in sun, and the water was a pointillist vision of glinting waves.

◆

A friend of a friend had given me the name of a professor at the University of the South Pacific. James was a mid-thirty-year-old who cherished the memory of the 1960s. It showed in his lank red hair, Zapata mustache, and octagonal spectacles. He wore an ele-phant-hair bracelet and tennis shoes with no socks.

James took me around the campus, which is shared and funded by a number of South Pacific island nations. There are three or four prestigious concrete buildings and several outlying structures of wood with corrugated iron roofs.

"This place was an air force base during the war," he told me. "As you can see, we're still using a lot of the old mess huts. Over there we have what I call a neo-traditional Fijian *bure*," he laughed, "and a Gilbertese *maneaba* of the same ilk. They had to make the walls out of cement to conform to Suva building codes. Down here's my favourite spot on campus. . . ."

He showed me a gully containing a small natural amphitheatre and a rusty metal movie screen.

"Imagine the poor old GIs watching movies here, being devoured by the bugs.

"Can you come for dinner tonight? Bring your archaeologist friend. We always like to see new faces."

That evening Derek and I made our way by taxi to James's address. He lived in a comfortable neighbourhood where the houses were set well back from the road on high ground among big trees.

"We rent this from the Methodist Church," he said. "I sometimes wonder what they'd make of our decor."

The walls were hung with ferocious masks and anatomically explicit wooden carvings from Papua New Guinea. James led us into the kitchen.

"Some bachelor *talatalas* [ministers] had the place before us— you wouldn't believe the pile of old corned beef cans we found outside below the kitchen window." He poured three large scotches and began cutting up a chicken—Fiji style, with a cane knife. Outside a *lali* drum beat out its sinister tattoo, summoning wor-shippers to church.

"Thought I'd try a Colombian recipe of mine." James threw chopped onion, garlic, and handfuls of green coriander leaves into a casserole with the diced chicken.

"My favourite South American city is Bogotá." He paused and smiled to see if we were surprised. "Wonderful Spanish colonial architecture, all green and white. I grew up in New Mexico, so I appreciate that. Of course, it can be a little rough, Bogotá—everyone I knew there got robbed, except me." He smiled again. "One friend of mine—I think he worked for the CIA actually—he got so tired of people breaking into his apartment and smashing the door that he just took the locks off. Every time he got ripped off he'd go out and buy new furniture, the word would get around, and two or three weeks later everything would be gone. Finally he just said piss on this, and lived in a bare apartment with no locks and nothing in it."

Two other guests arrived: an Australian economist, clean cut, and sporting a British accent acquired, remarkably, during one year at Oxford; and a "fellow Canuck," an art teacher from Medicine Hat, wearing a pink shirt and a surfeit of Navaho jewellery.

James emerged from the kitchen and brought us another scotch. "I gather you were in Peru," he said. "I was there myself in '76. The land reform was interesting."

"That's what this place needs," the Australian offered. "Take the land away from all the old half-wit Ratus and give it to the people."

"Which people?" said Derek. "The Indians?"

"Doesn't matter. The people are the people. It's time all this racial nonsense was broken down. It's getting exciting here now—the neo-colonial power structure the British left behind is starting to crumble. Just wait and see—there'll be plenty of changes here once all the good ol' darkies have died off. Nobody wants to talk about it to us, though. As far as the government's concerned we're just a bunch of commies."

James nodded. "Last month my office was turned upside down by the Special Branch."

"So you support the native lands policy?" the Australian said to me, as if he pitied my ignorance. I told him I hadn't been here long enough to say much about Fiji, although there seemed to be good reason for thinking that ownership of the land was what set Fijians apart from the social wreckage of native societies in Australia, the Americas, and elsewhere.

"Well, James and I are opposed to native property rights," he continued. "It's a reactionary concept. It implies that land can be owned. Land should belong to everyone in the name of the State. We've done some work with aboriginals in Australia. They talk about wanting to keep their 'traditional' lands and way of life. But it's all bullshit. It doesn't mean a thing. They don't hunt anymore. They just sit in their caravans, watch television, and eat corned beef. They wouldn't know how to go back to the old ways if we let them. The only way to help people like that is to get them into the mainstream of society like everyone else."

"What if they don't want to join?" asked Derek. (I could see he was starting to bristle. The scotches were making for a lively argument.) "You show me where forced integration has worked. The Canadians and Americans tried it for a hundred years. What gives us the right to impose our ideas of property ownership on other cultures? First we come along as capitalists. We say, 'These natives don't know what it means to own land,' so we take it away for the Crown or the settler government. Then the natives smarten up and learn how to claim back *their* land according to *our* criteria for owning it. Then you Marxists come along and say, 'Wait a minute chaps, it's all a big mistake. Nobody can own land, so we'll just hang on to it in the name of the State, thank you very much.' "

"What about the Fiji Indians?" James said. "They have a right to live here too. Why should the Fijians sit on all the land? It should be collectivized and divided up among those who want to work it."

"You know very well what would happen then. In a generation or two the Fijians would be dispossessed like all the other native peoples in the world. Do you want to open up a second wave of colonialism? Do you want to let the Indians finish the job the white settlers would have liked to do? Is that what you want—ethnic decay and disorientation, one more demoralized peasantry for a few corrupt commissars to lord it over? If you take away the constitutional protection of the Fijians they'll be overrun. And the way I see it, it's their country before it's anyone else's."

"Bourgeois romantic ideas of property rights!" the Australian snorted, turning to me.

I'd had three scotches by now and was ready to jump in with both feet. I suggested that non-Western peoples had every reason to be wary of Western monopolies on truth. European ideologies—

whether missionary Christianity, liberal capitalism, or Marxism—were all products of a patently ethnocentric utopian tradition. All shared the idea of human perfectibility and the attainment of some sort of paradise. But they had been developed in response to European needs and problems, and the last, particularly, was an attempt to redress social ills created largely by the first two. Marx's remedy had much to recommend it for societies based on the exaltation of the individual at the peril of the group; on the exploitation of an industrial or rural proletariat; on economic motivation by the stick of poverty and the carrot of greed. This type of society had been exported by Europe to much of the Third World. But Fijian society, it seemed to me, had successfully resisted its importation. To impose the materialist millennium here, regardless of cultural and historical circumstances, would be an act of cultural imperialism—no more defensible than temple burning or buying up land with bottles of rum.

It was time to change the subject or the evening would be a disaster. I asked James what had brought him to Fiji.

"It was a choice between coming down here to take this position at USP, or going professionally into the textile import business."

"What sort of textiles?"

"Oh, you know, weavings from Peru and Guatemala, batiks from Indonesia. Ideally, I suppose, I'd like to retire to Bogotá and live off textbook royalties."

♦

Pacific Harbour Resort and Cultural Centre, about thirty miles west of Suva on the Queen's Road, it not really a harbour at all. It has one of the few good bathing beaches within reach of the capital, a luxury hotel, and an open-air re-creation of ancient Fijian life.

I got off the bus too soon and found I had to walk for half a mile past the odd little villas built for lease as holiday homes to foreigners. All are exactly alike—concrete walls, faceted metal roofs—each on its bare plot of low-lying ground drained by deep ditches resembling moats. Foreigners wanting to spend, say, the Australian winter in Fiji may occupy their house for up to six months in the year; the rest of the time it sits empty or is rented to tourists. I could not imagine why anyone would want to stay here. The stark development, with its grid of ditches and perimeter fence, looked like housing for army officers, or perhaps a comfortable prison compound for deposed dictators, a humane alternative to the firing squad.

Beyond the villas you come to a large lily pond with tall trees hiding colonial buildings on the far side. Behind these are replicas of a chief's house, a Fijian fort, and a *bure kalou*, or spirit house, all built on a small island in a lake. The *bure kalou* is impressive. It stands on a stone-faced platform shaped like a truncated pyramid, and the door is reached by a stout tree trunk a yard thick, precisely notched with steps. The walls are about the height of a man, but from them rises a majestic thatched spire more than thirty feet tall, pewter-coloured and strangely glossy in the noonday light. The roof is capped by a ridge-pole that extends a yard beyond the gables, and from the ends of this, long *magimagi* ropes encrusted with egg cowries hang to the ground, like the braids of a straw Rapunzel.

I went back to one of the older buildings and bought coffee and a sandwich at the cafeteria.

"'Scuse me," said a portly figure at the next table, "can you puzzle this bloody thing out? Dunno if the film's woinding." I looked at the man's camera; it seemed to be all right.

"Where're you from? I'm a Kiwi," he said amiably. Then glossed himself: "New Zealander."

He worked for an international plywood company, I gathered, inspecting the Fiji operation. He asked what my "line" was.

"A writer, eh? I'll tell you something. I've travelled all over the South Pacific—I've known Fiji for seventeen years—and I'm shocked at how much the Reds are expanding in this part of the world. Take Vanuatu for instance—used to be New Hebrides. The silly blighters just opened up diplomatic relations with Cuba. Laying themselves open to all kinds of infiltration. And Western Samoa's getting Russian aid to build an airstrip. I'd write about that if I were a writer!"

I reminded him that Prime Minister Mara had just decided to let American nuclear-armed ships use Suva docks, and added that as far as I knew, the Cuban "ambassador" to Vanuatu visited there only once or twice a year. It seemed faintly ironic to be discussing superpower manoeuvres almost in the shadow of the heathen war temple. Ancient Fijian savageries acquired an endearing innocence.

"Anyway," I said, "if you were a poor Third World country, wouldn't you take aid from anyone and everyone?"

The Kiwi went silent. He glanced at me nervously, then continued fiddling with his camera. I think he had just seen another of his Reds.

◆

Every day, from Monday to Saturday, the fort is assailed by Fijian warriors; at other times pagan rites are enacted in the temple. The tourist audience watches from a punt equipped with cushions and a thatched roof. Sometimes the Pacific Harbour Resort, like several along the south coast, holds a firewalking performed by men from the nearby island of Beqa.

Unlike the hammed-up battles and sacrifices, firewalking is an unbroken tradition from pre-contact times. The ceremony is best described by John Bigay et al. in their fine monograph *Beqa, Island of Firewalkers*:

> The preparation for the firewalking begins with the digging of a circular pit, which is lined with large rounded stones. Then logs are piled on top and the fire is lit.
>
> After the fire has burned for 6 to 8 hours, the men of the village, led by the *bete* [hereditary priest], prepare the pit for the firewalkers. Using long poles with loops of great vines tied to the ends, the men pull the burning logs off the pit. . . . When the stones in the pit are level, the *bete* walks on them briefly in order to test their firmness. . . . When he is completely satisfied that everything is in order he shouts "O Vuto-O" and the firewalkers walk onto the glowing rocks. Each of them has a band of dry leaves tied around each ankle, and these leaves do not ignite.

The men spend about ten or fifteen minutes on the white-hot stones—long enough to discount the explanation that they walk too briefly to burn their calloused feet. Medical investigations have not been enlightening. The ability seems to involve trance or some other means of psychosomatic control, perhaps analogous to the practices of Muslim and Hindu ecstatic cults. (Fiji Indians also do firewalking—briefly on coals, not rocks—but there is no cultural link with the Fijian rite.)

Like the Luveniwai and other spirit cults now officially extinct, Beqa firewalking involves the gift of special powers from *veli*, the "little folk" or water sprites who are the offspring of Degei. The Fijian word for it, *vilavilairevo*, literally means "jumping into the oven." Symbolically the firepit is a large open *lovo*, or earth oven, and the ceremony is in many ways a flirtation of the raw with the cooked. The *bete*'s leadership is crucial; and the walkers believe they must observe certain tabus, including a period of abstinence from sex and coconut foods, or they will burn their feet. After a ceremony, special roots are buried in the pit for four days. These are later eaten by the walkers, and a portion is presented at the priest's house as an offering to the *veli*.

A legend tells how the ability to firewalk was first acquired by the Beqan ancestor-hero Tui Qalita. One day long ago Tui Qalita was digging for eel in a stream called the Namoliwai when he heard voices coming from a pool. Reaching into the water, he seized what he thought was an eel and pulled it out. But he had caught a tiny man, the Tui Namoliwai, king of the water sprites. The little god began to offer his captor various gifts in return for freedom, but none of the usual things—wealth, success in war and fishing— interested Tui Qalita, who was already the most powerful man on the island. Finally, Tui Namoliwai offered the gift of *vilavilairevo*. He prepared a firepit, taught Tui Qalita how to walk on it, and promised that the power would be passed down to the man's descendants. (The fairy god also offered to teach his captor how to bury himself in the oven-pit for four days and emerge unscathed; but Tui Qalita shrewdly decided not to overtax the god's generosity.)

Until 1960, firewalking was performed only rarely, on special occasions such as visits by royalty and high chiefs. Because of its infrequency and uniqueness the British did not suppress *vilavilair-*

evo with the other remnants of the old religion. Although the cult still has its hereditary *bete* (Tui Qalita's direct descendants) it is no longer regarded as a threat by Wesleyan Christianity. But what the British and the missionaries neglected to do, the almighty dollar may be accomplishing in a subtler way. In 1961 the firewalkers of Rukua village signed a contract with the Korolevu Beach Hotel to walk once a month for $400 a performance. This presented a problem: the tabu period on sex and coconuts was exactly one month. If the Rukua firewalkers were doctrinaire about this they would eventually make themselves extinct. The tabu was reduced to a fortnight.

In recent years Beqa firewalkers have performed as far afield as Canada and India. (It is said that the *veli*, whose presence is indispensable, travelled well in the *bete*'s hand luggage.) Commercialization has relentlessly eroded the mystical elements of the rite. The tabu period is now only a few days, the pits are smaller, and the performances sometimes perfunctory.

One wonders how much more secular the ceremony can become before Tui Namoliwai withdraws his protection and the firewalkers burn their feet.

◆

It was Derek's last night in Suva and he was in the mood for some nightlife. We had dinner at the Bamboo Terrace—a pleasant restaurant where one can sit outside on a colonnaded balcony and look down on the city's tree-lined streets. The street lighting is understated; the stars wink between the palm fronds.

"Too bad bureaucrats don't get holidays like writers," Derek complained.

"Remember, I'm not on holiday." But I was glad I had the prospect of another month in Fiji, instead of in an Edmonton office.

At Lucky Eddie's there were no tables to be had; we ordered scotch and drank it standing by the bar. We considered going somewhere else, but Derek said the Dragon was tough, and Senitiki had already warned us off Man Friday's, which had a big black foot painted on the door and a reputation for brawls.

The barman refilled our glasses. I read the label on the unfamiliar bottle: Black Cat Whisky, "blended from imported Scotch whisky and finest Fiji cane spirit." It did not admit to the proportions, but I was sure they favoured the Fiji economy, not whisky connoisseurs.

"I wish we could find a place to sit," Derek said. "My legs still hurt like hell from the hike."

"What?" I said (the music was loud). He repeated his words, shouting.

"You're welcome to share our table," came a female voice from behind my shoulder. I turned round cautiously, hoping it wasn't the multilingual Rosi. But no, this young woman was Oriental or possibly Indian, tall and slender, with a mane of long black hair clasped behind an elegant face with high cheekbones. We followed her through the crowd to a table by the wall. It was quiet enough to talk.

"My name's Nina," she said, "and this here's my friend Gladys."

We introduced ourselves. Gladys was coffee-coloured; she had short frizzy hair, a round face, and grey eyes.

"Don't think we're trying to pick you up or anything. It's just that I overheard what you said, and there's some creepy Indian blokes hanging around trying to chat us up."

"People think Fiji's a model of racial harmony," Gladys said, "but it isn't true really. We act friendly to Indians, but we can't stand them. I mean, some of them are all right—I have got some Indian friends—but on the whole they're none too popular."

Nina said she had just come home from a visit to Australia.

"I was in Sydney in July; God, it was cold. I didn't get out of bed till noon, and then I'd put the heating on and sit in front of it all day.

"Canada's ever so cold, isn't it? Do you ski? They say skiing's so expensive."

I tried to explain the difference between downhill and cross-country skiing.

"I've seen snow," Gladys said, "but I've never actually touched it."

Derek asked what they did for a living. They looked at each other and laughed.

"I wanted to go to university," said Nina, "but it's not so good.

The government favours Fijians. The Fijians think they're the only people with a right to live here. They get half the places at USP even if they don't really qualify. Indians get the other half. They only keep a few openings for other groups. The standard's so low anyway, I said to hell with it."

I asked her what group she belonged to.

"I don't know what I am really. Part Chinese, part Fijian, a bit of this and that. I'm a real fruit salad. Officially I'm an Other. Gladys is Part-European. There's probably one whole Fijian between us." They laughed. Nina's Fijian forebears had given her a generous mouth with slightly pouting lips, but she had the delicate build and long, straight hair of the Chinese. She wore a red sun dress, and her nails were polished to match.

This was interesting. The point of view of the Others was usually ignored in the Fijian/Indian dichotomy. People spoke much more frankly about race here than in Europe and America. Race in Fiji was accepted as a fact of life, and places of origin stood as the labels of ethnicity—it reflected the model of insularity imposed by geography in Oceania. In the Fijian language you defined yourself as *kai Viti*, "person of Fiji," *kai Idia*, "person of India," and so on. But what could a person of mixed race say? To be called an Other is merely an exclusion from the unmixed groups.

Nina's grandfather had come to Fiji from Hong Kong in the early 1900s and settled on Ovalau, not far from the old capital, Levuka. He opened a small store in a Fijian village and married one of the local girls. Nina's father was born to this couple. Her mother's family history was more confused, but the main elements were again Fijian and Chinese.

"It's hard to communicate in my family," she explained. "My grandfather only speaks Chinese and broken Fijian. My parents speak Fijian, English, and a bit of Chinese, and we—my sisters and me—only know English. My granddad's a very old man now, in his nineties. I wish I could talk to him, but I can't."

I wondered how it felt to be culturally a member of the global Anglo-Saxon civilization—even to speak like a London shopgirl—yet be descended from an island race of courtly cannibals and a people who built walls around themselves and meditated on the Tao.

Gladys was from Savusavu, a town on the south coast of Vanua Levu. It was one of the areas opened up by early planters in the days when a white man took a native wife or "wives." Most of Fiji's 10,000 Part-Europeans are descendants of these nineteenth-century unions, and today they outnumber Europeans (4500), Chinese (4500), and Others (1000). Even so, Part-Europeans and Others together form less than two percent of Fiji's population, and there are few interracial marriages nowadays. The peoples who came to Fiji have accepted the Fijian definition of groups by descent. Unlike Hawaii, Fiji is not a melting pot but an archipelago of racial islands.

"Are you married?" Nina abruptly asked us.

"Not me," Derek said.

"Not yet," said I.

"I thought you both would be. Most men are. I'm supposed to be getting married myself. Two weeks ago I was going to call the whole thing off. I don't love the guy, not really." She took a deep drag on her cigarette and blew the smoke neatly towards the ceiling. "But we're compatible, I s'pose."

"You don't sound very enthusiastic."

"That's what everyone says. His name's Terry. He's a New Zealander about your age."

"Are you marrying him so you can move to New Zealand?"

"God, no. I don't want to live *there*. I can't stand the cold. I'm not sure why. It'll give me independence—from my parents I mean—and it'll be an experience.

"It's funny; he's thirty-five, but he's so childish in many ways. I wrote to him not long ago and said I wished he'd grow up. He didn't like that. Wrote back and told *me* never to tell *him* to grow up. He does seem young to me, even though I'm only twenty-one. I was used to an older man. Before I met Terry I lived with Neil. He was Scottish, forty-five or maybe it was forty-six. People said I went with him because of his car—he had this beautiful Mercedes convertible—but it wasn't that of course. The first time I went out with him I didn't even know he had a car. He was good to talk to.

He knew so much about all sorts of things. I learned a lot, the time I was with him."

"Sounds like Maggie and Pierre," Derek said, adding "Trudeau" when she looked blank.

"Neil wanted to marry me, too," she continued. "My friends told me I was just throwing my life away on him. And it was true really, I *was* throwing it away. One day I told him I'd only marry him if he'd give me a two-carat diamond—and you know, a two-carat diamond is a big diamond. Of course I was only joking. But he went away on a business trip to Hong Kong and came back with a one-and-a-half carat one. Close enough, he reckoned, I suppose. That's when I decided I had better end it there and then. I've heard from friends that he's trying to sell the ring. I hope he gets a good price for it."

"Our friend Jack," Gladys said, "always teases Nina and me about the men we go out with. He calls us the TBs—that's short for Tycoon Bitches."

♦

Next morning I saw Derek onto the bus for Nadi, and made my way back towards the Grand Pacific.

In front of the Parliament buildings, on the side facing Victoria Parade, there are two bronze men. One is King Cakobau, sitting crosslegged atop a plinth commemorating the Cession of Fiji to Britain; the other, a bald, serious-faced man in formal *sulu* and morning coat, chest full of medals and honours, striding purposefully toward the sea. This is Ratu Sukuna, epitomized by his biographer as soldier, statesman, and man of two worlds.

Ratu Josefa Lalabalavu Sukuna was born in 1888, five years after the death of Cakobau. His father, brought up in the chiefly household of Bau, became one of the cornerstones of the native administration created by Gordon and Thurston—but not without difficulties reconciling the traditional rights of a high chief with the role of an imperial bureaucrat. He realized that the next generation of Fijian leaders should be able to operate in the white man's culture on equal terms. He hired a private tutor for his son in Fiji, then sent him on to boarding school in New Zealand. (The boy's exceptional ability had already been noted by several whites, including Brewster.)

Ratu Sukuna came back to Fiji for a spell as a clerk in the Colonial Secretary's office, and went up to Oxford in 1913. When war came he wanted to enlist; since the British army would not accept "coloured" men for duty in Europe, he joined the French Foreign Legion and fought in the trenches until wounded. In nine months' service he won the Croix de Guerre and the Médaille Militaire.

When the war ended he continued his law studies at Oxford and then read for the bar at the Middle Temple. Land and lineage being the axioms of Fijian life and culture, Sukuna made it his business to penetrate the alien concepts of land ownership that lay behind British thinking in this area. He came back to Fiji well qualified in property law, and took up the post of Native Lands Commissioner in 1922. Over the next three decades he used his expert knowledge of both native and foreign worlds to reform the landholding system devised by Gordon and Thurston, and, above all, to interpret those two worlds to one another. His work, involving endless public hearings all over Fiji, became in effect the way in which Fijian society defined itself. In the very process of codification the society undoubtedly changed, but the important thing was that it changed from within, under its own leaders. The changes may have been made under outside pressure, but not by foreign decree.

Critics have pointed out that the registration of lands begun by Gordon was based on a rudimentary understanding of what ownership meant in Fijian culture. The very act of codifying, or "freezing," a *status quo* was antithetical to the fluid and multilayered land-use rights of the native system. This was so, but Gordon, Thurston, and (later) Sukuna saw clearly that fluid land rights have nowhere withstood the onslaught of Western civilization. The only choice was to codify the land and lock it away, or see it transferred bit by bit from Fijian hands to foreign. Ratu Sukuna wrote:

> Had the Government prematurely granted the Fijian the freedom of the free or had colonial administration been the evil and discriminatory power it is sometimes represented to be . . . Fiji might now be occupying a position in trade midway between Hawaii

and New Caledonia . . . at the cost of a greatly depleted and impoverished indigenous population.

The present unrest between French settlers and New Caledonia Melanesians trying to recover their lost lands and autonomy shows how far and how clearly the first Fijian graduate had seen.

Ratu Sukuna was a high chief with blood about as blue as it can get in Fiji. His great-grandfather was Tanoa Visawaqa, father of Cakobau; other forebears included *tuis* of the important chiefdoms of Cakaudrove and Lau. Because of this, and because his plans for Fijian society did not fit with individualistic liberalism or left-wing ideology, he was often criticized as an arch-conservative defending the interests of a chiefly minority. These attacks were well aimed but culturally naïve. With the possible exception of western and interior Viti Levu, where the chiefly role had been less developed in pre-contact times, there was no way to dismantle the social hierarchy without destroying the integrity of Fijian culture. (Even Apolosi Nawai had arrogated the trappings of chieftainship to legitimize his claims to authority.) Culturally insensitive Western reformers—thinking in terms of a libertarian or Marxist model—saw (and still see) the native aristocracy as a class of despots exploiting the Fijian peasantry. Such an analysis is the product of our society, in which kinship is kept to the private sphere and the individual is the key to understanding political forms.

In Fijian culture the key is the kin group, descending from a common ancestor whose earthly representative and closest living relative is the chief. This man (or sometimes woman) is the legitimately constituted authority within the group and its delegated representative to other groups, whether foreign or Fijian. The main divisions in Fijian society run vertically, not horizontally: Fijians nowadays accept the principle of political equality *between* groups (other Fijian "tribes," whites, Indians) but resist the autonomy of individuals *within* the *mataqali* and *yavusa*.

If one must look for a Western analogy, these kin groups are closer to a family than to an electoral constituency. When outsiders insist that a chief should have no greater status than a commoner, it sounds to Fijians as it would sound to us if we were told by foreign "experts" that parents must have equal rank with children. In a harmonious Fijian kin group, as in a happy family, there are reciprocal mechanisms for representing and protecting the junior members, but a hierarchy of authority is essential to the cohesion and proper function of the whole. When family harmony breaks down the ultimate recourse is for the disaffected members to leave: this is exactly what happens in Fijian *yavusa*, although rarely. In 1948 Ratu Sukuna invited critics

> to reflect on the countries that have in recent times cast aside their own indigenous institutions and adopted the democratic form of government, and the people of which have soon found that democracy is for them an iron rule by one party. The consequences, violence and murder, misery and hunger, have shocked the world. Yet . . . it is being claimed that if we abolish the Native Regulations and the laws relating to Native Affairs—with them, of course would go Native life as we know it—we are emancipating the Fijian people. This is to argue that by removing institutions which people have laboriously built up through the ages and substituting nothing in their place we are setting the people free.

Long after he wrote those words, events in Africa have borne them out, along with the white man's tendentious but sadly accurate gibe "one man, one vote—once."

Fiji did evolve to independence and democracy in 1970, but it was a democracy tailored for local conditions. Though all are eligible to vote and stand for office, a complex electoral system keeps a representational balance between the different ethnic groups. As for the Fijians, they seem to be working out a compromise between democracy and aristocracy of a kind that should be familiar to the British. The hereditary power of the *ratu*s is gradually becoming more ceremonial than political; many chiefs are elected to high government office, but they increasingly observe the distinction between reign and rule.

The survival of indigenous political structure, and its successful translation into the constitutional chieftainship of today, saved Fiji from the Mobutus and Amins of Africa. Apolosi Nawai or another like him might have become such a leader if the traditional legitimacy of the chiefly establishment had not prevailed. Nawai was Sukuna's rival and antithesis. Both men had eyes for the future and the past. But where the one was mystical and inspirational to the point of delusion, the other built on foundations of scholarship, diligence, and common sense. Where Nawai had bravado, Sukuna had courage; plans instead of wild schemes; leadership by example, not demagoguery. Both had brilliance, but Apolosi was the trickster-teacher, Sukuna the sage.

Unlike the founder of the Viti Kabani, Ratu Sukuna did not see capitalism as a worthy option for his people. He did help those Fijians already drawn into what he called the "great octopus of the modern world" by establishing labour unions among miners and dockers; but his vision for the Fijian future was one of communal life in the village on the land. He has been criticized for not encouraging others to emulate his cosmopolitan career, but it is clear from his writings that he was not altogether happy in his bicultural fate. "Went to bed tired out by conforming to the demands of two entirely different social systems," he wrote in his diary in 1933, and in 1939 he pondered the "easy way out" offered by alcohol—a common temptation for those caught between worlds.

In advocating that the Fijian retain his attachment to the land, Ratu Sukuna was correctly and honestly representing the central values of his people. Apart from some success with co-operatives and the credit unions introduced by Governor Sir Ronald Garvey (1952–1958), Fijians have eschewed the business world. The qualities needed to succeed in commerce are not among those that Fijian culture admires. Even today, the economy of Fiji is dominated by foreign (largely Australian) capital and the entrepreneurship of local Indians and Europeans. Most Fijians believe that rapid urbanization, industrialization, and economic advance would cost them their cultural identity. They see land as more substantial than capital, subsistence farming more worthwhile than cash crops, and they have been able to continue in these "old-fashioned" ways by developing a political system that defends them.

Capitalists, liberals, and communists alike wring their hands over the lack of "development" of the natives. But the wisdom of the Taukei may be seen next time the world economy falters or fails. A people who grow their own food on their own land and can defend themselves from others have little to fear from the peristaltic progress of the octopus.

Ratu Sukuna, twice knighted, died in 1958, not long after his seventieth birthday. He died at sea during a voyage to Britain— fitting perhaps for a man who loved the ocean and spent much time sailing between islands.

♦

"I remember Canada well," Gorky said, his eye on the G.P.H.'s plump Tongan barmaid. "Let me see—that musta bin the year of Our Lord 1979. An artist friend of mine took me to this topless, bottomless place in Vancouver. The only thing you can do after a night like that"—he regarded me with the air of a doctor about to impart bad news—"is get a long rest and make sure no friendly critters are infesting you."

Gorky was having trouble holding his drink. The glass was in his left hand, both elbows were on the bar, and the right hand had a strong grip on his left wrist. At the apex of this unsteady triangle was a rye and ginger to which Gorky periodically lowered his head. I had deduced that this two-handed technique was the result of a long day's drinking, but Dr. Gorky was eager to disabuse me.

"My little problem here, you understand, is the result of some friendly critter just trying to get blood. I was gathering plants up near Rakiraki when this scorpion or spider, or whatever, lets me have it on the left wrist, and I'm left-handed, see. My assistant, who is a very nice fellow but also one of these darned preachers they have so many of around here"—Gorky lit a cigarette, took one drag, and coughed into the ashtray, scattering its contents— "he thought I deserved it for upsetting the local ghosts. Anyhow, to cut a long story short, they told me at the hospital this morning that my arm isn't completely shot, although for a few days I'm going to be as limp wristed as all these thweeties here." He rolled his eyes in the direction of the Grand Pacific's androgynous waiter. "So I told the *talatala* to go and get in touch with his spirits and let them know they goofed up in trying to punish this particular white man. So you see there's hope for me after all, although that might be a mixed blessing, depending on your philosophy."

I was waiting at the Grand Pacific Hotel bar to meet Dr. James and two councillors from Rabi Island at six o'clock. Rabi is in the northeast corner of the Fiji group, about two hundred miles from Suva by air. Its inhabitants, who call themselves Banabans, are a Micronesian people resettled in Fiji after their home island was destroyed by phosphate mining. "If you want to see British colonialism in its true colours," James had said in our heated discussion, "go to Rabi and talk to the Banabans." He had offered to introduce me to two of their leaders, who were in Suva. Apparently these councillors were also Methodist ministers. It was damnable luck to run into Wendell Gorky: *talatalas* don't drink and he was a living banner for their policy.

I tried tactfully to remove myself to a distant corner of the lounge. Gorky straightened himself as I got up, and said in the tone of a radio announcer:

"And now a final message from dear, lovely, soon-to-be-frozen Canada. This is not, mind you, a product of the Canadian Broadcorping Castration, however. . . ."

He began singing to the tune of "My Bonnie Lies over the Ocean":

> My father's a French missionary,
> My mother makes synthetic gin,
> My sister sells love for a dollar,
> My God, how the money rolls in. . . .

I saw James approaching from the lobby, and briskly went to meet him.

"Let's sit over here," I said. "There's a drunk at the bar we'd better avoid."

"Ronald, I'd like you to meet Reverend Taatu and Reverend Rongorongo, members of the Rabi Council of Leaders."

We shook hands and sat down at one of the glass-topped wicker tables. Both men wore the typical dress of a *talatala*, or minister (the Fijian word means "messenger" or "one who is sent")—white

shirt, formal black *sulu* of good cloth, black sandals—and carried
leather briefcases. But here their resemblance to Fijians ended. The
Banabans, being Micronesians, are similar in appearance to "classic"
Polynesians, with straight black hair, golden skin, and somewhat
Asiatic bone structure. Reverend Taatu was about thirty, slim,
athletic, robustly handsome. Rongorongo was no older, but huge
and jolly, with brilliantined hair, which made him look rather like
a Mexican *maître d'hôtel*.

"Rongorongo is taking a degree with us at USP," James explained. "We've been looking at the British exploitation, and Japanese atrocities during the war."

"Please excuse us," Rongorongo said to me, "if we
are . . . suspicious towards outsiders. We have sometimes not been
treated well in the past, so we feel we must be . . . cautious. You
must take no offence."

They didn't appear to be at all suspicious. Indeed, there was an
engaging candour about them that seemed almost naïve. We had
been talking only five or ten minutes when they invited me to visit
Rabi and the discussion turned to travel arrangements.

The waiter appeared. I offered drinks.

"I'll have a scotch," said James. "What about you, Reverend
Taatu?"

"I would like a Coca-Cola, please, if that is all right."

"We are not allowed to drink by our church, you see," said
Rongorongo, "because we are . . . holy men." He always hesitated
before saying the key word in a sentence. The habit must have
begun, I suppose, when Rongorongo wasn't sure of his English.
Now his vocabulary was faultless, but the charming mannerism
remained.

"There's only one thing that is worrying us about you," he said
after the drinks arrived. "You are not from the . . . CIA?"

"?"

"Just a joke, just a joke. Sometimes we worry about Dr. James
because he is an . . . American. No offence, Dr. James. You see,
we Banabans are highly suspicious. But you will find it easy to
come and visit us. We understand how it is for people from other
countries. They do not know the . . . customs. Ourselves, too.

A Russian came to Rabi last year. We had heard so much . . . propaganda about Russians that we were expecting something not human, or perhaps someone yellow or . . . red. But this Russian was white! Like a European. We said, 'You can't be a Russian.' We had no idea the Russians were Europeans."

I recalled Ratu Lemeki's surprise that French and Germans were indistinguishable from English. Here again was that quaint notion that every nationality has its peculiar physical type.

"If you come to Rabi," Rongorongo continued, "you will have no worries. You can trust us—we are men of God."

Before I could think of a suitable reply, I saw Gorky advancing like a malign Javanese shadow puppet across the lounge, singing in the style of a radio jingle:

> Christianity hits the spot!
> Twelve apostles, that's a lot,
> Jesus Christ, a Virgin too,
> Christianity's the thing for you!

Mercifully he changed course and left by the door that leads to the swimming pool.

"He is a friend of yours?" asked Rongorongo, beaming. "Dr. James told us you were travelling with a friend."

"No, no, that's not him. My friend just went home to Canada. That's someone we happened to meet on the plane."

"Very . . . interesting," Rongorongo said inscrutably. "I hope he feels better soon."

6
▲▲▲
RABI

There is only one flight a week to Rabi, but the Banabans have an alternate route involving air, land, and sea. We had just completed the aerial leg of the journey and were lunching at Savusavu, Vanua Levu. Around an oilcloth-covered table in a Chinese restaurant sat Rongorongo, two other Banabans, myself, and a Nigerian (Rev. Taatu had already returned home). Outside, the sun lay brilliant on the white coral street; distant mountains, a deep olive green, rose behind the lighter fringe of a coconut plantation across the estuary. The bow of an old wooden schooner, bleached by the sun and riddled with ship-worm, reared from the water like the last moments of the *Titanic*. So this was Savusavu: I could see why Gladys had been seduced by Suva (and tycoons). There was little here but nineteenth-century memories, and the genes of white planters lingering in the blond mops on dusky children.

Saho, the Nigerian, was a colleague of James's; the two of them were doing "a little applied economics," trying to help the Banabans assemble a claim for damages committed by the Japanese in World War II.

"They need a victory, any victory," James had said to me in Suva. "If the Japanese would just give them a fishing boat, or something like that, it would be a major boost to their morale."

He had also lent me *Treasure Islands*, by Pearl Binder, an emotional account of the troubles that began for the Banabans in 1900. Until then they had lived in relative isolation on a tiny island that stood alone on the equator, in the middle of the western Pacific, some sixteen hundred miles northwest of Fiji. Its nearest neighbours were Nauru, two hundred miles to the west, and the Gilberts, three hundred miles east. The inhabitants called it Banaba, "Isle of Rocks." The British imaginatively renamed it Ocean Island.

As things turned out, Ocean was a better name: Banaba was made not of inert rock but of phosphate of lime—easily processed into valuable fertilizer. Within eighty years most of the island was taken across the sea and spread on the fields of Britain, New Zealand, and Australia. Many peoples in the world have been driven from their lands, but the Banabans were the first to have their country dug from under them.

After lunch Rongorongo, Saho, and I got into the back of a battered Chevrolet. The Rabi Council Chairman, a huge man in a bright pink shirt, and the Secretary, genial but inarticulate from his underhung jaw and surfeit of beer, shared the front seat with the elderly Indian driver. The car ploughed its way up the so-called Hibiscus Highway—about sixty miles of dirt road along the coast of Vanua Levu's Natewa peninsula. I tried to see what I could between the three men and a pair of orange plastic angel wings mounted on the taxi's bonnet. We passed through endless coconut plantations, kept free of undergrowth by cattle browsing beneath the palms. Behind us a wake of fine dust drifted off into the ranks of trees. Villages were few and small, but the road always had a skin of asphalt wherever there were dwellings. People, mainly Fijians, came to their doors and waved. Occasionally you saw copra-drying furnaces, like abandoned steam engines in the bush; but there was usually a pennant of smoke at the funnel and the accompanying incense of burning husks. In places the road met tidal inlets with bush-capped mushrooms of eroded coral standing in the glaucous sea.

Our destination was a small bay near the tip of the peninsula. The tide was low. We had to walk across a mudflat to a launch anchored in shallow water fifty yards from the beach. There was a shoreline fetor of salt and rottenness. Movement on the mud caught my eye—a furtive, sidelong ballet performed by dozens of tiny dancers holding shields to their faces. They were crabs. Each had one prodigious claw almost equal to its body size, and they ran brandishing these with a dry, staccato clack, like the snapping of false teeth.

A beard of weeds was growing on the launch's hull, but the strong motor soon propelled us out to sea. Beyond the reef, the water becomes an extraordinarily deep and lucid sapphire, far bluer than the sky.

Like anything truly beautiful, Rabi gets lovelier as you approach. What is at first a hazy green lozenge on the horizon breaks into folded drapery of different shades: the bottle green of pristine forest, coconut groves the colour of young wheat, and dark cliffs dropping to a beach whose brilliant yellow extends beneath the water and gives an opalescent border to the sea.

◆

"I hope you will be comfortable here," Rongorongo said. "This man is the caretaker. Caretaker doesn't speak much English, but he will take care of you anyway. I will see you at dinner in two hours."

"Rongo," said Saho wearily, "do we have to make speeches tonight?"

"Of course. You would like to express a few words . . ."

"I said I would only come this time on one condition—that it would be all work and no speeches. You do it for us."

"I will be honoured to translate."

"These people love speeches," Saho told me as soon as the Reverend had left. "And eating. Eating and speeches."

"Can't they do what the Fijians do—appoint a spokesman to take care of the formalities for us?"

"They don't do things like that here. When in Rabi do as the Banabans do—that's their philosophy. It's very admirable but I have a hard time with it. For one thing, I'm a very small eater—I need very little food—but they get upset if you eat less than three helpings of everything."

"Caretakah!" Saho called in the imperious manner of an African chief. The man quickly appeared, old, with bloodshot eyes and sagging cheeks that made him look like a faithful mastiff.

"Caretaker, I want some beer. Last time I came I ordered beer. Where is it?" The old man beckoned Saho to follow him to the kitchen.

"*Bia!*" Saho repeated, pronouncing it in the Fijian way. The caretaker opened a large kerosene fridge and stood aside.

"Look at this," Saho said to me. "Two bottles! Ha! That will last me about ten minutes. He doesn't understand a beer drinker's needs."

I suggested we buy some more.

"There are no bars here—not even a bottle shop. The Rabi co-op store sometimes has beer but it will be closed now."

Before the British bought Rabi for the Banabans (with Banaban money) the island belonged to Lever Brothers, the soap and margarine multinational. Where we were staying had once been the headquarters for the white manager of Rabi's copra plantations. The building fell into a ruinous state over the years, but the Banabans later rebuilt it as a residence for visitors with official business on the island. A large dining room serves the Council as a meeting and banquet hall; and there are four spacious bedrooms, a kitchen, and bathroom. My room had a double bed, dresser, wardrobe, and lace curtains in the windows; the walls were a cheerful pink.

Saho and I opened the beers and sat on the veranda, admiring the residence's superb setting. It stands on a ledge cut into the steep hillside of the island, about three hundred feet above the shore. A long flight of stone steps (a relic of Levers' days) leads down through a series of garden terraces overgrown by bougainvillaea thickets and rows of frangipani trees.

It was sunset now. To the west, across five miles of ocean, the dark mountains of Vanua Levu, "Great Land," rose in silhouette against an orange sky. The sea answered this colour with swirls of pink and red like incandescent glass. Below us was the old company wharf and a weathered warehouse on the rocky shore. From the village came sounds of a chainsaw, men building, children's voices, and a rooster's crow.

"James told me there were no chickens on Rabi—no livestock at all, in fact?"

"James isn't always right," Saho observed drily.

Despite the African's overbearing manner toward the caretaker, I found myself liking him. He was about my own age, trim and smartly dressed in khaki shorts, a white polo shirt, and an expensive pair of gold-rimmed spectacles. His father, he said, had been a district commissioner under the British in Nigeria. Saho was studying abroad when Gowon seized power, and had seldom been home since. He taught for a while in Montreal, then, like James, got a post at the University of the South Pacific.

"James is a good fellow but he exaggerates," Saho continued. "The Banabans are not as demoralized as he thinks. The younger generation now see Rabi as their home. It's the older ones, the ones who remember back before the war—they do nothing but talk of Ocean Island. They believe they can go back. They even talk of taking soil and water there so they can rebuild it. It has become a symbol."

"Something like Africa to the Jamaicans?"

"A bit like that, but it hasn't gone so far. I was in Jamaica, up in the hills. When they found out I was African they wanted to talk about Jah Rastafari, the 'living god' Haile Selassie. Ha! I had to be careful what I said—they didn't want to hear that he was firstly dead and secondly a tyrant."

The sky was darker now. When the sun had set, a crimson glow lingered like the presence of a great city over the horizon. To the east it was already navy blue, pierced by a few stars. The tropical new moon lay on its back above a mango tree, a bright dish offered to the night.

◆

Dinner was a buffet, served in the residence hall and attended by the Chairman, Secretary, four other councillors, and their wives. The men wore cotton trousers and open-necked shirts, the women voluminous print dresses (derived from the Mother Hubbards of the missionaries) and strings of plastic beads. Rongorongo arrived, dapper in formal *sulu*, black sandals, and white shirt.

The Chairman got to his feet and began to make a speech in the Banaban language (though he spoke good English), pausing after each paragraph for Rongorongo to translate:

"Chairman wishes to welcome you here, and to thank you for coming through all the . . . hardships of aeroplane, taxi, and boat. He begs you to excuse any inadequacies of the . . . facilities here on Rabi.

"Chairman wishes that you will enjoy your stay here with us, the Banabans, and that the people will help you with your important work of interviewing and writing about the Banaban people.

"We call upon Our Lord that he may help us find wisdom and truth, and guide us in the many tasks we have to perform."

Saho then rose and did his best to reply. (The important thing, he had told me, was to mention everyone, especially God, and remember to thank specifically for everything.) When he had finished I did the same. Rongorongo managed to make our halting efforts sound poetic in his language—clearly he was drawing on a long tradition of formal oratory. He concluded by saying grace, and then sat down beside Saho.

"The food is on the table!" Rongorongo said, and beamed enthusiastically.

"After you, Rongo," Saho replied.

"No, after you," said Rongorongo.

"After you!" Saho repeated.

Finally, the Chairman prevailed upon us to fill our plates first. On the table were dishes holding vast amounts of sausages, tinned fish, hard-boiled eggs, tinned tomatoes, fried chicken, roast goat, rice, and potatoes. The caretaker, meanwhile, had started a noisy generator; the residence was brightly lit. I felt the Banabans discreetly yet intently watching to make sure I ate enough. Every time our plates were even half empty, we were exhorted to fill them again.

More speeches ended the meal; then Chairman and councillors politely left, saying that their wives were tired. Rongorongo and Saho drank tea and discussed how they would go about their project. They had bought a tape recorder and were planning to interview those who remembered the war.

"This is a very unhappy business, you must understand," Rongorongo said. "For example, there is a woman living here today who saw her father's head cut off with a sword when she was only a teenage girl. Most people prefer to forget such things, but I think it is important we find out the truth. That is why I think it is necessary that I come with you, to translate but also to . . . reassure. If you talk to them alone sometimes they may exercise their right to . . . distort. But if they see a man of God there, they will have to tell the truth."

My gaze strayed round the room, and I was cheered briefly by its uninhibited décor. The windows had curtains striped in jade, aqua, blue, and mauve—the colours of a reef—and the light-blue walls were stencilled with a gold and green paisley motif. But above the dining table hung a map of Banaba and photographs of Ocean Island being devoured: trees falling to bulldozers; machines gnawing hungrily at pinnacles of rock; ore cars on railway tracks running across a lifeless moonscape; and, over everything, a shroud of fine white dust that gave a spectral quality to these images of progress.

♦

Since archaeological work on Banaba is now impossible, no one will ever know for how long the island was inhabited. According to the oral histories of the Banabans, there were three successive waves of occupation in prehistoric times. The first people are said to have been a small dark-skinned race of Melanesian type. Then came an Asiatic people from far to the west, who intermarried with the first group and eventually came to regard the island as "the first of all lands, the navel of the universe and the home of the ancestors." The third people, apparently related to the second, arrived from Beru in the Gilberts (now Kiribati). These latecomers regarded the earlier folk as Bu-n Anti, the "Breed of Spirits," but nevertheless found their women human enough to take as wives. On such a small island the three races soon mingled to form a "Micronesian" people typical of that part of the Pacific. ("Micronesian" is as dubious as "Polynesian" and "Melanesian" if used as an ethnic label, but it is a convenient geographical term for the countless small islands and archipelagoes that lie north of a line drawn from Samoa to Mindanao.)

Over several centuries between the coming of the Beru people and the arrival of Europeans, the Banabans developed a distinctive culture. Unlike the hierarchical Fijians and Polynesians, they had no king or paramount chief. Political power was vested in councils of elders who met to discuss formal business in the *maneaba*, or meeting houses, of each hamlet. All four (originally five) districts into which the island was divided did have "chiefly" families, but their status had more to do with ritual than with actual power. The "chief" of Tabwewa, for example, because of his descent from the spirit folk, had the right and duty to be the first to board foreign vessels. There were similar hereditary rights in the other districts, and within each hamlet, but any authority these rights conferred was restricted to the matter in hand.

The Banabans lived by fishing and the cultivation of food trees: mainly coconut, pandanus, and wild almond. Land was owned individually and inherited by children from their parents. Land was also the chief medium of exchange whenever an important debt or obligation had to be discharged. It had many of the functions of money in our own society, and consequently was fragmented into numerous small plots. Early in this century the British lands commission registered 2749 individual holdings. At that time there were only 700 Banabans, though there may have been thrice that many before contact. Some families were richer in land than others, but powerful mechanisms ensuring its circulation seem to have prevented gross inequalities. Land was capital—a direct measure of a Banaban's prestige—but anyone could make a daily living from the sea.

One commodity, however, was often in precarious supply. Ocean Island had no ponds or streams, and would have been uninhabitable were it not for the presence of about fifty underground caves containing reserves of brackish water. These *bangabanga* were the special province of women, whose right and duty it was to collect the water in coconut shells. Caves were owned communally by hamlets, but the use of them was strictly managed by committees called the "kindred of the well."

Besides a developed sense of both private property and communal obligation, Banaban culture seems to have drawn a clear distinction between the sacred and the profane. Secular business took place in the *maneaba;* religious rites and ceremonial feasts in honour of the deified ancestors were held in the *uma-n anti*, or spirit houses. The building types were similar—a large hall with a high thatched roof supported on stone pillars, the sides open to admit air and light.

Most Banaban lineages regarded Nei Tituabine, whose earthly form was the giant ray, as tutelar goddess of the island. Men practised a solar cult that involved the capture and taming of sacred frigate birds, symbolic of the sun. The birds were caught and kept on large stone-faced terraces overlooking the sea. These massive and presumably ancient constructions were similar to the terraced *marae* temples found throughout Polynesia. Some of them belonged to specific *uma-n anti*, and they were also used for feats of endurance, magic, and initiation rites.

Though idyllic in some respects, the Banaban world was a fragile one, vulnerable to hurricanes and droughts. In his book *Disconcerting Issue*, anthropologist Martin Silverman characterizes Banaban culture as "maximizing options": the social structure had to be strict enough to hold together through long periods of Draconian rationing yet sufficiently flexible and innovative to rebuild itself after a cataclysm, such as the drought of the 1870s, when three quarters of the population died or fled the island.

Banaba both nourished and demanded the principal Banaban virtues: courtesy, dislike of violence, respect for individuality, resourcefulness, and a strong sense of reciprocal obligation. These qualities would be tested to the utmost by the man-made disasters of the twentieth century.

◆

Once or twice during the night I was awakened by heavy rain thrumming on the iron roof and dripping onto the broad-leafed plants that grow around the residence. At dawn came the usual country sounds—chickens, dogs—and snarling combat between a watchdog and a mongoose. (Like the mynah bird, the mongoose is an Indian species that has burgeoned in parts of Fiji. Having killed the snakes and ground-nesting birds, it thrives nowadays on chickens' eggs.) Unable to sleep any longer, I pulled on my jeans and went into the bathroom across the passage. I turned on the basin tap; the water flowed for half a minute, then stopped. There came a knock at the door and the caretaker's voice:

"Water, he finish."

I found Saho and Rongorongo on the veranda.

"Good morning," the *talatala* beamed. "I hope you are not inconvenienced by the water—the lack of it, to be precise. Our Superintendent has invited you to take breakfast at his house. He has a shower there and you are welcome to use it."

Rongorongo explained how there are four *talatalas* on Rabi, one for each village, but the minister of Tabwewa is the leader of the island's Methodist Church.

"We others have to be obedient," he added. "Otherwise, we are . . . excommunicated!"

The path to Tabwewa was wet underfoot. Cool drops fell on us from the trees, but the sun—up for more than an hour—was already warm. People waved to the minister from their tidy concrete-block homes, built by the Rabi Council with phosphate royalties. Above us, in a location on the hillside similar to that of the residence, loomed an enormous whitewashed building more like a cathedral than a Methodist church. It is an austere modern structure with a tower pierced by a tall cruciform window; and it stands imposingly on top of six stone-faced terraces jutting out from the slope of the hill. Rongorongo said these were built without machinery by volunteer labour. I guessed that their resemblance to ancient *marae* was more than mere coincidence.

The Superintendent welcomed us in fluent Oxford English, but compared to Rongorongo he was a man of few words. His manner was an engaging blend of shyness and assurance. After giving us time to shower and shave, he invited us onto the veranda, where there were some wicker chairs around a table. The house stands near the church and commands an equally fine view. The ocean below was a flat steel grey, strewn here and there with dissipating mist. You could hear the shouts of three men fishing from a small boat anchored on the reef.

"You know, I am a fisherman," said Rongorongo. "My father taught me how to dive and use a spear gun. We pass on the skills to one son—it is a secret. Diving is the most important thing for a man, even today. When a girl meet a boy, her parents will ask her, 'Can he dive?' If not they will say, 'That boy is a . . . ' We have a word like 'poofdah'—too much like a woman."

The Superintendent's wife brought a large pot of tea and a plate piled high with toast and slices of cheese. She set them quietly on the table, then retired. Rongorongo was asked to say grace by his superior. After a decent interval he resumed his train of thought.

"Nowadays education is also good, but the best of all is to be a minister! When you are a single minister many girls seek you out. Not openly—they are very modest—but they have their ways. You are very popular until you make your . . . decision. Then many people are disappointed."

"Is it the prestige?"

"Right! The prestige, yes, that's it. Right. But not only the prestige. With a *talatala* they know they are . . . guaranteed for life. Guaranteed home, guaranteed food. Because, you know, if a man goes fishing—like those men down there—always the first fish he catches he brings to the minister. They believe if they do not do that they will not catch anything. It is a . . . superstition but it works to our advantage. Also the women know that a minister will never beat them."

"Does much of that go on here?" Saho asked.

"Not a lot, but it happens. We don't approve of divorce. If I have a married daughter and she is beaten by her husband and runs to me, I must always send her back. With a heavy heart, but I must send her back. It is the custom. Her protection is her brothers and other male relations.

"Let us suppose one night I come home drunk and I hit my wife. The story gets out, and next day her brother comes to see me, and he will say, 'Next time you feel like hitting my sister, hold your fist! Hold your fist and save it for me. And perhaps you will enjoy it, because I shall give you a good . . . opposition!' I must not only apologize. I must tell him if he wants to hit me he should go ahead. In this situation you must stand and take it without fighting back, because that is the position of the woman—she is too weak to resist."

"What happens if you do hit back?"

"If you hit back at the brother you are finished. More will come and you are . . . within an inch of a dead man!"

When Rongorongo saw that everyone had finished eating, he turned to us and said:

"It is customary, now that we have enjoyed the Reverend Superintendent's hospitality, to say some words to express our . . . appreciation."

I began to get to my feet but Rongorongo stopped me:

"No, no, that is not necessary, because this is not a public occasion. You may say a few words . . . sitting down."

I was grateful for the cues. Already there had been several occasions when the loquacious minister saved us from violating Banaban etiquette. Unlike the Fijians, who put foreigners in a kind of social quarantine while a spokesman goes through the form, the Banabans try to educate outsiders in their customs. Both strategies affirm the integrity of native culture and show a healthy lack of awe for foreign ways.

This time I slipped into the cultural gulf. We each made a speech of thanks. I tried to mention everyone and everything of relevance; but as soon as I had finished, a cloud crossed Rongorongo's jovial face.

"Excuse us," he said ironically. "Excuse us our . . . superstitions. We are very superstitious. We think it is right to give thanks to Our Lord."

◆

During the year 1900
There came, there came to Ocean Island
The company, the BPC*

*British Phosphate Commission, at that time actually the Pacific Islands Company.

Oh, look here and see, you people of the world!
What a clever race the white-skin is
To confuse the price of phosphate
To our ancestors of long ago! . . .
So look here and see, you British!
How you set a bad example
To us learners of the ways of the world!

This is part of a song performed for Queen Elizabeth in 1977. It was sung and danced by Banaban women with the skill, beauty, and smiling gracefulness that they have always brought to their historical epics. The message, however, was clear. The Banabans had been taken advantage of by a people who—according to their own ethics—should have known much better.

On May 3, 1900, Albert Ellis of the Pacific Islands Company arrived on Banaba. He had already seen a piece of phosphate rock from the island, and he thought there could be more. The Banabans had had some contact with white people for about fifty years. In the great drought of a generation before many had been forced to sign aboard the dreaded "blackbirding" (labour recruiting) ships. A few eventually returned from Queensland and Tahiti, and some of these then worked for the Methodist missionaries who arrived in 1885. But by 1900 fewer than half of the Banabans professed the new religion, and most had not yet learned the shame of their bodies, which the churchmen encouraged in order to save souls and sell cloth at a profit.

As was customary, the chief of Tabwewa greeted Ellis; and Ellis, like other Europeans before him, imagined that this man was the King of Banaba. The white men strode about the place, drilling holes and analyzing the results on the spot. Ellis was good at his job: he concluded that Ocean Island was almost pure phosphate, that the whole island could be mined away, and that this might take eighty years. In all three things he was absolutely right.

Ellis was also good with Pacific natives: he was smiling, ceremoniously courteous, generous with paltry gifts. Through the offices of a faulty interpreter he got the "king" to let his company "lay tramlines or do any work on their land provided the coconuts

and gardens were not interfered with." The "King" signed an agreement giving, among other things, "the said Company the sole right
to raise and ship all the rock and alluvial Phosphate on Ocean
Island." The rights were granted for 999 years in exchange for £50
per annum in trade goods.

The king who was not a king can have had little idea of what he
was signing. No doubt a pen was thrust in his hand and he made
the sign of the cross to please the Christian strangers. Certainly he
had no jurisdiction over any lands on Banaba except his own. Ellis,
on the other hand, must have known very well that he had got the
Banabans to give him a licence to destroy their country in return
for a pittance in overpriced trinkets and third-rate tinned food. Not
satisfied with this, he made so bold as to hoist the Union Jack
(without authorization from Britain) and inform the Banabans that
they were now *kain Engram*, people of England.

The British government was at first unamused by Ellis's pre-
sumption. In 1892 it had made the Gilbert and Ellice Islands a
protectorate, and found the farflung group profitless to administer.
There was no wish to extend this colonial burden across an extra
three hundred miles of empty ocean. The Pacific Islands Company,
however, had friends in high places. On the board of directors in
London was one, Lord Stanmore. Before getting his barony on
retirement from the colonial service, Stanmore had distinguished
himself as Sir Arthur Gordon, first governor of Fiji and defender
of native rights. Under his governorship Fijian lands were made
inalienable and the natives thereby saved from becoming wage slaves
on white plantations.

But by 1900 all that was twenty years in the past; and Gordon,
it seems, had been transformed into a businessman as well as a
baron. He understood immediately the importance of the Ocean
Island find, and persuaded the Colonial Office to run up the flag
there before some other foreign power did. The government soon
realized that on Ocean Island lay the means to subsidize the empire
in that part of the Pacific. In September 1901 a British admiral
followed Ellis's illegal raising of the Union Jack with a legal ceremony. To the Banabans, no doubt, it was equally mystifying.

The Pacific Phosphate Company (as it became in 1902) descended on Banaba with machinery and personnel, including hundreds of Chinese and Gilbertese workers. By 1909 some two million tons of phosphate had been mined and 240 acres—almost one sixth of the island—destroyed. The company failed to keep even the minimal obligations to the Banabans that it had allowed itself in the original agreement: food trees disappeared with the land; natives were charged far higher prices than whites at the company store; and distilled water, which Ellis had promised the Banabans in return for the firewood to make it, was sold at such a price that the inhabitants had to continue drinking from *bangabanga* increasingly polluted by the mining.

When the Banabans finally refused to lease any new land, the company tried to exert pressure on them through the British resident commissioner. He, however, suggested that the company should offer the Banabans better terms and, since it was obvious that mining would eventually consume the whole island, should start a trust fund that would allow them to buy a new home when Banaba was finished. The company's answer was to get Lord Stanmore to press for the commissioner's dismissal. In 1913 the man was removed and sent to an even less desirable post. This happened to every resident commissioner of Ocean Island until 1920: all three tried to defend the natives from abuse—as it was their sworn duty to do—and all left Ocean Island with their careers, and illusions, in ruins. Too many powerful people were making too much money. The company could not be touched.

Meanwhile the company's shareholders were reaping unheard-of profits: annual dividends of 50 and 60 percent at a time when a tenth of that was considered a good return. In 1909 questions were first asked in Parliament, and in 1913 the Colonial Office sent out E. C. Eliot to replace the sacked commissioner and negotiate a new agreement with the Banabans. He managed to get them slightly better royalties, and the company some more land—though not as much as it wanted. Then he turned his attention to a task he innocently supposed had little to do with the phosphate issue.

In 1915 the Gilbert and Ellice Islands Protectorate (including Banaba) was converted into a colony. The change went through quietly enough: more important things were happening elsewhere; Eliot and the islanders thought it would probably be for the better. (The Banabans still had such faith in the ultimate goodwill of their colonial rulers that they gathered £10,000 worth of copra from their remaining coconut trees and gave it to the war effort.)

Nobody but the company and its friends in London realized that the change in status undermined what little sovereignty the Banabans had left. From now on, a portion of their royalties was secretly diverted for administering the colony as a whole (this portion ultimately reached 85 percent). Company lawyers could advance the argument that the Banabans owned only the *surface* of their island; all other rights conveniently belonging to the Crown; and in a colony, of course, the Crown could invoke the law of compulsory purchase to force its citizens to sell their land.

◆

After breakfast Rongorongo, Saho, and I were collected by a rusty minibus with the words RABI COUNCIL OF LEADERS stencilled on the door. At the wheel was a gaunt young man whose thin mustache and long black hair made him look like an Oriental pop star. The other front seat was fully occupied by the Council Chairman.

"This is Joseph, the Island Manager," the Chairman said. "He takes care of everything—the copra, the accounts, the cars—all practical matters."

Joseph drove quickly but skillfully over the narrow sandy road, shouting the day's order of business above the engine's roar: first, interviews with elders in Tabiang, then lunch at Buakonikai. The island has a garden-like quality enhanced by the spacious nature of the villages. Each house stands on a quarter acre, among fruit trees, coconuts, and flowering shrubs. There is no formal clustering around a village green or church—people live along the island's only road, down by the beach, or on the lower slopes of the hills. The ideological foci of the communities—the churches and meeting halls— occupy imposing locations on the edges of the settlements. This somewhat suburban pattern derives from the ancient Banaban practice of living in loosely structured districts.

Rabi is a long, rather narrow island with a crest of forested hills along its spine. The four villages (or districts) have the same names and many of the same traditions as those that formerly existed on Banaba. Three have been built along the northwest shore: Tabwewa, the northernmost, at the old Lever headquarters; Uma, in the middle; then Tabiang, which has the airstrip. Buakonikai lies farther south. The layout is different from oyster-shaped Banaba, but the greater isolation of Buakonikai (whose name means "amid the bush") has been retained. The far side beyond the ridge is devoted to coconut plantations. Tracts of these are reserved to each village, and some people prefer to live there in outlying hamlets. Rabi is nearly ten times larger than Ocean Island, so there has been room to spare, even though the Banaban population of about three thousand is now greater than ever in the recorded past.

Joseph stopped in front of a neat bungalow and let us out. Saho and I followed the Chairman and Rongorongo, removing our sandals at the door, entering stooped. Unlike the Council residence and the Superintendent's house, where Europeans are often entertained, there was no furniture here except for an expensive Sony video cassette recorder and television on a stand in one corner. The lack of tables and chairs was evidently from choice, not poverty. The floor was covered by fine pandanus mats; a dozen elderly men and women were sitting crosslegged along the walls. Family photographs and bright calendars decorated the room, but British royalty (*de règle* in a Fijian house) were conspicuously absent.

We were shown where to sit. One by one the other occupants crossed the floor and shyly shook our hands. Rongorongo made a speech explaining the purpose of the gathering (though this was already well known), and was answered with a welcoming speech from the owner of the house. Two women came in from the kitchen with biscuits and sweet, milky tea mixed in the pot. The room filled with the clatter of teacups and softly murmured conversations.

To begin, Rongorongo announced, four ladies would sing a song recounting the first Japanese bomb attack on Ocean Island. Four dignified and portly women, all of them grandmothers, put frangipani wreaths in their long grey hair and sang, still sitting cross-

legged, swaying from side to side with the lilting tune. This was
not mere entertainment but the ancient medium of the verse epic—
a fragment of the old South Seas expressing a modern catastrophe.
The words told how three warplanes flew over in formation, their
symmetry was beautiful to see, and they wore strings of beads
beneath their wings.

The "beads" soon fell to earth and exploded on the commissioner's residence, though nobody was killed. It was December 8, 1941:
the day after Pearl Harbor. Three months later the British left,
having systematically destroyed the phosphate plant. The Banabans
and several hundred Gilbertese workers were abandoned with the
pious hope that they could survive well enough on their native
resources. But at least half the food trees on the island no longer
existed, the fishing grounds had been disrupted by forty years of
mining, and the people had come to rely on Western supplies from
the company store.

In August 1942 the Japanese occupied the island. They failed to
revive the phosphate operation and were soon faced with serious
famine among the natives. Recognizing that Banaba could never
again support a self-sufficient community of any size, the Japanese
deported the starving inhabitants to other parts of Micronesia and
put them to work growing food for the war effort. This involved
cultivating pumpkins with human excrement—a practice normal
in Japan but loathsome to the islanders. Atrocities occurred. One
hundred and sixty Gilbertese were massacred by machine gun; all
the lepers were put in a boat that was deliberately sunk; many
people were mutilated and beheaded. In three years of war, about
five hundred Banabans—or one third of their total number—died.

After the song, Saho and Rongorongo sat down opposite the old
man and began to ask him questions: *Did you see the Japanese sacking
people's houses? Did you see anyone tortured or killed?* The Chairman
talked to me quietly while the others did their work.

"I was just a schoolboy when the Japanese came to Ocean Island.
I remember one funny thing that happened. The Japanese made
us grow pumpkins for them to eat, but we ourselves were hungry
all the time. One day two Banaban men were stealing a pumpkin
when a Japanese guard came along. What could they do? They had

to attack. One grabbed the guard and held his arms behind; the other drew back his fist to punch the Japanese and knock him out. Well, the Japanese moved his head like this—to one side—just when the fist came towards him, and the punch knocked out all the teeth of the Banaban man behind." The Chairman laughed silently; then his broad face became grave.

"The Japanese punished those men by dropping heavy stones on them. There were other things much worse than that. Sometimes they cut off the women's breasts, and they crucified them by tying them up to trees at crossroads with their legs apart. Everyone who passed by was forced by a guard to look at them."

♦

During my days on Rabi the Chairman often talked to me quietly in the houses and meeting halls while the others were busy with their work. I found him to be a man of surprising contrasts. He was a fundamentalist preacher, but spoke at length about his people's ancient beliefs. He said he'd had only six years' schooling, half of that in Japanese: "I should apologize for being Chairman with so little school, but they elected me anyway." There was no need for this diffidence. Unlike other fundamentalists I've met he had a lively and eclectic mind; he was interested in language, culture, and the contradictions between experience and faith.

"I myself was well treated by the Japanese," he told me. "I learned to speak their language and they made me a pupil-teacher. That was on Kusaie in the Carolines—after they took us away from Ocean Island. It make me sad that several of us can speak Japanese, English, yet we have forgotten our own tongue. What you hear us speaking nowadays is not really our Banaban language. It is Gilbertese—similar to Banaban but not the same.

"Many people came from the Gilberts to work on Ocean Island, and everything—the government, the church, the Bible—all were in Gilbertese. Over the years we stopped speaking Banaban; today we know only a few phrases."

He gave me some examples and followed them with the Gilbertese equivalent. Although I understood nothing, it was clear that the differences were considerable. There are political implications in this: when the Gilbert Islands became independent (as the Republic of Kiribati) in 1979, Ocean Island was made part of the new country, very much against the wishes of the Banabans.

"We are a different people from the Gilbertese, but they say we are not because we speak their language. But that is only a new thing." The Chairman became quite vehement. Saho, taping an interview nearby, had to ask him to speak more quietly. The big man, who resembled somewhat those statuettes of the Chinese god of plenty, took this with equanimity and fell silent. Later the soft voice resumed.

"The Bible say that all languages of the races of man were confused long ago at the tower of Babel. You have read some anthropology. What do you think of that?"

I said that from an anthropological point of view such stories were the myths and legends of the Hebrews. They were symbolic ways of explaining the world, not necessarily any truer than the myths of other peoples. He said nothing for some moments; I was afraid I might have caused offence, but he was thinking.

"In the beginning, our old stories say, Banaba was inhabited by people who were not human. They were half spirit, half man. Then the first true man and his daughter came by canoe from Beru [in the Gilberts], and the leader of the spirit people said, 'Give me your daughter to be my wife.' But he took only the woman's eye; he wrapped it in leaves and put it in the ground for three days. And on the fourth day the eye grew into a girl! In another story, the great eel came out of the sea and married a Banaban woman. These things happened at Uma, my own village. I don't know if they are a legend, a fairy tale, or what. . . ." He looked at me inquiringly, as if to gauge my reaction, then continued.

"The descendants of the spirit people live in the village of Tabwewa. They are the true natives of Ocean Island. Once a year we hold games, and Tabwewa challenges all the others, who, they say, are foreigners.

"In the old days we did not have powerful chiefs like the Fijians have. We had speakers for each village. According to Banaban custom the election of Council should be done by the speakers.

Nowadays we do things in the way of Western civilization—everybody have one vote—but we know who the speakers are. When we welcome someone very important here, like the Prime Minister of Fiji, it is not Council Chairman who greets him at the dock but the Speaker of Tabwewa. He must put a garland of flowers and coconut leaves over the visitor's head. This is because in the old days we made sorcery, and the garland protect him from the ghosts. Now we no longer make sorcery, but if we did the ghosts would say, 'Who is this stranger? We have not been introduced to him!' And they would kill him if he did not wear the garland."

He paused and stared out the window, where palm trees were thrashing in a sudden breeze.

"When the missionaries came to Banaba," he added, "they told us all our old stories were lies."

◆

The road to Buakonikai is a raw, red gash through the jungle, like a Brazilian dream of progress. It swings inland and winds over the hills of Rabi's interior. The night's rain lay in puddles on the clay surface and ran down the bulldozer cuts that serve as ditches.

"The British built the road for us a year ago," Joseph said. "Their consciences must have been bothering them; they gave us two million dollars, for this and the secondary school."

Until then the only way to Buakonikai had been by sea. The village is admired by the rest of Rabi for its independence and the progress it has made with jungle farming learned from Fijians.

Joseph stopped the van abruptly at the top of a ridge and told me to bring my camera. Through a gap in the bush I looked down on a luminescent bay. Orderly ranks of coconut trees stretched back from the turquoise water, and on the far shore the houses of the village were visible among the palms. Above, on a wide terrace, stood the white eminence of a church as great as the one at Tabwewa.

"Buakonikai is very proud of that church," Joseph said. "The people dug the terrace from the hill with shovels and wheelbarrows." Although it lacked the stone facing of Tabwewa's terraces, the artificial platform looked much larger. There was even room for a playing field in front of the minister's residence.

The *maneaba*, or meeting house, of Buakonikai is a large wooden structure resembling an old railway station. It stands near the water with other relics of the Levers' empire—a wharf and some huge primitive machines, slowly disintegrating like fallen colossi. Inside you can see marks on the plank floor where the building was once divided into offices and storerooms. Now it is furnished only with mats, the shutters and doors are always open, and one or two old windows that have kept their bars make silent comment on Rabi's transformation.

Small groups of people were seated around the periphery of the hall, quietly talking. Elderly women had one wall to themselves; old men another. The younger men were gathered at the far end, where Reverend Taatu, whom I'd met in Suva, and three others were playing a game that involved cards and the movement of chequers on a board.

After speeches and introductions Saho and Rongorongo began to interview the women. There was a feeling of peace in the decrepit but spotlessly clean hall. The softly spoken conversations, the wind in the trees outside, and the resinous smell of coconut husks smouldering beneath trays of copra: these things conveyed a sense of the community of which the *maneaba* was the social heart. Two adolescent girls, very beautiful with their waist-length hair and pink school frocks, brought me a sliced papaya, some biscuits, and a pot of tea. When I tried to share this with those seated near me, they made it clear that the "snack" was just for me.

I had scarcely finished it when more women began arriving with rice, potatoes, three kinds of fish, a beef stew, sausages, greens, and steamed breadfruit. They set their dishes on a trestle table. Rongorongo gave advice on etiquette:

"Saho, Ronald, every woman here has prepared something and they watch very closely to see what you will eat. Therefore it is important that you take from everything, so no one will be offended."

"Rongo," Saho said wearily, "we aren't like you. We are very small eaters. They have just given us tea and biscuits—that would have been quite sufficient for me."

"You are offended by the food?"

"Of course not. The problem is the quantity. We aren't accustomed to eating this way."

"We are only on this earth for a very short time," the *talatala* replied. "Who knows how long? Maybe we will die tomorrow. The Bible tells that in Paradise there is no feasting, because it is a . . . spiritual world. We must eat what we can in this life because we will be spirits for eternity." Regret in Rongorongo's voice implied that the absence of table pleasures in the next world was a stiff test of his faith.

After lunch Reverend Taatu showed me his church. The style of the building—it must have been the creation of an Indian architect in Suva—is a remarkable blend of Christendom and Orient. Corbel arches and pointed transom windows blend with the English plan and spire. Inside I was startled to find a gigantic skeleton of steel joists and pillars.

"When our parents built this church," Reverend Taatu explained, "the architect said it was very strong. Now we have been told that it needs bracing against hurricanes."

The steel framework was massive enough to build a major bridge. I hoped that some Suva slicker hadn't talked the Banabans into an unnecessary expense. The minister pointed out that the joists will support an upper floor; two buildings will be made from one: the church above, and church hall below. Fifty thousand dollars has been spent on the steel; an equal sum will be needed to finish the job.

"It is very costly, but we thought we had better take no risks."

Unlike other districts of Rabi, which include minorities of Catholics, fundamentalists, and perhaps even a few pagans, Buakonikai is wholly Methodist. The church was built a generation ago by every able-bodied man giving two days' labour a week. As in mediaeval Europe, congregation and community are one: the church is Buakonikai's cathedral, a monument to strength.

◆

The first half of the twentieth century was, for the Banabans, a period of catastrophic change. Since the white man's arrival they had been indoctrinated by his missionaries, exploited by his commerce, and abandoned to his foes. There was a time span of only two generations from the loss of primaeval isolation to involvement in a global war.

Paradoxically, perhaps, the new religion gave them a rallying point when everything else was in ruins. It is clear that pagan Banaba exalted virtues very similar to those which Western man calls civilized: individual responsibility, communal conscience, and hatred of violence. (The white man's abhorrence of the body was something new, but the Banabans, like other Pacific islanders, humoured it as a tabu of the foreign faith.) There was therefore much in Christianity that the Banabans could admire; and it had the advantage (so they thought) of giving them membership in an ethical system shared by the outsiders with whom they were forced to deal.

The Banabans always assumed, and perhaps they still do, that the people at the top of British civilization—the high officials, judges, and the monarch—were good Christians who could be expected to obey the laws of God. This was not merely naïvety: the only alternative to believing in the ultimate decency of the interlopers was to assume the outside world was ruled by chaos—a belief that could not give the Banabans the ideological anchor they needed. By a happy historical accident, they received a Nonconformist brand of Christianity, which provided a model of legitimate dissent, a precedent for the "loyal opposition" style in which Banaban complaints to the government were expressed.

Banaban Methodist ministers emerged as the new leaders for the times. The assumption of power by youth can be disruptive in a society where political control has always been vested in the elders; but Banaban culture provided a mechanism for the change. The old men had traditionally deferred to young males, known as *rorobuaka* (warriors), in military matters. Bloodshed on Banaba was forbidden, but the warriors were allowed to engage enemies at sea. The struggle with the phosphate company and the British—essentially a fight with outsiders for land—was seen as a fitting theatre for the "warrior" generation. Thus Banaban custom sanctioned the inescapable fact that only younger, more acculturated people could oppose the foreigners effectively—even though this spelt the end of real power for the gerontocracy of elders and hereditary speakers.

Pastor Rotan Tito, the man who became the principal Banaban statesman for most of his life, was born in 1900, the very year that Ellis discovered the riches of Ocean Island. He came from a prominent Buakonikai family with extensive lands. His mother was one of the first Banaban women to protest the destruction of food trees; his father was an early convert to the Wesleyan faith. Rotan Tito was educated at the Methodist college on Tarawa in the Gilberts, and then became minister of his village. He was a man of great personal courage, as he demonstrated years later by demanding better treatment for his people from the Japanese. But long before that, when still in his twenties, he was the leading Banaban in dealings with the company and the new resident commissioner, the famous and infamous Arthur Grimble.

The phosphate issue died down somewhat during Commissioner Eliot's term on Ocean Island (1913–1920) because of his efforts on the Banabans' behalf and the effect of the First World War. However, after that war the British, Australians, and New Zealanders took over the neighbouring island of Nauru, formerly a German possession.

Nauru was geologically identical to Banaba but three times larger. (Both were submerged mountaintops on which had grown coral reefs followed by immense deposits of fossilized bird guano up to eighty feet thick.) The imperial government decided to exploit the two islands for the greatest benefit of Britain and her colonies by transforming the phosphate company into a Crown corporation under joint British, Australian, and New Zealand control. The British Phosphate Commission (BPC), as it now became, was to be run on a "non-profit" basis, selling fertilizer at cost to subsidize the empire's farmers.

For the Banabans it was business as usual. The new corporation proved to be every bit as intractable as the old company. While the BPC subsidized millions of white imperial subjects around the world, it could not bring itself to give fair, let alone generous terms to the owners of the few acres in the Pacific that made all this possible.

In 1925 the BPC wanted to acquire another 150 acres, or one tenth of Ocean Island. (Eliot's 1913 agreement had obtained 250 acres at £50 per acre and a royalty of 6d, or £0.025, per ton of raw phosphate.) This time £100 per acre and 9d a ton were offered. Grimble told the BPC that the Banabans would not accept these prices; he suggested doubling the offer. The Banabans, led by Rotan Tito, had set a much higher value on their homeland. They asked for £5000 per acre—a figure which Grimble's superior, the High Commissioner for the Western Pacific, considered "not unreasonable" in light of the fact that an acre yielded £40,000 worth of phosphate, even at the BPC's artificially low prices.

The two sides were hopelessly far apart. Without consulting the Banabans, Grimble did his own negotiating with the BPC, recommending a "minimum" of £150 and 10½d. He then tried to use his knowledge of the Banabans' culture to break their solidarity and win over a faction to these terms. The islanders stayed united behind Rotan Tito and refused to sell anything. Instead they fought one unrealistic proposal with another: they dropped the acreage demand and offered to sell the phosphate at £5 per carload. Since a car held roughly a ton, and an acre produced about 30,000 tons, they were now in effect asking for £150,000 per acre. Grimble was furious. He punished the landowners for exercising the right to keep their property by banning all games on the island and imposing a dusk-to-dawn curfew.

◆

Sir Arthur Grimble, as he became, is known to millions for his beguiling books *A Pattern of Islands* (1952) and *Return to the Islands* (1957). In these, and in many radio broadcasts, he presented himself as a benign, paternalistic figure ruling his simple native "children" for their own good in the best of all possible worlds, the British Empire. He was an amateur ethnologist of note, a would-be poet, and a "writer of magnificent fiction." Unfortunately for the Banabans, he was not a man to sacrifice his career in their defence.

Before becoming resident commissioner on Ocean Island in 1926, Grimble had spent twelve years in the colony. His advancement was not as rapid as he would have liked; in his own words he was "left with a depressing sense of talents gradually atrophied for lack of exercise." He was married, but saw his wife and children for a total of only nine months between 1920 and 1930. There is no doubt his job was hard, particularly for a Cambridge-educated man with literary ambitions. Loneliness and intellectual isolation were exacerbated by recurring gastric illness.

In Grimble's favour it must be said that he had a genuine affection for the Gilbertese (though perhaps less for the Banabans); that his ethnological research is regarded as first rate for its day; and that he defended native culture, especially dancing, against puritanical missionaries. But from the way he consistently underestimated the ability of his charges to think and act for themselves, and from the host of petty regulations with which he complicated their lives, it is clear that the view of empire he ridicules on the first page of *A Pattern of Islands* was not far from his own.

> The colonial possessions, as everyone so frankly called them, were properties to be administered, first and last, for the prestige of the little lazy isle where the trumpet-orchids blew. Kindly administered, naturally—nobody but the most frightful bounder could possibly question our sincerity about that—but firmly too, my boy, firmly too, lest the school-children of Empire forget who were the prefects and who the fags.*

By 1928 Grimble had had enough of Ocean Island and its stubborn inhabitants. Sick, lonely, and frustrated, he wanted to pull off a coup that would earn him transfer to a better post. He noted the fate of his idealistic predecessors and decided to impose a solution to the phosphate problem. When the BPC pressured the British Secretary of State into suggesting compulsory purchase, Grimble readily concurred. Despite the fact that there was long-standing *de facto* recognition of the Banabans' ownership of minerals as well as trees (i.e., subsurface and surface rights), the islanders were dispossessed of everything but their topsoil by the stroke of a pen in London.

---

*Junior boys used by seniors as personal servants.

The BPC now saw no reason to be generous. They made an offer even lower than before, and Grimble agreed. (Disturbed by his subordinate's failure to defend the Banabans, the High Commissioner in Suva later restored some of the lost revenue to the natives.) There was then a farce of "compulsory arbitration" enacted by a colonial official from Tonga and the BPC's own Ocean Island manager. It was left for Grimble to persuade the Banabans to accept the iniquitous terms, or simply sign the order to alienate their property. Obviously it would look much better for him if he could force the islanders to agree. On August 5, 1928, he wrote the following letter:

To the People of Buakonikai,
Greetings,
   You understand that the Resident Commissioner cannot again discuss with you at present as you have shamed his Important Chief, the Chief of the Empire. . . .
   Because of this I am not writing to you in my capacity as Resident Commissioner but I will put my views as from your long-standing friend Mr. Grimble who is truly your father . . . you must choose LIFE or DEATH.
   I will explain my above statement:

POINTS FOR LIFE
   If you sign the agreement here is the life:
1) Your offence in shaming the Important Chief will be forgiven and you will not be punished;
2) The area of the land to be taken will be well known, that is only 150 acres, that will be part of the Agreement;
3) The amount of money to be received will be properly understood and the company will be bound to pay you, that will be part of the Agreement.

POINTS FOR DEATH
   If you do not sign the Agreement:
1) Do you think that your lands will not go? Do not be blind. *Your land will be compulsorily acquired for the Empire.*

If there is no Agreement who then will know the area of the lands to be taken?

If there is no Agreement where will the mining stop?

If there is no Agreement what lands will remain unmined?

I tell you the truth—if there is no Agreement the limits of the compulsorily acquired lands on Ocean Island will not be known. 2) And your land will be compulsorily acquired *at any old price*. How many pence per ton? I do not know.

. . . And what will happen to your children and your grand-children if your lands are chopped up by mining and you have no money in the Bank?

. . . you much choose LIFE or DEATH. There is nothing more to say. If you choose suicide then I am very sorry for you but what more can I do for you as I have done all I can.

I am, your loving friend and father,

Arthur Grimble.

P.S. . . . If the Agreement is not signed consideration will be given to punishing the Banabans. And the destruction of Bua-konikai Village must also be considered to make room for min-ing. . . .

Despite the threats, the Banabans refused to sign. Rotan Tito sent a letter of protest to London, where it gathered dust in a drawer. Grimble signed the purchase order and mobilized colony prisoners (from other islands) as special police. Banaban women clung to their trees as the bulldozers advanced; the police beat them and tore them away. Rotan Tito later wrote:

We were willing to die for our lands at that time, but we respected our elders' word of advice under the Banaban Custom that to shed blood is prohibited on their island.

We followed such advice then with my anticipation and trust in the Sovereign of Britain, that he would readily help us when he is able to hear the true position of the Banabans on their homeland. . . .

Arthur Grimble's letter presumably shocked the Banabans of 1928 as much as it did the British public when the Banabans produced it at their London court case in 1976. By that time Grimble had been dead twenty years and was not able to defend himself; but his letter was unequivocal. A resident commissioner had threatened the people under his care with the destruction of their village and lands if they did not sell their birthright to a Crown corporation for a song. It destroyed overnight the avuncular image that Grimble had so assiduously cultivated for himself. He was not the only one to blame, of course. He was the instrument, the broken reed, used by ruthless financial and political interests to achieve their ends. The stench from Grimble's letter must pervade not only his books but many panelled rooms in London.

◆

Saho and Rongorongo held their last interviews in the Catholic church hall at Uma. This building is another modern *maneaba*, about a hundred feet long by fifty wide, with freshly painted white concrete walls and floral linoleum beneath the pandanus mats. Three electric guitars were hanging on the wall.

You can distinguish Rabi's churches by their attitude to dancing: the fundamentalists allow none; the Methodists grudgingly permit traditional performances; but the Catholics are so liberal as to hold Saturday-night hops in their hall. Joseph, the Island Manager, is himself a Catholic and leader of the band.

"We keep the place well lit," he said. "The parents sit around the walls and keep an eye on things. No girls are allowed outside with boys. But they have a good time. We play all the new songs. Tell me, where can I get a book with the words of the latest hits? We copy the music from tapes, but we have trouble following the words."

I glanced across the room. White-haired men and women were sitting crosslegged below the Yamaha guitars. Saho and Rongorongo quietly questioned them about the Japanese; it seemed that their conversation could not possibly belong to living memory.

"Uma has many churches," the Chairman told me, as we shared a plate of biscuits and a pot of tea. "Most of the Catholics live here, and so do many members of my church, the Assembly of God.

"I was brought up in the Pentecostal faith, but I had to leave because a lot of them were breaking their vows. They were smoking and drinking, also dancing." He nodded with a grin in the direction of the instruments. "I began to testify. I preached everywhere—in Tabwewa, in Tabiang, in Buakonikai, in Uma. At first nobody came. They mocked me. But after six months we had eight members and we built our first church—a Fijian *bure*. Two years later we had eighty members, and we built our present church of concrete block. Now we are two hundred. My church is still the smallest one on Rabi. But I think it does not really matter." He pointed to the roof. "We all worship the same God."

He fell silent for some minutes. Again I could hear the questions being asked on the far side of the hall. *How long were you in solitary confinement? Did anyone actually witness that man beheaded?*

"After the war ended," the Chairman said, "the British collected us and showed us pictures of an island they said was Rabi. We saw a beautiful river with rows of houses on each side, and they told us that our homes on Ocean Island were destroyed. We said yes, we would like to go to Rabi, but when we got here we found it was all a trick—there were no houses, only tents. Two years later some of us went back to Ocean Island and we found what they had said about our villages was also a lie. Our houses were still there, and we could have mended them."

I asked why the Banabans had voted to stay on Rabi when a referendum was held at that time.

"We decide to stay here because we saw that they would mine away Banaba no matter what we said. We had no rights there anymore. Here there is no phosphate, and we wanted to be left in peace.

"But that does not mean we have given up. Some of us have gone back to Ocean Island. They are planting trees. One day, with God's help, it will be like it was before—but that will not be for the people of my generation, or even my children's generation, to see."

When it was time for lunch, a long mat was unrolled down the middle of the hall. More people arrived; women brought bowls of hot food, which they set on the mat between rows of plates and glasses. The quantity and variety were staggering: beef, chicken, spinach with corned beef, rice, noodles, *dalo*, local greens, and cakes for dessert. The women and men seated themselves crosslegged on opposite sides of the mat; there must have been at least fifty people altogether. Rongorongo gave thanks to the Lord, and the banquet began.

Saho and I were provided with knives and forks; most of the Banabans used only spoons and their fingers, helping themselves to enormous handfuls of rice. But this was done with such grace, the people bending gently forward from the waist, that their feast had the rhythm of a seated dance. I tried to imitate their posture—it was almost of yogic severity, with both knees kept very low. Saho, however, arranged himself in an African pose: one foot tucked beneath him, the other planted firmly on the floor with the knee raised toward his chin. Elderly ladies opposite began to giggle; one said something to the Chairman. He waited a moment, then whispered in my ear:

"She laughs because you can sit like us, but Dr. Saho is having difficulties." Clearly, it was a corrective joke. Saho's posture—a disaster had he been wearing not shorts but a *sulu*—was in Banaban etiquette the equivalent of an open fly.

◆

In 1909 the Ocean Island resident commissioner, Quayle Dickson, had proposed that the phosphate company should open a Banaban trust fund against the day when little or nothing of Banaba would be left. The company vigorously resisted the suggestion at first, but later saw the wisdom in granting the Banabans the means to settle elsewhere: it would be much easier to mine away the island if its tiresome natives were removed.

As the fund slowly accumulated, so did pressure on the Banabans. In 1928 Grimble suggested they consider an empty island in the Gilberts; suspecting his motives, the Banaban leaders refused. But by the late 1930s, Rotan Tito began to favour the idea of buying an island in the Fiji group. He hoped it would allow the younger generation to revive traditional culture, while giving himself better access to High Commission headquarters at Suva. However, he made it very clear that purchase of a new home was not to weaken the Banabans' rights on Banaba, or to imply that all of them would move. He liked the sound of Wakaya, about fifty miles northeast of Suva, but the British thought it too small.

Meanwhile, Lord Leverhulme (alias William Lever) foresaw the Japanese threat to the Pacific and began selling off his coconut estates. In 1941 the High Commission bought Rabi from him for £25,000 (Australian) taken from the Banaban fund. The Banabans were told about their new island in March 1942—just before they were abandoned to three years of hardship and exile. They could have spent the war safely on Rabi, had a ship been available to take them there.

After the war it was a different story. When the British found that the inhabitants had already been removed from living inconveniently on top of Ocean Island's riches, they made sure the Banabans went straight to Rabi with no chance of seeing, let alone resettling, their ancient home. The High Commissioner wrote:

> . . . It is essential that the B.P.C. should lend the Government a vessel for the purpose of transporting the natives. . . . This request is made with confidence, since the removal of the Banabans and the settlement of the Banaban question is even more to the essential benefit of the B.P.C. than the Government.

The Banabans were told that Ocean Island was completely uninhabitable, and that they must go to Rabi for at least two years, after which they could choose where to live. At the same time, the BPC began recruiting three thousand workers to be housed on "uninhabitable" Banaba.

The islanders' first experience of Rabi was not a happy one. Their only housing was army tents, for which they were later charged A£12,000. The hurricane season was unusually severe, with day after day of cold torrential rain. The Banabans now numbered 703, and they had with them 300 Gilbertese spouses and friends. Forty old people and several children died of influenza and pneumonia before the weather eased.

Rabi had been conquered by the Tongans in the mid-nineteenth century and later sold to Europeans by the chiefs of Taveuni. The sale was among those upheld as lawful after Fiji became a British colony. Because it had been worked for decades as a private plantation, there were few people living on the island, and none who could claim it as their home. Rabi was more fertile than Wakaya, and, at twenty-seven square miles, big enough for any foreseeable increase of the Banabans. In the long run it was the better choice, but to the war-shattered Ocean Islanders arriving there in December 1945 it seemed large and threatening.

While the Banabans were still disoriented, the BPC began to press for a mining agreement, and a negotiating session was called for January 1947. The attitude of the London Colonial Office is revealed by these minutes for December 4, 1946:

4. It seems to me that a point for conversation is whether we should warn the Fiji Government that we are quite definitely going to the talks in January ready in effect to ditch the Banabans if this proves necessary.

The British High Commission suggested to the Banabans that they hire a specialist to advise them on the intricacies of the phosphate business. They did so, paying his fee in advance. The man failed to turn up at the critical stage of the negotiations. The BPC officials said that he was ill; but this was odd because he had been seen having lunch in Suva that very day. Later it was discovered that the advisor had been told not to go to the talks—by the British High Commission.

The Banabans had little room for manoeuvre, and they feared another compulsory purchase order. They hesitated for a while, but signed the new mining agreement when the BPC marginally improved the offer. Many land titles and other documents had been lost in the war; most of the adults had to visit Ocean Island and mark their boundaries as best they could.

While they were there something momentous happened: Nei Tituabine, the tutelar goddess of the island, appeared to some people of Uma. "So you Banabans are not all dead," she said. "I have been looking for you." When the Banabans returned to Rabi she went with them, and it is said that the health of the people immediately improved.

◆

Midway between Tabwewa and Uma there is a settlement still known by the Fijian name Nuku. It is here that buildings of a pan-Rabi nature have gone up, including a small post office, an island meeting hall, and the new secondary school.

Saho had been asked to give a speech at the school, after which we were invited to a lunch cooked by the senior girls. There were Indians, Fijians, and Banabans on staff. Headmaster Teiwaki was a stocky thirty-year-old with a wide Mongolian face and thick black hair.

"Before this was built the older children had to board in Suva," he told me. "It was expensive for the parents and destructive of our culture. Now all the children can stay on the island until they are ready for higher education.

"I hope our young people will look forwards—to Rabi—and not only back to Ocean Island. This, now, is Banaba."

The schoolchildren were waiting crosslegged on a concrete classroom floor, the boys in white shirts and dark shorts, the girls in pink dresses. Saho had agreed to talk about opportunities at the university in Suva, but as he warmed to speaking he began to lecture about the need to question assumptions. The matless floor was hard on the children's bony legs, but their attention never wandered. Whether they followed Saho's lofty argument or not, they gave Banaban respect to the spoken word.

I wondered how it was for them to grow up in this society of paradoxes: faith and disillusionment, naïvety and resourcefulness, rapid change and adherence to a continually redefined tradition. The "warriors" were in charge now, but from the children's point of view was the society not rigidly authoritarian? The role of the Church on Rabi was almost theocratic, although the rule of the Methodists had been balanced somewhat by the choice of a fundamentalist chairman and a Catholic manager.

I had seen a graffito scrawled in charcoal on an outside wall: SEX IS MY GAME, EVIL IS MY TASTE, DEATH IS MY LAST. Just the bravado of some adolescent malcontent, perhaps. But the words—the repudiation of puritan virtue and its heavenly reward—seemed an ominous challenge to Rabi's being.

Later that day I saw something much more hopeful at the school— a performance of traditional Banaban dance. It was an evening of golden light on the village palm trees and the wild green hills above Tabwewa. The air was still, soft, filled with the sound of frogs and the smell of wood fires. On the way to the school Teiwaki garlanded us with *leis* of frangipani petals, woven by the schoolgirls. They were masterpieces, those *leis*, so skillfully entwined by diligent fingers that they might have grown to their circular form; when worn, their perfume was intoxicating.

And then, the dancing. The young girls in their *leis*, thin vests, and raffia skirts—all that was intoxicating, too. But its sensuality was innocent and joyful—swaying thighs were waves, rotating knees the preening of birds, beckoning fingers the ripple of coconut fronds. To begin, the dancers sat—two rows of girls, behind them the boys. They danced by swaying from the hips, with arms outstretched, chanting the music as they did so. Then they rose and performed an intricate ballet; the two lines flowed through each other, broke up, and rejoined in changing configurations. Ballet was not the right comparison. Western dance is so often a matter of fits and starts, of tiptoe dashes, sudden swoonings, and abrupt pirouettes. This had none of that disjunction: it was sinuous; it flowed; its movements were inspired by waves and wind, by birds in flight and the gliding of fish through the reef.

"The last dance," Teiwaki said, "is a kind of Banaban hula, done by three of our naughtiest girls. You could say it is a celebration of the body."

Three lithe beauties (who, I was sure, were not really naughty at all) appeared in wide, bell-shaped grass skirts like eighteenth-century crinolines. These they shook with the hips while their arms waved above their heads. Faster and faster they went, gyrating about the floor. The fronds of the hula skirts parted now and again, always in unison, to show an extraordinarily rapid but controlled flexing and quivering of the thighs. From Teiwaki's remark and the laughter of the audience it was clear that this dance had some erotic connotations, but there was never a hint of lewdness. It had the sensuous virtuosity of a flamenco but none of the repression, the gaiety of a cancan without its prurience. While the adults laughed, the small children—too young to guess at any symbolism—were shrieking with delight.

◆

In 1947 the Banabans signed away the remaining 671 acres of Ocean Island and voted to stay on Rabi. They then turned their attention to the British legal system, in which they still had a touching faith.

In the post-war years the Banabans had before them the instructive model of Nauru, the larger, luckier phosphate island that managed to buy its freedom from the BPC. The Nauruans had also been bombed and abused by the Japanese, but after the war their island came under the trusteeship of the United Nations. In 1968 they achieved independence; two years later they bought out the BPC, and then hired the corporation—on *their* terms—to continue working the deposits. The Nauruans got rich. They bought an airline and choice real estate in Australia (including Nauru House, the tallest office block in Melbourne, known locally as "Birdshit Tower"). Nauru is the smallest republic in the world (eight square miles) and it has the world's highest per capita income. For the Nauruans the "cargo" has arrived, and is likely to remain, at least until their phosphates run out in the 1990s. By then they should have enough capital to see them through to doomsday. But unless they buy a new island or rehabilitate their old one, the Nauruans will always be utterly dependent on the world civilization which, in its small way, their island has helped to build.

The Banabans, poorer and with a deep sense of grievance, have two advantages over the Nauruans: a new island on which they can easily support themselves and a collective purpose to their lives. While the Nauruans began sinking into a sybaritic world of junk food, luxury automobiles, tax-free alcohol, and heart disease—a parody of the Western dream—the Banabans began legal proceedings in London against the British government and the BPC. The case became the longest in the history of British civil law, and, at three quarters of a million pounds, one of the costliest.

On my last morning Joseph took me to see a copy of *Go Tell It to the Judge*, a documentary film on the case and its issues first shown by BBC Television on January 6, 1977—shortly after judgement was reached. We drove to a house in Tabiang and were greeted by a young Indian. He had married a Rabi woman and settled on the island (several Banabans have married members of other groups). The living room, as usual, was empty of furniture save a video recorder and TV set.

"Where you from, sah?" the Indian asked me.

"Canada."

"Canada, oh yes, Canada. I have relations in Vancouver and I was wanting myself to move there. But then I meet one Banaban girl and I think I will stay. You marry a Banaban, safe from Fiji government because Rabi Council have the power here. Banaban womans very pretty, nice long hairs, and all very friendly people. Not like Indians. I don't like my own race! I don't like my own race at all."

He grinned and waved his hand toward the front yard, where there were some pieces of steel and an arc-welding plant.

"My profession is welding, but I like to open a supermarket here. Banaban peoples know nothing about money. Here only small stores, price very high. With supermarket lots of sales, plenty profit!"

Joseph produced a video cassette and put it in the machine. About a dozen people had gathered to watch; as their voices fell, the hiss of the television competed with the insect din outside.

There were two suits in the Banaban case: one over the BPC's unfulfilled contractual duty to replant trees in mined-out areas; the other claiming £21 million from the British government for breach of trust in diverting phosphate revenues to subsidize the Gilbert and Ellice Islands colony and the farmers of the empire.

The case took six years to assemble, seven months to hear, and four months for the judge to decide. In the course of the trial the judge and lawyers made an unprecedented journey to see for themselves the destruction on Ocean Island, and the clouds of acrid dust from machines that were not yet silent. (The deposits finally ran out in 1980—exactly as predicted in 1900 by Albert Ellis.)

The Banabans got little satisfaction from the court. The judge, Sir Robert Megarry, found that they were indeed entitled to financial compensation from the BPC, but failed to say how much. "The damages shall not be token, not minimal but not large" was his Delphian utterance. He left it for the Banabans themselves to negotiate a figure with the BPC—as if they had not already done enough one-sided bargaining with that corporation. As for the suit against the Crown, the judge found that the Banabans might well have a moral claim, but they could expect no award from the court because the Crown was not legally the Banabans' trustee. In other words, this Crown which had run up its flag, created a colony, and done what it would with the natives' land and wealth had been all the time in the enviable position of holding power without responsibility!

The BBC documentary accomplished more for the Banabans than the legal apparatus of the decayed imperial power. Millions of Britons watched *Go Tell It to the Judge*. They saw Rotan Tito standing like a Nagasaki survivor in the white dust and glaring desolation that had once been Buakonikai. They saw men who still believed in the God the British had foisted on their empire, and in the justice they had said could be found beneath the Union Jack. And they heard Grimble's shameful letter.

The public was outraged. The BBC and members of Parliament were flooded with letters. Questions were asked in the House. Eventually a special commissioner was sent to the South Pacific to investigate. Britain, Australia, and New Zealand dug deep in their national coffers and offered the Banabans ten million Australian dollars on an *ex gratia* basis—that is to say, without admitting any liability.

The Banabans are not impressed. Too many questions are still unanswered. What compensation will the BPC pay? Will Banaba ever be reconstructed? Worst of all, what security of possession do the Banabans have over Ocean Island now that Britain has made it part of Kiribati?

Where is my land?
This is my land.
My grandparent says
This is my land
But I don't know.
I am a child,
And have just been born.

7

▲▲▲

LEVUKA

After Rabi, Suva seemed a meg-
alopolis. I shared a taxi into town from the airport with three
Banabans, whom the driver tried to cheat. They handed the man
a roll of cash and told him to take out his fare; he began counting
off fives and tens as if they were ones; the Banabans said nothing.
I wasn't sure if they had failed to notice or simply could not bring
themselves to protest. They acted as if money embarrassed them,
as if to guard it were not worth the loss of dignity involved.

One night at the Grand Pacific; then off to see Levuka, Fiji's
capital until 1882, on the island of Ovalau. I was up and out of the
hotel by six. The streets were empty but for lonely joggers—all of
them Fijian. I walked briskly down Victoria Parade to the Pacific
Airlines office, where buses to the airport leave on each half hour.
Clouds above Parliament were already peach-coloured in the early
light, the buildings a leaden grey. The harbour was absolutely still,
a sheen of reflected hills and clouds, with the hulls of anchored
ships turning golden in the first rays of the sun.

The bus took the King's Road through shabby Raiwai and Raiwaqa, then prosperous Indian suburbs where the houses are built
on tall concrete posts (the ground floor is walled in and developed

as the family grows). A short stretch of country was followed by
the long iron bridge across the Rewa to Nausori and the delta
flatlands. This fertile, low-lying plain was once the powerful chiefdom of Rewa, Bau's main rival in the mid-nineteenth century; but
now it is given over to commercial rice and sugar farming. Nausori,
like Nadi, is a predominantly Indian town—in Fiji, flatlands, Indians, and airports go together.

By half past seven I was aloft in a Dehavilland Twin Otter bearing
the orange and white livery of Fiji Air and the name *Tui Manu
Levu*, "King Hawk." Other passengers were reading the morning
papers but I spent the short flight gazing down. The delta looked
like an experimental garden, its neat strip fields and grid of red-
earth roads broken in places by patches of bush, fallow, and meandering streams. Here and there, either intact or evident in crop
patterns, you could see ring ditches and circumvallations of ancient
fortified towns. At one time there were hundreds of them (by no
means all contemporary), but modern agriculture and settlement
are fast erasing these traces of the endless native wars. A pity: Fijian
fortifications were among the most sophisticated and effective ever
built. The moats and berms, elaborate wooden ramparts, parapets,
tortuous entrance galleries, and rows of poisoned stakes were virtually unbreachable until the advent of firearms. Such villages fell
to starvation or treachery, seldom to direct assault.

At the edge of the delta came some low hills followed by a fringe
of mangroves and open sea. I realized as the plane left the Viti
Levu mainland that our course was taking us over the royal island
of Bau. It lay not half a mile from the shore: a twenty-acre islet
occupied by many houses, a triangular green, and several large
buildings. Most interesting of all was its shoreline—too regular to
be natural, and set with indentations like the edging of a postage
stamp. These were the stone-built docks for the great canoe fleet
with which Bau's twenty acres once subdued much of Fiji's seven
thousand square miles. The feat was proportionally comparable
to the rise of the Aztecs on their muddy islets in the lakes of Mexico; or, for that matter, to the influence of the British Isles on the
world.

◆

The plane's route—NNE from Rewa over Bau to Levuka—followed the axis of central Fiji's nineteenth-century politics. While Bau and Rewa struggled for hegemony in Fijian affairs, the relationship Bau's monarchs established with the early white settlers ultimately guaranteed the island dynasty's emergence as the foremost native aristocracy. In that relationship a "tribe" or people known as the Levuka played the major supporting role.

According to tradition, the Levuka were original inhabitants of the island now called Bau. They were fishermen, subject to the Bau people, who lived in those days nearby on the Viti Levu coast. In the mid-eighteenth century the Levuka offended their masters and were displaced from Bau island by the ancestors of the present Bauans. The fisherfolk scattered to Lakeba (where the *Argo* was wrecked *circa* 1800) and the coast of Ovalau, where their tui founded the village that became Levuka town.

The Levuka, however, remained vassals of Bau, and in return were granted certain privileges including the right to act as the Bauan Warlord's ambassadors. It was in this capacity that they brought some cargo and at least two white men from the *Argo* wreck to Bau. One of these was Oliver Slater, who soon discovered the sandalwood on Vanua Levu; the other was a shadowy figure known only as Na Matai, "The Craftsman." He lived at Bau for a few years and prospered by claiming to be in touch with the shade of Vunivalu Banuve, victim of the "long disease," the first great plague of foreign origin.

In 1808, about five years after the accession of the new Vunivalu, Naulivou, the Levuka brought another foreigner to Bau. (By that time Na Matai had joined Banuve permanently in the spirit world, after dying from a surfeit of kava.) He was a Swede who had spent some time idling in Tonga with fellow "beachcombers"—the castaways, deserters, escaped convicts, and marooned undesirables who became the principal culture brokers in the early contact years. His real name was Kalle Svenson but he soon became known in English as Charley (the) Savage. He had signed aboard a brig bound from Tongatapu for Sandalwood Bay but was wrecked on a reef about a hundred miles east of Viti Levu. After a pleasant sojourn with a local chief, Savage was taken to Bau as a gift for the Vunivalu.

Bau was a rising star in Fiji politics but she was still outshone by Rewa and Verata (a coastal chiefdom immediately to the north). At that time most Fijians knew nothing of firearms. (They had indeed taken some gunpowder from the *Argo*, but held it in awe after what happened when they used it as body paint and tried to dry themselves by the fire.) Charley salvaged some muskets from his wreck and realized that he could make himself a *deus ex machina* in the local wars. He showed the new weapon and his command of it to Naulivou, and then went with Bauan war parties against outlying strongholds of Rewa and Verata. Savage was like a time traveller appearing with an automatic rifle on mediaeval battlefields. He would pick off the enemy chiefs and leave the Bauans to pursue with the usual mayhem that attended a Fijian rout.

Savage held the esteem of his hosts by observing important Fijian customs while daring to break minor tabus with lordly style. Naulivou judged his man well: he raised him to the title *Koroi na Vunivalu*, the "Warlord's Killer," and gave him highborn women; but he made sure no male children survived birth.

In 1813 the Killer met his end. He and some other beachcombers underestimated the natives in the sandalwood region of Wailea on Vanua Levu—they failed to keep up a rotation of fire, and were overwhelmed when their shots were spent. The Waileans knew that muskets had to be reloaded. So pure was the victors' hatred that they restrained themselves from dashing Charley's brains out on the spot. Instead, they drowned him in a pool, to save his skull for a drinking cup. His body was cooked and eaten, and the long bones kept for making sail needles.

Charley Savage left no written record, but a contemporary, the enterprising Scotsman William Lockerby, wrote a fascinating journal of fourteen months in the "Feejee Islands" from 1808 to 1809. This has considerable literary and ethnographic merit, and is candid about its author's behaviour. Like most sandalwood traders, Lockerby took part in local wars for the sake of obtaining a cargo; when this failed he was not above threatening the natives with magic of his own invention:

I then took some long grass and bound it round several of [the Fijian's] breadfruit trees; this done, I made a pile of stones before a pond of fresh water which was before his door; and then told him whoever should eat of the breadfruit would die, and that the same fate would meet the person who should wash himself in the pond. . . . All this I assured him was . . . because he would not let me have the wood.

Two days after this incident Lockerby records the following:

May 18th [1809]. A canoe came alongside of the ship, belonging to Highley Bay. ["Highley" is L's rendering of Wailea, where Savage was later killed.] It brought a present for Captain Scot, which it may be supposed could not be accepted. It was the entire body of a man who had been cooked upon hot stones in the ground. The bearers of it said it was one of their enemies, and added they thought they could not have brought us a more acceptable present; particularly as it was cooked in the manner they are always done when they make presents to their principal chiefs. We told them to throw it overboard; this they would not do; and left us saying we were afraid to eat our enemies.

Notwithstanding the above passages, Lockerby, like the best of the beachcombers, was sympathetic to Fijian culture and healthily irreverent toward his own.

During that period their conduct towards me, and their general character . . . made me consider them in quite a different light than in that of cannibals. . . . They differ from other [natives] in being very desirous of keeping their skin clean. Their hair is [dyed] different colours, so that one half of their heads will appear white and the other black at the same time. In war they are fearless and savage to the utmost degree, but in peace their disposition is mild and generous towards their friends, and the affection they bear towards their relations is very seldom found among Europeans. . . . The women are remarkably handsome, and have all that delicacy of form and softness of voice and man-

ners, which distinguish female from the other sex in every part
of the civilized world. Their virtue might be set as an example
to nations who pride themselves on being far removed from them
in knowledge and refinement.

♦

Beyond Bau the plane traversed a seascape of outstanding beauty.
The water varies, according to depth and currents, through an
infinite range of blues and greens—aqua, navy, turquoise, alfalfa,
and emerald—with white and gold aurae surrounding every reef-
borne island. In other places there is no land, merely a reef, treacherous to shipping but offering to the sky a swirl of hues beneath a
film of water and a ring of foam.

Suddenly a forest rose to meet the aircraft as it crossed the heights
of Moturiki. I looked down on green peaks and chasms traced with
mist. Then came a narrow strait between this isle and its larger
neighbour, Ovalau. From the air you can see that Ovalau is the tip
of a large volcano. The island is approximately round, and sunken
in the middle like a fallen soufflé. A mountain ring rises steeply
from the sea and encircles the caldera. At one time the interior
must have held a crater lake, but the Lovoni River has broken
through the rim to the southwest. The mountains acted as a cultural
barrier—when the east coast was settled by the Levuka, and later
their white adherents, the central basin remained in the hands of
the Lovoni people who originally controlled the whole island.

Immediately upon landing I felt the languor of the place. There
is a half-hour taxi ride from the airstrip to Levuka, but the Indian
drivers do not hustle here: they fill their cars by strict rotation and
the fee is fixed. The road skirts the southern shore, passing through
coconut groves and tiny villages almost in the shadow of the hills.
To the right the ocean stretches away, empty but for circles of
sticks and stones in the shallow water of the reef. These are fences
that trap unwary fish with each ebb tide. Dark children wearing
tufts of sun-bleached hair waved to us as they paused from gathering
the catch.

It was still early when we reached the town, and a stroll down
the main street confirmed what others had told me—Levuka is

"dead." The former capital of Fiji now has only fourteen hundred people, a drop of almost three hundred over the last ten years. I searched in vain for an open café or restaurant. It seemed that even the Chinese had left. At length I came to a large clapboard building set back from the road beside a creek. The words ROYAL HOTEL were painted in huge letters on the corrugated iron roof.

"Excuse me. Are you serving breakfast?"

"Breakfast?" A look of incomprehension passed across the weathered face of an old, mostly white woman who appeared after I had spent five minutes knocking, coughing, and treading loudly up and down the boards of the veranda. There was no lobby, desk, or bell; and the doors to what looked like the lounge were shut.

"It is breakfast time, isn't it?" I glanced at my watch. It was eight-thirty.

"Are you staying here?" the woman asked suspiciously. She had come down from the first floor by an external staircase flanked by a large sign: HOUSE GUESTS ONLY. NO VISITORS ALLOWED UPSTAIRS. Evidently the Royal, Fiji's oldest extant hotel, had changed from the days when Levuka had an ocean-wide reputation for whoring, gambling, and every other kind of frontier entertainment. (It is said that ships found the port by following the line of empty rum bottles floating out.)

The woman unlocked the doors and preceded me into a cavernous lounge furnished with rattan chairs. The floor sagged under the weight of a grand piano, there was a fine barkcloth *masi* on one wall, and overhead hovered a squadron of ornate but crippled fans. The woman disappeared into the back without a word and left me for a quarter of an hour. I considered leaving, but the chair was comfortable. A sea breeze came in from the veranda and played with the torn lace curtains; it roused the stale odours of floor polish, tobacco, and insecticide, and brought with it a rhythmical croaking of frogs. The woman returned.

"Breakfast is one dollar fifty," she said, as if it had taken her all this time to calculate the figure.

"What is it?" I asked.

"?"

"What do you serve for breakfast?"

"Breakfast is pawpaw, bread, fried egg, and tea. I'll call you when it's ready."

I decided to explore. The next room held a full-size billiard table; on the walls were a cue rack and scoreboard, a magnificent eight-legged *tanoa*, and faded photographs of sports teams. CRICKET MATCH. GARRICK HOTEL, SUVA, VERSUS ROYAL HOTEL, LEVUKA. AT LEVUKA JANUARY 1st 1949, I read. There was no mention of which team had won.

The dining room housed a collection of Japanese dolls in glass cases. Above the kitchen door gaped the jaws of a shark, its teeth raked backwards to allow no escape, like a mediaeval painting of the mouth of hell.

◆

In 1815, two years after the killing of Charley Savage, Oliver Slater was clubbed in his sleep. The sandalwood era died with the man who had started it: the wood had been cut to the point where the stands would never recover. For the next ten years few ships called at Fiji, and with the resulting shortage of gunpowder and musket parts the influence of the remaining beachcombers declined. Some survived as handymen and court jesters, but others ended as a chiefly dinner when their tricks no longer amused.

After exhausting sandalwood, South Pacific traders turned to a new and unlikely product. This was the *bêche-de-mer*, or sea cucumber, a reef-dwelling marine slug which in some species grows more than a foot long and three inches thick. It was highly prized in China for its flavour and imagined aphrodisiac qualities.

Bêche-de-mer trading required an approach very different from the grab-and-run tactics of the sandalwooders. The smelly cargo took time to gather and even longer to cure by a boiling and smoking process. Fijians had to be induced to fish for the creatures and spend weeks preparing them; large curing sheds had to be built near the beach. It was obviously not in the traders' interest to encourage local wars—their plant and cargo were too vulnerable. A more stable pattern of contact slowly emerged: the whites exchanging iron tools and other useful goods for Fijian services. There was a need for men who could operate as honest brokers in both cultures.

In 1824 a young New Englander named David Whippy came to Fiji. Straight in his dealings and good at languages, he soon made friends with the Tui Levuka and settled on Ovalau. He supervised the curing of *bêche-de-mer* cargoes and made sure his native hosts got hard steel tools in return—not the cheap soft iron usually foisted on Stone Age peoples. Whippy's presence at Levuka attracted other whites; the town developed into a trading post where Fijians could obtain foreign articles at a fair price, while whaling and *bêche-de-mer* ships could put in for supplies under the protection of the Tui Levuka and his powerful suzerain, the Vunivalu of Bau.

By 1840 Levuka had a "foreign" population of about two hundred; thirty or so were British and American, the rest their native women and half-caste children. For the most part these people were industrious—they planted gardens, set up workshops, and built boats. Commodore Wilkes of the United States Navy, who came to survey the islands in that year, remarked that he had "met with no better disposed whites throughout the voyage than we found there."

But the settlement was not without problems. In 1841 the Lovoni of the interior fell on the town by night and burned it to the ground. Three years later the whites suffered a further setback, partly of their own making. The long war between Bau and Rewa had broken out the year before. It had been the policy of Levuka settlers to stay as neutral as possible in native wars, but one of their number became embroiled in the dispute and involved others. Ratu Seru Cakobau, the new *de facto* power of Bau, angrily expelled all Europeans from Ovalau for what he saw as disloyalty, and the Tui Levuka had no option but to agree. Thus began a five-year exile in an undesirable spot on Vanua Levu, but it saved the whites from massacre when the Lovoni attacked again in 1846, killing four hundred natives in the space of an hour.

Cakobau eventually relented and allowed the Europeans to rebuild their town. He had missed the convenient trading post and needed munitions for war. But the Levuka that re-established itself lacked the integrity of the early years. It began to acquire a reputation for brawling, drunkenness, and racial discord. A British official commented in 1858 that the white population "did nothing to civilize or improve the natives; on the contrary they have in many instances fallen to a lower level. Whenever they can obtain spirits, most of them drink to excess." Some settlers were notorious for swapping a musket or two for young Fijian girls to use as concubines and household slaves.

By the early 1850s, the outside world was buffeting Fiji with political and economic pressures that the chiefs could no longer contain. David Whippy was outranked now by John Brown Williams, the American consul and commercial agent from 1846 to 1860. Williams, who hated Cakobau, tried to poison the Bauan's foreign relations by filing against him inflated claims for property losses suffered by Americans (especially Williams himself). United States warships periodically threatened the Vunivalu with dire consequences if he failed to pay. Meanwhile the unscrupulous consul made massive pseudo-legal land grabs of a sort only too familiar to America's own natives.

Cakobau was saved from losing the war with Rewa only by last-minute Tongan intervention. But the Tongans also had imperial designs and were quietly setting up a government in the Lau group and other parts of eastern Fiji. It seemed to Cakobau that the only way out of all these problems was to call on a benign foreign power to annex the islands. In 1858 he turned to W. T. Pritchard, the newly arrived British consul at Levuka, offering Britain sovereignty over Fiji and a grant of 200,000 acres of land if she would settle the American claims and confirm Cakobau as paramount chief.

London sent two commissioners to investigate. One made an exhaustive study of Fiji's potential for agriculture, and turned in a glowing report on the prospects for cash crops such as cotton. The other commissioner, concerned with political issues, was less favourably impressed. He doubted Cakobau's authority to make such an offer, and recommended against annexation on the grounds that Fiji might be more burden than benefit to the British Crown.

It took almost four years for the first offer of cession to be weighed, and at last rejected in 1862. But during those years the possibility of British rule attracted more whites to Fiji, kept the Americans at bay, and restrained the Tongans from a final campaign against Bau.

The Tongan leader Ma'afu was never able to fulfill his boast "I shall be chief of Bau, and Cakobau shall cook for me." Cooks had very low status in the South Pacific; to make your enemy your cook was the next best thing to cooking him—a threat that Cakobau and Ma'afu, both Christians by then, could no longer use.

♦

Beach Street, Levuka's main artery, follows the shore between a crumbling seawall and a row of wooden storefronts that might have been transported here from the Wild West. The hills crowd the town against the ocean: most of the side "streets" are in fact steep footpaths and flights of steps leading to clapboard villas and overgrown flower gardens. I climbed all the reputed 199 steps of Mission Hill, hoping for a panoramic view. The early settlers denuded the hinterland to deny marauding Lovoni any cover—but that was more than a century ago and now the mountainsides are thick with trees. I could see little of the town below—just a few silver roofs glinting behind palms and giant thickets of pink and yellow frangipani. Above, the heights of Ovalau's rim were capriciously hidden, then revealed, by fickle clouds.

Levuka's outskirts have the half-occupied look of a place whose population has collapsed. The buildings are not exactly abandoned, but a house is now only a storehouse, an ornamental garden a vegetable patch, and a family mansion the lonely dwelling of a grandmother. Because of the high ratio of property to people, or perhaps as a legacy of the lawless past, there are more "Keep Out" and "No Trespassing" signs than I can remember seeing anywhere. Sometimes they are written in Fijian, an ominous SA TABU ("it is forbidden") guarding a stand of coconuts or a gutted car.

Tabu: I saw the same word outside the Catholic church. The building is a simple wooden structure, no different from the "motor garage style of Fijian Methodism" decried by Ratu Sukuna, but a concrete tower has been added, supporting a clock and a neon cross. At the foot of this stands a large notice board bearing bright-red letters in two languages: CHURCH OF THE SACRED HEART, VALE NI SORO NI UTONA TABU. The translation into Fijian seemed sinister and not quite right, like the sign seen by Lowry's demented consul in *Under the Volcano*. It is true that *tabu* means "holy," but it carries the connotation of "forbidden" or "set apart"; and *vale ni soro*, "house of atonement," somehow added to the weight of guilt. ¿LE GUSTA ESTE JARDIN? ¿QUE ES SUYO? ¡EVITE QUE SUS HIJOS LO DESTRUYAN! You like this garden? Why is it yours? We evict those who destroy!

A sketch made in 1854 shows Levuka as a village of thirty or forty thatched houses surrounded by an embankment and overlooked by a cannon on top of the bald rock outcrop known as Battery Hill. Mission Steps had ended in private gardens and a muddy field; I decided to return to the shore for a closer look at the rock—there might be a good view from there and perhaps some remains of the gun emplacement. As I descended, the scent of tropical flowers yielded to the reek of seaweed and fish.

I walked northwards along the beach. The tide was out, exposing stretches of mud, sand, and coral. Far off in the shallows three women fishing with a net were silhouetted against the ocean glare. Fijian women keep their clothes on in the water—apart from their heads of hair the draped figures looked like Grecian statues revealed by the ebb. There was an interesting wrack of artifacts below the seawall: axles of ancient trucks, colossal gears and tubing from a steamer, old motors seized into abstract rusted forms. Some of these things were being used as anchors for small boats, but even the living craft seemed neglected, and I wondered how many would lie on the mud until they, like others I saw, were nothing but a keel and a fence of ribs. Levuka had been lulled asleep by its memories, by waves crashing on broken walls, and the stealthy tread of a returning forest.

Battery Hill rises like a Nazi helmet from the sea; the road has to squeeze beneath it on a narrow causeway. There was no obvious way to climb up: I would have to ask. Approaching slowly were an old man the colour of *café au lait*, crippled and leaning on the shoulder of a blond but otherwise tawny girl—the only people I had seen on the road all morning.

"Can't tell you, mate." the man said. "It's a long time since I wanted to go up there. Maybe Jenny knows. Do you, Jenny?" The child shook her head. "See them blokes sitting by the big house in the village there?" the man continued. "They'll know."

Situated between the foot of the hill and a small creek were the dozen houses of Fijian Levuka. As far as I could tell they occupy the same spot as the early town shown in the engraving. Nowadays the houses are of wood, and the largest has a tall pyramidal roof of the fluted brown aluminium often used by neo-Fijian buildings at tourist resorts. Several young men were relaxing on the village green.

"*Ni sa bula*," I said.

"*Ni sa bula vinaka*," the men chorussed affably.

"Would it be all right if I climbed the hill behind the village here?"

"Of course," said the Fijians, eager to please, but they looked puzzled when I asked the way.

"Is there a way up? Do people go up there?" I repeated.

"Oh yes, people go up there, but not very often. Ask that old man, he'll show you." They pointed to the cripple receding down the road.

"I already have—he told me to ask you."

At this the Fijians laughed. They called to a middle-aged woman washing clothes in a tub behind the chief's house. She smiled at me and thought for a moment.

"I don't think I have ever seen anyone go up there," she said. "Only goats. They can climb, but for people it isn't safe."

"Yes," the men agreed. "Only goats."

♦

After the first offer of cession was finally rejected in 1862, the flow of settlers to Fiji faltered briefly, but then swelled to a flood as the American Civil War brought a boom in cotton prices. By 1866 there were five hundred whites in Fiji; by 1870, two thousand. Levuka of the 1860s was a town of power without government, wealth without accountability; it swarmed with confidence tricksters and "bush lawyers"; every second building was a bar.

A chaotic state of affairs was not to the advantage of the more established settlers. They needed some form of government to ratify and safeguard land titles, protect property, and keep the natives from avenging white encroachment. To these ends, the settlers devised several short-lived, gimcrack regimes with native chiefs as figureheads and the real power in European hands.

In 1865 an agreement of confederacy was signed at Levuka. Cakobau was elected President and given as his salary a yearly cask of oil worth £23. Six other high chiefs, including Ma'afu, joined the government; but within two years it split along Fijian versus Tongan lines. In 1867 the whites decided on the less ambitious project of creating a Kingdom of Bau, intended to control Viti Levu, Ovalau, and whatever other parts of Fiji remained outside Ma'afu's comparatively efficient administration.

Since about 1850, Cakobau had been known among Europeans as the Tui Viti, or "King" of Fiji. The title apparently originated in a letter addressed to him by the British consul-general at Hawaii. It had no precedent in Fijian tradition, but tallied with the Bauan chief's ambitions. Cakobau's use of it, however, brought him troubles: the whites found it convenient to imagine that there was one native monarch whom they could hold responsible for debts and damages.

Unlike Tonga and Hawaii, Fiji had never been a united kingdom. Many high chiefs were called Tui, but the title was always qualified by the name of a people or place to which it was confined. Fijian political structure was a labyrinthine edifice of interlocking fealties—on Ovalau, for example, the title Tui Levuka was defined territorially and belonged to the paramount chief of the Levuka settlements on that island's coast; but the Vunivalu of Bau was also Tui Levuka in his capacity as overlord of all the scattered Levuka clans, wherever they happened to be living. War, intermarriage, and migration had created any number of quasi-feudal hierarchies open to differing interpretations of precedence. Even where Cakobau's authority was recognized, his rights varied widely in quality and degree. Abstract titles meant little without the physical exercise of power.

But the settlers thought in terms of European culture. Why shouldn't they make Cakobau a "real" king and set themselves up as his ministers? The Vunivalu, for his part, saw no harm in it: he needed white support against his rivals, especially the subtle Ma'afu.

On May 2, 1867, the new king's subjects gathered at Bau for the alien ceremony of coronation.

> All went well until the solemn act of crowning; but when the King took the crown—a contrivance of zinc, made by a carpenter in Levuka at a cost of four and a half dollars, and resplendent with such gems as the stores could supply—and placed it upon his bushy head, the absurdity of the scene was irresistible; a titter threatened to develop into unrestrained laughter, and uproar was averted only by the King's natural dignity of deportment.

The British consul at Levuka refused to recognize the kingdom, and warned British nationals (about 90 percent of the whites in Fiji) not to jeopardize their citizenship by serving under it. The regime proved unable to collect taxes or enforce its laws; and a disastrous campaign against the eaters of Reverend Baker exposed the hollow nature of its sovereignty. Cakobau himself seems to have been under no illusions—it is said that he wore the crown only once, and later threw it in the sea.

Although many whites were content with the absence of effective government, relentless pressures continued to build against the blithe anarchy of Fiji. Foreign banks would not advance loans against titles that had no legal sanction; the islands lacked a proper currency and postal service; and, notwithstanding Levuka's notoriety as a haven for "blackbirders," labour was in short supply.

Blackbirding, in theory, was a form of indenture recruiting by which Pacific Islanders were induced to work as migrant labour in Queensland, Fiji, Tahiti, or Peru. The hirer was supposed to pay his workers in cash or goods, and have them returned to their home islands on the expiry of their "contract." In practice, the traffic was often mere kidnapping and enslavement by ruthless press-gangs prowling the ocean from unregulated ports such as Levuka. Most of the workers came from remote parts of Melanesia and Micronesia; Fiji planters preferred them to local natives because, being socially isolated, they were much more easily controlled. Whites who had no need for island labour themselves profited by servicing the trade.

The ugly traffic soon attracted the attention of a British government under increasing pressure from anti-slavery societies to stamp it out. The Fiji settlers again moved to create an autonomous regime that would meet their needs and keep meddlesome philanthropists at bay.

In 1871 a faction of Levuka residents once more conspired with Cakobau; this time to make him king of all Fiji. An article in the *Fiji Times* (then only two years old) made it clear what many expected from the Fijians:

> We do not require their talent, the white man will bring that; but we require their sanction because in mere brute force . . . we are not more than a fiftieth of what they are and we also require for purposes of government their money contributions. In all other respects, the European will rule . . . and if the prominent figure be a native whether in the form of a king or president, it is only a puppet, the strings of which are pulled by the white men.

The Lovoni people of Ovalau's interior provided the occasion and the means to launch the regime. For a while they had acknowledged the hegemony of the Vunivalu, but gradually they became unruly, and made the final break by eating a minor chief loyal to Bau. Cakobau waged a long campaign but failed to achieve decisive victory. A surrender was eventually arranged with the intercession of missionaries; it seems that Cakobau then seized the Lovoni, after they had laid down their arms, and sold them to labour-hungry planters. With £1100 thus raised, he and his white collaborators funded the new government. Cakobau was proclaimed King of Fiji on June 5. (For reasons that are not clear, Ma'afu gave his support. Perhaps he recognized the need for native unity to contain the settler threat.)

In August, a House of Delegates met at the Levuka Reading Room to draw up a constitution. Whites and natives were represented, but the latter soon drifted away from proceedings whose language and purpose were equally obscure. The amateur politicians created a document far more elaborate than the 1867 Bau constitution, but no better suited to Fiji's conditions. When the session closed three weeks later King Cakobau addressed the House with the words "Fiji is a dark land, and we look to you for light as to law and civilization."

It was a forlorn hope. Most whites had little concern for indigenous Fijians except as a source of cheap labour, and the unseemly wrangle between the government's supporters and opponents was far from enlightening. One member had this to say of Cakobau and the other chiefs:

> What are they but niggers and hill men? Is it not an insult to this House and to every white man in the country to have an old nigger like the King set up, as he is being set up. King indeed! . . . he would be more in his place digging or weeding a white man's garden.

Despite greater acceptance among settlers, the new Cakobau government suffered from many of the same weaknesses as the first. A cabal of Levuka whites—some of them fugitives from the writ of other nations—refused to honour laws or taxes. The more articulate sheltered behind arguments of citizenship and jurisdiction; most were simply racists and ne'er-do-wells. Early in 1872 they formed a local chapter of the Ku Klux Klan and barricaded themselves in a ramshackle hotel called Keyse's Place.

Matters came to a head when a white planter, wanted for murdering a Fijian chief, sauntered into town and dared the government to touch him. An armed squad emerged from the Klan stronghold and demonstrated in the streets, but it failed to arouse public support and was dispersed without bloodshed. Cannon at "Parliament" (the Levuka Reading Room) were trained on Keyse's Place, which stood on wooden pilings farther down the waterfront. The standoff continued.

King Cakobau called a meeting in the town square and gave a timely warning to the whites:

> We Fijians understand revenge, and the law of the club. You white people said such things were cruel and savage. You wanted

civilization, and you brought us laws. Now there are divisions among you, and an appeal to force. If you resist the law, and force us to settle matters in our old way, there will be a war of races.

◆

Lunch at the Royal Hotel. Two elderly men were playing draughts at one of the veranda tables. They stopped their game when I came in, craning their necks at me like anxious turtles.

"Good afternoon," I said. The men blinked and resumed play.

I took out my notebook and began to bring my journal up to date. This drew another silent inspection from the turtles, but passed the time until the woman I had met earlier appeared.

"Yes?" she said, in a way that denied all recognition yet managed to convey "What do you want this time?"

"A large Fiji Bitter. Cold one, please."

The woman chatted with the old men before going to get the beer; from the way they spoke it was clear that the turtles were hotel residents: retired planters, I guessed. Obviously the Royal was the sort of place where transients were not really wanted. When the beer came it was warm, and there were fly spots on the inside of the glass.

I had hoped to strike up conversation with an old-timer at the hotel, but there were no customers besides the draughts players, and they left when I ordered a sandwich and a second beer. There had been characters enough drifting through Levuka in the old days—men with Runyonesque names like Harry the Jew and Cannibal Jack.

Harry, or Henry Danford, arrived in Fiji in the 1840s. He found a niche with the cannibal hill folk of Namosi, northwest of Suva, and there lived in the style of an early beachcomber long after civilization claimed the coast. Life was in fact hazardous for him among newly Christianized Fijians—hearing his name they imagined he was kin to the killers of Jesus, whose death they were eager to avenge. Harry was not really Jewish at all, but had earned the nickname for sly dealing and surprising skill with a billiard cue when there was money on the game. He witnessed many of Consul Williams's fraudulent land titles and spent his later years on seven hundred acres he had managed to alienate for himself near Pacific Harbour. By the time he died, in 1889, the district was well stocked with the progeny of Harry's several dozen wives.

Cannibal Jack had wider horizons. Born William James Diaper (or Diapea) in Essex, England, he was orphaned young and raised by relatives. They educated him at Dedham Grammar School, which produced a worthier pupil in the painter John Constable. Diaper ran away to sea at sixteen and arrived in Fiji about 1840, having taken the name Jack Jackson. He befriended a son of the Tui Macuata and settled at Somosomo, on Taveuni. When the old Tui died Jack eloped with one of the younger widows (ostensibly to save her from the customary strangling cord) and added her to his *ménage* of three other "wives."

Soon after this he shipped out to Manila, sold a load of tortoiseshell for £1000, and spent most of the proceeds travelling luxuriously in India and China. By 1844 he was back in Fiji, making bullets for Cakobau. Somehow he offended his host and had to flee to Lakeba, where he took more wives and left descendants who still bear the name Jeksoni.

His career throughout most of the 1850s is obscure, but he spent enough time in New Caledonia to become "earnestly desired by the French . . . for selling arms and ammunition to revolting natives." He followed the same trade in New Zealand during the Maori Wars, and from there returned to New Caledonia. Finding the death penalty still on his head, Jackson hastily departed in an open boat which he sailed fourteen hundred miles to Samoa. He tried to live quietly for a while on Savaii, working for missionaries, but they found him "very objectionable" and expelled him for "insulting language to the girls and women."

Unlike Harry the Jew, Cannibal Jack was a handsome man, and many were susceptible to his charms. One night in an Apia tavern he arranged with a certain Mr. and Mrs. Lawton to get them a passage to Fiji. He collected the fare in advance and picked up the couple in a small boat, which they assumed to be the tender of a ship offshore. But Jack himself took them all seven hundred miles in the tiny craft, and spent much of the trip making love to a willing Mrs. Lawton while her husband was forced to steer.

Again he tried to settle down, bought land, and applied unsuccessfully for a job with the Cakobau government. By 1880 he was destitute, "loafing about the beach at Levuka." When he left for the last time, he did so true to his style.

A German firm advanced him materials to build a cutter. As soon as it was finished he "paid the debt with the fore-top sail," making off to the Loyalty Islands, where he stayed until his death in 1891. Jack claimed he was blown out to sea while on a trial run—but the fact that he had filled the boat with passengers and provisions casts doubt on this excuse.

♦

On Levuka's waterfront today nothing remains of Keyse's Place or the Reading Room. A photograph shows the latter to have been a small but surprisingly elegant Victorian pavilion surrounded by a balcony and capped with a fine Fijian thatch in the style reserved for the houses of gods and chiefs. It was a fitting symbol for the regime that used it as a parliament: this foreign structure sheltered beneath a native canopy.

The building stood on Niukaubi Hill, a peninsular knoll now occupied by the war memorial. I climbed the steps and read the eroding marble names—many from the "Great War," a few from the Second, all European. (The Fijians have their own memorial opposite the Catholic church.) Weeds were thrusting up between the flagstones; someone had left a cigarette packet and two banana skins.

At the south end of town Beach Road acquires a narrow block of buildings on its seaward side. The main wharf is here, the post office, customs house, and an old wooden store that might have been standing when cotton and Cakobau were kings. Again, that Wild West look—a long, rectangular false front with the words MORRIS, HEDSTROM LTD. painted in illusory relief. At Suva, Nadi, and elsewhere, "MH," as it is known, has become a modern department store selling everything from can openers to video cassettes; but the old building at Levuka was abandoned for some years until the Fiji National Trust restored it as a museum and library.

Inside there is a small collection of Fijian artifacts, frontier Victoriana, and old photographs. One corner is devoted to circulating books—a lot of Agatha Christie and Beatrix Potter. And such innocence: where else nowadays would the shelf marked "Adult Books" hold Greene and Dostoyevsky? The librarian sold me some facsimile excerpts from the early *Fiji Times*. The paper's first edition was datelined "Levuka, Saturday September 4 1869"; like most journals of the period, its front page was given up to advertising.

A Mr. Robertson begged "leave to inform the inhabitants of Fiji that he is established at Levuka as CHEMIST & DRUGGIST" with an impressive stock of "English, American, and French Patent Medicines." These included Kennedy's Medical Discovery, Fish's Hair Restorative, Dr. Hunter's Eradicator, and something called Uterine Catholicon. The last two were probably abortifacients. For women who already had babies, there were "nipple shields, breast tubes, and pap boats," while for clients interested in hard drugs Mr. Robertson could supply Cocoaine [*sic*], Baker's Pain Panacea, and Poor Man's Friend.

Beyond the Morris, Hedstrom museum stand the gleaming metal buildings of the fish cannery, Levuka's only thriving industry. Like the *bêche-de-mer* on which the town was founded, the fish processed here are shipped mainly to the Far East. Ironically, this Japanese-run factory exports high-grade tuna while Fiji imports—from Japan—tons of inferior tinned mackerel and sardines.

A cat was sunning itself on the seawall, inhaling the cannery's reek, chin lifted and eyes half closed, like a Frenchman sniffing a cognac. It was black with a white front and paws, the sort Fijians called a *talatala ni vusi*, or "clergyman of cats." I approached calling "Puss, puss, puss," but the animal ceased its reverie and ran away. Maybe it feared culinary interest: I am not sure that cats are still relished in Fiji, but there are certainly very few of them about.

I continued walking south. The breeze, though fishy, was cool; afternoon sunlight deepened the colours of tangled vegetation and

the turquoise sea. Whenever the wind fell still the air was invaded
by the chirruping of insects, who paused as they heard my tread,
then resumed behind me like a hundred squeaky wheels.

The road runs in a gentle sweep between the shore and hills.
After about half a mile you come to Nasova, where the Deed of
Cession was signed in 1874. A flagpole and recently built *bure* mark
the site of Cakobau's Parliament House, completed at a cost of
£1140 in his government's final year. Opposite, on a grassy point
overlooking the sea, stand three stones enclosed by a white picket
fence. These commemorate Cession, Independence (1970), and the
centenary of Cession in 1874. The largest is a smooth boulder, as
nature formed it, except for the addition of a plaque:

> THE INSTRUMENT CEDING
> TO QUEEN VICTORIA, HER
> HEIRS & SUCCESSORS, THE
> POSSESSION OF, AND FULL
> SOVEREIGNTY & DOMINION
> OVER, THE FIJIAN ISLANDS
> AND THE INHABITANTS THEREOF,
> WAS SIGNED HERE
> ON THE 10TH OCTOBER 1874

◆

Cakobau gave his public speech of warning on March 9, 1872; a
few days later the Premier (prime minister), a former auctioneer
named Burt, resigned. The King, Ma'afu, and other chiefs—supposed by many to be puppets—took the initiative by appealing to
the one man they hoped could save the government. He was John
Bates Thurston, a cotton planter of unusual ability and views.
Unlike others of his period and race, he did not believe that Fiji
should become a white man's country, and he despised "rampant
Anglo-Saxons," or white supremacists.

Thurston had not wanted to get involved in the regime—he
recognized the specious constitution for what it was, and would
have preferred to influence events as British consul (a job he had
held before in an acting capacity). But the consulate was already

occupied by the insidious E. B. March, who, among other things, was a pillar of the "British Subjects' Mutual Protection Society"— a euphemism for the Ku Klux Klan.

Thurston realized he could no longer live quietly on his Taveuni plantation, untouched by events at Levuka. In May he joined the cabinet as Acting Premier, and later became Chief Secretary. From 1872 to 1874 he had the formidable task of steering the Cakobau government through an endless financial crisis, the intrigues of the Klan, and demands from other whites to get on with what they saw as the real business of the regime—the opening up of the country and unhindered exploitation of its people. The strength of his hand was tested soon after he took office. Two Klan members had been imprisoned for assault; the rest tried to release them from jail. Thurston armed two hundred men, many of them Fijians, and had Keyse's Place surrounded. Battle was prevented by the captain of a visiting British warship. Instead of siding with the consul, he advised the extremists that British subjects had to respect the laws of the country in which they lived, and drove home the point by assuring the King of British sympathy. The Klan was cowed, the government given a whiff of outside support: Thurston had won the first round.

E. B. March was recalled early in 1873, but by that time financial problems had brought the regime to the brink of collapse. Almost everyone—from the white extremists to Thurston and Cakobau— now favoured annexation by Britain; an enquiry was sent to London on January 31. In February, massacres on the north coast of Viti Levu culminated in a settler revolt and a costly (but successful) campaign against the hill folk.

In June the government fell in a vote on the budget and a wrangle over native electoral rights, which the House wanted to withdraw. The King dissolved Parliament; he, Thurston, and other ministers continued ruling by decree. Again there were tax revolts and street demonstrations; again, peace was restored through the intervention of British naval captains. The government created by and for the whites was now almost universally opposed by them. "Justice to the Fijian nation is of more consequence than cotton growing," wrote Thurston. His enemies replied that they would never submit to "unconstitutional ministers and their nigger-loving government," and ridiculed the King as "Cockaboo Rex."

Thurston and Cakobau now realized that the best hope of protecting Fijians from a settler takeover was to offer the kingdom to Britain, with conditions safeguarding native interests. A formal request for annexation was sent to London. The British government was loath to take power in a country that might soon explode, as New Zealand had, in a war of races. On the other hand, Fiji's location was strategically important, and since most of the Europeans there were British, Britain was involved whether she liked it or not. Two commissioners were sent to the islands at the end of 1873; but by the time they began their investigations both Thurston and the King were having doubts. Cakobau feared that cession might bring a flood of the dangerous foreigners, while Thurston was trying to write a new constitution that would give natives the majority of seats in Parliament.

The commissioners found that most settlers wanted annexation, that the King's ministers were politically isolated, and that the Cakobau regime had accumulated an international debt of nearly £90,000, which it could never hope to repay. Cotton prices had collapsed; plantation owners were consoling themselves with "gun-barrel rum" distilled illegally to avoid liquor taxes; some Europeans were talking openly of a war between black and white for the land. "Should Her Majesty's Government decline to accept the offer of cession," the commissioners reported, "we can see no prospect for these Islands . . . but ruin to the English planters and confusion to the Native Government."

Cakobau and Thurston wavered for three months. Eventually the King and other chiefs saw that they had better cede Fiji before the country slipped from their grasp. "If matters remain as they are," Cakobau said,

Fiji will become like a piece of driftwood on the sea, and be picked up by the first passer-by. The whites who have come to Fiji are a bad lot. They are mere stalkers on the beach . . . if we do not cede Fiji, the white stalkers on the beach, the cormorants, will open their maws and swallow us. By annexation the two races, white and black, will be bound together, and the stronger nation will lend strength to the weaker.

In September 1874 Sir Hercules Robinson, the Governor of New South Wales, arrived at Levuka to make the final arrangements.

Saturday, October 10, was a day of driving rain and oyster skies; the ceremonies had to be postponed until mid-afternoon. At about half past two, Cakobau, Ma'afu, and eleven other high chiefs signed the deed in the Council Room at Nasova. Outside on the *rara* the flag of the Kingdom of Fiji, with its scroll and motto *Rerevaka na Kalou ka doka na Tui* ("Fear God, Honour the King"), was solemnly lowered.

Unfortunately, some white residents of Levuka had passed the morning in premature drinking celebrations, and were in a mood unfitting for the dignity of the occasion. One man tried to trample the old flag, another to bury it, yet others to make off with it as a souvenir. British naval officers quickly restored order, as they had done so many times before; the royal standard was then raised to a twenty-one-gun salute.

The next edition of the *Fiji Times* printed the full text of the Deed of Cession and the following proclamation:

Unto Her Majesty Queen of Britain—
We, King of Fiji, together with other high chiefs of Fiji, hereby give our country, Fiji, unreservedly to Her Britannic Majesty Queen of Great Britain and Ireland; and we trust and repose fully in her, that she will rule Fiji justly and affectionately . . .
Done at Levuka, this tenth day of October, in the year of Our Lord one thousand eight hundred and seventy-four.
Signed: Cakobau R., Tui Viti and Vunivalu

8
▲▲▲
SUVA

"**D**id you see the Miss Gay Fiji event?" the woman at the hotel desk had asked when I returned to the Grand Pacific from Ovalau. "Some of the guys were really beautiful—lovely clothes."

Suva was humming with Hibiscus Festival, an eclectic fair, pageant, and parade. I poured myself another cup of the GPH's vapid coffee and opened the paper. There had been an accident with the Ferris wheel set up in Albert Park: it had jammed in operation and developed a dangerous twist; the fire brigade eventually released the riders, though some had sat aloft for hours. Below this was a syndicated item under the heading "It's a Mad, Mad, World":

> Religious piligrims are flocking to see what they believe is an image of the Virgin Mary [on] . . . the side of a house in Texas.
> Huge crowds have stood in lines several blocks long the past few nights to see the image reflected from the bumper of Mary Ibarra's 1975 Chevrolet when she turns on her porch light.

A chrome apparition of Our Lady—*Nuestra Señora del Chevrolet*. What could be more Texan than that?

After breakfast I strolled across Albert Park to see the carnival installations on my way to the Fiji Museum. (At ten o'clock I had an appointment there with the well-known anthropologist Marshall Sahlins, who was visiting Fiji and had kindly agreed to give me an interview.) The park was uncharacteristically debauched, littered with corn cobs, ice-cream sticks, and paper cups; a slightly putrid smell arose from their rotting on the damp turf. Along the side of Cakobau Road stood an instant shantytown—coconut shies, betting tables, shooting galleries, and food stands. Whiffs of candy-floss and curried snacks mingled with the odour of trampled earth. GENUINE INDIAN & GUJERATI FOOD, said a sign. There were few potential customers about at this hour, but some of the gambling games were open.

"You, sir, sit down here, sir; win plenty money!" a tout called with such mercenary zeal that I wondered to what extent his enterprise supported charity, as it claimed.

There was more local ingenuity at the fairground. Merry-go-rounds were made of old axles and wooden boxes naïvely cut out and painted to resemble horses. One, with twenty-four seats, was powered by a lawnmower engine. The stricken Ferris wheel stood abandoned and askew. It was driven through the differential of some antiquated British lorry. Hand levers were attached to the original brakes for slowing and stopping the wheel. Apparently a drum had seized and the ponderous contraption had buckled under its momentum.

Beneath a flotilla of vivid hydrogen balloons, Radio Fiji's mobile broadcast had already begun the day. The Big Ben chimes of Parliament were banished by reggae and wailing Indian songs invading the park from a bank of speakers.

I crossed Cakobau Road and entered Thurston Botanical Gardens. You could still hear the music but it was softened by the leafy canopy of trees that must have been standing here long before Fijians saw their first *valagi*. When Suva became the capital in 1882, it was Thurston who made sure the ancient village site remained untouched. At the same time he founded the first botanical garden on a hill above the town. In 1913 the collections were moved the present location, but not until 1976 were the gardens honour of their founder. They are a fitting monument

Fiji were his great enthusiasms. Even the belated acclaim seems suited to his self-effacing style. Thurston has only recently been recognized as a chief architect of Sir Arthur Gordon's generous policy towards Fijians.

♦

I found Dr. Sahlins at work in a small office next to Fergus Clunie's. A greenish gloom filtered in through a window behind the desk. The trees surrounding the museum have virtually smothered it. Sahlins himself radiated an American vigour from his tanned skin and witty eyes. On the phone he had sounded wary (academic suspicion of journalists is too often justified), but in person he was affable.

"I'm working more with history right now, but from a cultural perspective," he told me. "It's been said that the Bau-Rewa war of the last century was probably the biggest ever fought in the Pacific until World War Two. It was something like the Peloponnesian War—naval power versus land power—though I wouldn't want to take the analogy too far."

Marshall Sahlins has written several important books on Pacific culture and anthropological theory; these include *Moala: Culture and Nature on a Fijian Island* (1962), *Stone Age Economics* (1972), and *Islands of History* (1985). I began by asking his views on Fijian religion: how well had the culture survived the destruction of its old beliefs; indeed, had those beliefs really been destroyed; and how much anthropological work was being done in this field today?

"If we look at early accounts of the conversion to Christianity," Sahlins said, "we find that some people thought the old gods had left Fiji, but others believed that the gods themselves converted. This is interesting because if the gods converted, then they're still around and they're still Fijian gods—even though they may be good Wesleyans like everyone else. It's a very flexible idea.

"The missionaries destroyed the temple system and put churches in its place, but the folk religion, if you want to use that term, is still strong—especially curing and sorcery, things like that. *Mekes* are still composed by an inspirational process—the songs are 'given' ɔ the composer in a dream or vision. There's a lot of stuff out there but nobody's working on it, as far as I know. The anthropologists have mostly been working out in the boonies, on the small islands. Nothing's being done on the big chiefdoms; nothing's being done in the west."

Fergus poked his head around the door. "There's tea made," he said. I got up and returned with two mugs of Sela's sweet and milky brew. (I would never make tea like that for myself, but it brought back so many memories of motorcycle rides and roadside cafés in the England of twenty years ago that I enjoyed every drop.)

"I'm interested in how religion and other cultural factors shape history and politics," Sahlins continued. "The Bau-Rewa wars ended in a kind of stalemate when Cakobau converted to Christianity. After that there were no more big power struggles between the Fijian chiefdoms. This wasn't just because the missionaries encouraged pacifism—Cakobau and the others knew very well that Christians fight one another often. It was more complicated than that—the old religion and the old warfare were part of a cultural system. With the overthrow of the war gods came the end of what Fijians regarded as the just causes of war.

"Then of course there were strong cultural factors in the relationship of the British and the Fijians. You might not think so at first glance, but they had a lot in common. They were both societies that understood the meaning of ceremonial and hereditary rank. The British came here with their knights and lords and their governors in fancy uniforms with those floppy-feathered hats, and the Fijians loved it. The Fijians respected chiefly style—the structure was familiar to them even if the details were not. The British, in turn, found the Fijian style very winning. The Fijians had respect for authority, impeccable manners, but also a fundamental sense of dignity—they were 'Nature's gentlemen.' "

Sahlins swung his chair around and peered through the thicket outside the window. The fly screen was spotted with small spiders' webs and patches of moss. "Some museums buy special equipment for maintaining a humid atmosphere," he said, "but here they have the opposite problem." The notebook in my hand felt limp as cloth; I had forgotten the crackle of paper. Music from the park fell silent long enough to hear the Parliament clock chime its half-hour tune.

"What about modern politics?" I said.

"The part that interests me is to watch how the leaders—almost all of whom are chiefs—combine new means with old alliances. The Prime Minister is Tui Nayau, or high chief of Lau. His wife is Tui Dreketi—high chief of Rewa in her own right. It's interesting how Lau and the east have been up and coming through the twentieth century. The same thing was happening in the last century—if Cakobau hadn't made a deal with the British, Lau and Cakaudrove might have taken over Fiji under Ma'afu's leadership."

I asked what he thought of the view that it was time to dismantle the chiefly establishment and the landholding system. Was tradition hindering the ordinary Fijian's progress?

"People have been saying that for more than a hundred years; and if you look at who says it, it's usually those who want to get their hands on the land. You don't hear many Fijians talking that way. There are certainly problems in Fijian society. There seems to be more theft, more drunkenness and violence—not only in Suva but in the villages too. I think a lot of this is linked to thwarted expectations, but I don't agree that the answer is to dismantle the traditional structure and certainly not the social relations among the ordinary people. Societies everywhere are under intolerable pressures. If we compare Fiji with other countries of similar background, things look pretty good here. The existing structure has prevented the wholesale disorientation that's sadly so common in the developing world." He paused for a moment and turned again to the window.

"I guess I have to quarrel with that word—'development,' " he resumed, "whether from a capitalist or a Marxist point of view. Development ideology is the religion of the twentieth century. It's the new shibboleth. No one wants to talk about the misery caused by economic envy. Development, if it's not to be socially destructive, should include arts, poetry, history—non-material aspects of culture.

"As for the landholding system, it may be far from perfect; but if land is made alienable in Fiji, the Fijians are finished."

♦

Fijians nowadays regard the Deed of Cession as their Magna Carta, the foundation of their constitutional rights. But the importance of all such documents lies more in subsequent interpretation than in the written words. Like other treaties between native peoples and the British Crown, the deed meant very different things to the two sides.

When Cakobau finally surrendered Fiji he did so "unconditionally"—he himself said that conditions were not "chieflike." To the British this meant that Fiji was theirs, with no strings attached besides a few spoken assurances that Fijian interests would not be neglected. To the Fijians the word *vakaturaga*, "chiefly" or "chieflike," meant something quite specific: Fiji was presented to Queen Victoria as a *ceremonial* exchange.

In the quasi-feudal Fijian polity this implied that the ultimate fealty of Fijians now went to the white queen; in return the white queen was expected to give protection from external enemies and to mediate internal disputes. For these services the new ruler would be entitled, as was a paramount chief, certain *lala*, or tribute in goods and services. The exchange did not mean that the very ground of Fiji now belonged to foreigners.

The Deed stated that all lands not already the bona fide property of foreigners, and not actually used or occupied by a chief or tribe (and not needed for their "probable future support"), would be vested in the British Crown. If Cakobau had been able to see how similar treaties were being interpreted in, say, Canada, he might have been deeply disturbed. There, an archipelago of small reserves was deemed sufficient for the Indians, while the rest was taken by the Crown. If this interpretation had been applied in Fiji, the natives would have been left with a few hundred thousand acres, and the British with four million.

Luckily for Fijians, Sir Arthur Gordon, Governor from 1875 to 1880, deliberately misread the Deed to their advantage. He made the unusual, possibly unique assumption that all land not yet taken by settlers belonged, in the full sense, to the natives. Elsewhere in the world the career of the Anglo-Saxons has been an unrivalled land-grab since before the days of Beowulf. Any land worth taking, which could be taken, was taken. Even "wastelands" (but inhabited wastelands) like the Canadian Northwest were seized by the Crown in the spirit of Pope Alexander's infamous division of South America. Why was Fiji different?

A cynic might point out that the British were temporarily chastened by the Maori troubles, and that almost half the best arable land in Fiji lay within the percentage that *was* successfully alienated. These points are part of the context but they do not amount to an explanation. Sooner or later, events would have taken a more familiar turn were it not for Gordon and Thurston—two romantic idealists blessed with each other's support and the chance to practise their beliefs. It may be unfashionable to emphasize the role of individuals in history, but on a remote group of islands with a small white population the scope for discretionary action was wide. And behind all this lay the Fijians—not only as potential adversaries but also in the way their society resisted disintegration and stimulated the better qualities of those who came to rule them. Gordon wrote:

> If I could get the natives twenty-five years start I would have no fear whatever for their future. . . . As it is they may be unable or rather I may be unable to withstand the demand of the planters for more land and more labour, but thus far all looks well. A change at the Colonial Office or a change here might bring into play forces which would quickly exterminate the native population.

He and Thurston, who held various posts before becoming Governor from 1888 until his death in 1897, devised the British Empire's first system of indirect rule (though Lord Lugard later got the credit for inventing it in Nigeria). They governed the Fijians mainly through traditional chiefs confirmed as officials of the Crown; they prevented further alienation of land by registering it under communal ownership based (partly, at least) on native structures; and they allowed the Fijians to pay taxes by cultivating communal plots and selling the produce through a government marketing agency. These measures respectively saved the natives from insensitive white officials, land swindlers, and having to raise cash by working away from home. The taxation system was so successful that many Fijian communities received cash refunds for the excess value of their produce over assessment.

Gordon got the Fijians their twenty-five years, but only just. Governor Sir Everard im Thurn (1904–1910) listened to the local settlers and decided it was time to grant Fijians the same liberties that had destroyed the Maoris. His lifting of the ban on native land sales was eventually stopped by top-level intervention from Lord Stanmore (Gordon), but im Thurn's successors continued a slow assault on the semi-autonomous Fijian administration throughout the 1920s and '30s. Culturally myopic British bureaucrats began tinkering in the names of progress and integration; native officials were downgraded or displaced by whites; many Fijians began to feel that they were losing control of their country and their culture.

Ratu Sukuna had chafed under this process for years, and when the Second World War broke out he recognized immediately the opportunity presented.

Until the *Pax Britannica*, Fijian society had constantly reaffirmed itself through the act of war. Except for rare "total wars"—such as the one between Bau and Rewa—native fighting had been largely a chivalric ritual designed to strengthen the group by transforming boys into men, and supplying the warriors, chiefs, and gods with a flow of their favourite food: enemy dead. If the end of the Bau-Rewa War in 1855 marked the close of ancient Fijian politics, the Second World War brought their rebirth in a modern form ninety years later.

In 1940 Ratu Sukuna was commissioned to raise a native military force. He recruited the men province by province, with their own chiefs as officers—thus reviving old loyalties within the framework of a national war effort. The Fijian troops quickly distinguished themselves, especially as stealthy jungle fighters in the Solomons. Many won medals for bravery, but relatively few were captured or killed: the ancient battle skills were successfully translated into a modern idiom. (However, one man, a little too closely in touch with ancestral practices, had to be restrained from preparing two Japanese dead for a cannibal feast.)

Fijian performance in the war had profound effects on the independent Fiji that emerged a generation later. The natives' brilliance, not only as fighters but in organizing themselves for every aspect of the war effort, convinced the British that they should be allowed a greater say in government. In 1945 the Fijian Administration was reconstituted with Ratu Sukuna at its head and a majority of natives in key positions. It was given new powers and responsibilities, and ultimately became the model for the Fiji government of today.

The war also influenced subsequent history in another way: whereas eleven thousand Fijians volunteered for service, fewer than three hundred Fiji Indians did so. There were good reasons for this—the Indians resented discrimination in Fiji and the continued rule of Mother India by Britain. They did not see why they should serve the imperial order. On the contrary, they organized cane strikes to press for better conditions at the height of the Pacific War in 1943. The grievances were genuine, but the tactics seriously damaged the future position of Indians in Fiji. At best, their indifference suggested that they identified far more closely with India than with their island home; at worst, that they were disloyal, even subversive. And by standing aside in the war, the Indians ensured that the army and police force of the new Fiji would be overwhelmingly Fijian. The Fiji whites, as disgusted with the Indians as they were impressed by the natives, closed ranks with the latter and became staunch defenders of Taukei claims to primacy in future constitutional developments.

◆

The hallway of the Parliament building was empty, the information window closed. The mock-marble walls nowadays look more like the stained and polished concrete that they are. A plaque by the door announces that the foundation stone was laid on May 12, 1937, the coronation day of George VI; another, farther in, gives a list of all the governors and their dates. After reading these I went down to the office in the basement where weeks ago I had bought some maps for the Nadrau hike. The same woman was there—a friendly Fijian with a flower-print dress and buoyant hair-do stuck with yellow combs. Was it possible to see the House? I asked.

"I don't think they're sitting at the moment," she said. She turned to a colleague. "How can this man get into Parliament? Is it locked?"

"Go back upstairs, walk around the side, and knock on some of the doors at the back. Someone there will help you."

I thanked them and followed their directions. The third door I tried opened. A small, balding Indian in an immaculate suit greeted me.

"You wish to see Parliament?" he said, beaming. "Just one second; I'll get my keys." He searched his desk, found what he sought, and stood up triumphant. "Here we are. Come with me, please. I'm afraid they're not sitting now, but if you like I can show you the chamber.

"My job here," he said "is . . . well, actually I am wearing two hats. I am Clerk to the Upper House and at the same time Assistant to the Lower House. In most countries you cannot have loyalties to both Houses, but here"—he gave a shrug that was almost Gallic—"both Houses use the same Chamber anyway."

He unlocked a tall wooden door. Our footsteps echoed as we entered; the room smelled like a church. At the far end were the public benches, with a sign on the wall inviting people to exercise their rights by attending. A gallery above these was divided into a section for the press and a booth for translators.

"When we became independent in 1970 we were given all this translation equipment. You said you were from Canada—it was a very generous gift from the Canadian government, I believe. We were going to have simultaneous translation in English, Fijian, and Hindi. But I'm afraid we haven't had to use it yet. So far all our members have been able to speak English. But if ever we get someone who understands only Fijian or Hindi I am sure it will be most useful."

On the wall below the press gallery hangs a portrait of Ratu Seru Cakobau, Tui Viti. At the other end of the chamber, behind the Speaker's chair, are four large paintings of British royalty: Queen Victoria, George V, Queen Mary, and Edward VIII. (The last choice was a little odd, I thought.)

"Allow me to show you the woodwork," said the Clerk. The woods in here are very symbolic. You see, we have one kind of wood from almost every country in the Commonwealth, but unfortunately I don't think there is any from Canada. What kind of wood is Canadian?"

"Pine, cedar, maple . . ."

"Maple is syrup, surely?"

"It comes from a tree. Good wood for furniture."

"Of course, yes, excuse me. Long time since I was a schoolboy. Now, the Speaker's chair is Indian teak, the desk is English oak, the members' benches are Fijian *yaka*—a lovely wood, very lovely; see the grain here." He ran his hand over the members' horseshoe table: the surface resembled mahogany, but was a light golden colour shot with dark streaks.

"In the meeting room at the back there is a table with even nicer grain; I'll show you presently. Where was I? Ah, the dispatch boxes, they're New Zealand kauri, and the Division Glass stand over there"—he pointed to a colossal egg timer supported in carved gimbals—"is Australian mahogany."

"You sound like you must be interested in cabinetry," I said.

"Yes, my hobby. I find wood is so relaxing. Can you not feel it here? There is a tranquillity which comes from the wood."

He was right; the Chamber had a soft golden texture that seemed to emanate from the benches and panelled walls. The style of the woodwork was simple and angular, like the building itself, but in this medium there was none of the forbidding austerity of the concrete façade.

"The only thing I can't show you, I'm afraid, is the mace. It is only here when Parliament sits."

I would have liked to see this. It was originally Cakobau's finest war club, known in its early days as the "Blood-Bather." It served as the mace in the short-lived assembly at Levuka; and in 1874, at the Cession ceremony, Cakobau presented it to the Queen's representative with the following words, translated by John Bates Thurston:

. . . The King desires, through Your Excellency, to give Her Majesty the only thing he possesses that may interest her. The King gives Her Majesty his old and favourite war-club, the for-

mer, and, until lately the only known, law of Fiji. . . . The King
adds only a few words. With this emblem of the past he sends
his love to Her Majesty, saying that he fully confides in her and
her children, who, succeeding her, shall become Kings of Fiji,
to exercise a watchful control over the welfare of his children
and people, who, having survived the barbaric law and age, are
now submitting themselves, under Her Majesty's rule, to civilization.

In 1932 Cakobau's mace, suitably embossed with silver, was returned to Fiji; it has served in the legislature ever since.

◆

Unlike most colonies, Fiji was shy of independence, and democracy
came late. Universal adult suffrage was not established until 1963—
the first time Fijian members of the legislature were directly elected
rather than being appointed by the Council of Chiefs. Even then,
the electoral process was not so much demanded by Fijians as
imposed on them for the sake of international opinion. Indians, by
contrast, had elected some token members since 1929.

In the late 1960s the British prepared to divest themselves of the
colony. The question, of course, was to whom should they hand
over power? Many Fijians thought it was a simple matter: the
sovereignty relinquished by the Taukei in 1874 should be returned
to them in 1970. The Indians, at 50.5 percent of the total population, demanded a democratic system based on a general (non-
racial) voting structure by which they hoped to achieve a permanent
majority.

Two main parties emerged: the National Federation Party, mainly
Indian; and the Alliance Party, supported by Fijians, Europeans,
Others, and a few conservative Indians. The Alliance was (and is)
led by Ratu Sir Kamisese Mara, Paramount Chief of the Lau islands, and the elected member for Lau-Cakaudrove-Rotuma. He
managed to hold Fijian support while advocating a moderate, multi-
racial society.

The question of whether voting should be based on racial bloc
or universal principles was resolved by devising a complex system

in which each elector belongs to two rolls, one restricted to his communal (racial) group and one national or common. There are three communal rolls: one for Indians, one for Fijians (including other Pacific Islanders resident in Fiji), and one for Europeans and other minorities. The lower house, or House of Representatives, has fifty-two members: twelve Indian, twelve Fijian, and three "general" (European, etc.) elected on communal rolls; and a further ten Indians, ten Fijians, and five general members chosen by the common or national roll.

The upper house, or Senate, has twenty-two members appointed by the Great Council of Chiefs, the Prime Minister, and the Leader of the Opposition. As in the British system, the Senate may delay legislation but cannot ultimately prevent its passage (although there is a kind of chiefly veto on laws affecting only the Fijians and their land). The official head of state is Queen Elizabeth II; she is represented in Fiji by the Governor General, who is appointed on the recommendation of the Prime Minister. Ratu Sir George Kadavulevu Cakobau, great-grandson of Fiji's King, held this post from 1973 until his retirement in 1980. The Governor General's role is largely ceremonial, but under certain conditions he may intervene in politics—as he did after the 1977 elections.

In the first post-independence elections (1972) the Alliance Party won thirty-three seats, the Federation nineteen. The Alliance's strong showing was due largely to success in winning the more moderate Indian vote away from the Federation, but the cost of this was a suspicion among some Fijians that Ratu Mara was going too far in his multi-racialism and was undermining the security of the Taukei. These fears coalesced around the person and policies of Sakiasi Butadroka.

Butadroka was expelled from the Alliance Party in 1973 for adopting a "Fiji for the Fijians" stance. He continued to sit in Parliament as an independent member, then formed the Fijian Nationalist Party. In 1975 he introduced a motion calling for the repatriation of Indians to India at British expense. The motion was roundly condemned by the Prime Minister and many other speakers from both sides of the House, but it inflamed the Indians' deepest fears—

fears already rekindled by the example of Idi Amin's treatment of Uganda Asians just three years before.

In the 1977 elections Butadroka became the champion of the less privileged and less sophisticated sectors of the native population. These people—mainly westerners, unemployed townsfolk, and low-status villagers—saw themselves being left behind by the growth of the Indian business sector. (The effect of foreign, largely Australian, capital was more important but far less visible than the ubiquitous Indian stores and bus companies.) They feared that having survived the threat of European domination, they would now be outbid and outbred by the Indian parvenus.

When the election returns came in, the Alliance won twenty-four seats, the Federation twenty-six. Butadroka was the sole elected member of his party, but he had split the Fijian vote and thus given victory to the Indians. (There was one Independent, who sided with the Federation.)

Opinions vary on what happened next. It seems that Siddiq Koya, the Federation leader, had not really expected to win; he was overawed by the prospect of being Prime Minister. Instead of forming a government, he vacillated and finally proposed to Ratu Mara that they join in a coalition of national unity. This Mara wisely refused. Co-operation with the Indians would have been a political gift to Butadroka.

Meanwhile, Koya's lack of resolve caused members of his own party to question whether he should remain as leader. Indian unity, always fragile, began to crumble. On April 7, 1977, Governor-General Cakobau made a final appeal to the Federation to form a government "forthwith"; he then reappointed Ratu Mara as Prime Minister of a caretaker government to take office until new elections could be held.

The decision was controversial, but the Alliance did not let its opportunity slip. The party began a major overhaul of its machinery in preparation for the next campaign. The Federation, however, continued to suffer from internal disputes; and Butadroka went too far with his racist rhetoric and was jailed for breaking the Public Order Act. When the September vote came in, the Alliance won thirty-six seats, the Federation fifteen. There was one Independent. Butadroka (who was allowed to run) lost his seat.

The Fijian Nationalist Party failed to reappear with any strength in the elections of 1982, but the issues it had raised helped to create a climate of acrimony and polarization. Both major parties now relied more than ever on their ethnic constituencies: if the superficial debate was about political and economic issues affecting Fiji as a whole, the real contest centred on unifying each racial community behind its political establishment. In this atmosphere, the Australian Broadcasting Commission made a television documentary exposing what appeared to be a Nixonian scheme concocted by Alliance supporters for the undermining of opposition groups. Fiji itself has no television network, but the Federation tried to capitalize on the programme by circulating video copies throughout the country. The opening words of the documentary characterized Fiji's elected leaders as the descendants of chiefs who "clubbed and ate their way to power"—a remark so offensive (and so hypocritical, coming as it did from a settler nation which had exterminated most of its natives) that it discredited, in Fijian eyes, not only the programme but also those who had gleefully distributed it. There were slurs and counter-slurs: Indians were called "foreigners" and "dogs"; racial animosity was the highest it had been since 1975. Butadroka no longer called for Indian expulsion, but he and others suggested a constitutional amendment to reserve at least 75 percent of parliamentary seats for Fijians.

The result was close: the Alliance won twenty-eight seats, the Federation twenty-four. All minor parties effectively disappeared. It was clear that Fiji elections are about the balance of power between races rather than about abstract issues. There was, in any case, very little difference in political orientation between the contestants. (Even the WUF, a western Fijian splinter group shakily allied to the Federation, reaffirmed the Taukei values of village and tradition, though they attacked—as westerners have always done—the hegemony of eastern chiefs.)

Since the 1982 elections racial friction has eased; and a royal commission investigating the more serious allegations of both sides has been sensibly ponderous in its task. It would be very wrong,

I think, to conclude that integration would be the salvation of Fiji. This is almost always an outsider's view, inspired by the inappropriate models of South Africa or the southern United States. Race may be a problem in Fiji (mainly at election time), but it isn't nearly so sinister a problem as in countries where ethnic differences are ignored or denied.

The so-called melting-pot philosophy too often ends in the forced acculturation of weaker groups to the ways of the stronger. The peoples of Fiji are seeking ways to be equal but different. Even if it were possible to produce an authentic hybrid culture in Fiji, neither Indian nor Fijian is willing to hazard his ancient identity for such an unlikely result.

◆

In Suva it is easier to stay than to leave. My time in Fiji was running out, but I was contenting myself with a little library work and barfly journalism at the Grand Pacific. I met some interesting people: a descendant of the *Bounty* mutineers; a Tongan minister of agriculture; some diplomats from Papua Niugini (as they spell it); and a California beauty disappointed in the Pacific.

"I like to be very free with my body," she told me over her gin and tonic, "but there are no nude beaches here. The Fijian women keep their clothes on in the water—I just don't believe it."

"You're a century too late."

"Or too early." Then she sneezed. "Wow! That's an allergy sneeze!" She jumped off her stool and stared with accusation at some hibiscus flowers on the bar. "I'll have to go," she said.

Wendell Gorky, it seemed, had left the country.

"He was in here one day with his friend the *talatala*," the barman told me, "*talatala* drinking orange juice, Dr. Gorky drinking rum. Later on I hear Doctor tell the *talatala* he feel like going home. And you know, I never saw anyone move so fast. That *talatala* went straight down to Air Pacific, got tickets right away, and put Doctor on the plane before he sober up and change his mind. Quiet here since then."

I had not yet been to Bau. Once, after leaving Aseri's village, Derek, Senitiki, and I had stood on the jetty at Bau Landing and looked across the half mile of water—grey under driving rain—at the tiny isle with its sparse mop of tossing palms. There is no regular boat service, and, even if there were, tourists are not encouraged to tramp the chiefly soil. One cannot just go to Bau, Senitiki had said; some sort of permission was required.

For several lazy days I told myself I didn't really need to go. I had seen the island so clearly from the air that I was sure I knew what its twenty acres held. But the desire to go there nagged at me. Tiny Bau was a presence out of all proportion to its size. It could not be ignored. I felt I had to stand on Bau and gaze across to the mangroved mainland coveted by Cakobau.

Among the "temporary" wooden sheds which house outgrowths of government ministries behind Parliament, there is a small black and white sign: FIJIAN LANGUAGE DICTIONARY PROJECT. Marshall Sahlins had suggested that I go there to meet Paul Geraghty, a linguist working on a new and definitive lexicon of all major variants of Fijian. I decided to call on him and ask if he knew where one could obtain permission to visit Bau.

Geraghty was a slight, trim figure in white shirt, khaki shorts, and bare feet. I glanced around: all the office staff had bare feet; there was a row of shoes parked by the door; I had forgotten my Fijian manners—my sandals were still on. Geraghty is famous in Fiji for his command of some thirty local dialects. His English accent was hard to place—I thought I could hear New Zealand mixed with North Country, and something else.

"I'm Irish actually," he said, "but educated at Rugby. I suppose there's some Fiji English on top of that by now—it comes with the job. I must have been here seven years by now."

How long would it be before the dictionary was finished?

"Don't ask me that," he said. "It's a bit like painting a bridge, you see. When we get to the end the language will have changed and we'll have to start all over again. But we hope to have a preliminary volume out next year—just on Bauan, whatever that is." He smiled at me quizzically.

"I thought Bauan was pretty standard?" I said.

"Depends. Depends what you mean by Bauan. You see, the missionaries came here and wrote down what they thought was

Bauan, but nobody bothered to go to Bau to see what was being spoken there. The missionaries weren't allowed on Bau itself so they settled on Viwa, which isn't far from Bau, of course, but the Bauan used there was partly a trade language, a coastal *lingua franca* that seems to have Rewan and Bauan parentage.

"As for written Bauan, I'm afraid that was a creation of the missionaries. They didn't do a bad job, but imagine the problems they faced trying to translate the scriptures into a language not their own. Several of my Fijian friends will privately admit there are long passages of the Fijian Bible that they don't understand a word of. Isn't that right, David?"

Geraghty introduced me to Tevita (or David) Nawadra, the dictionary's editor, a powerfully built Fijian. He wore a formal *sulu* of dark cloth, and, at six foot four or so, looked colossal beside the spare Irishman; a receding hairline enhanced his august expression.

"Tevita's from Bau himself," said Geraghty.

"You don't really need permission," Nawadra said when I asked about visiting Bau, "but you should have an invitation. If you can wait a few moments I'll make a couple of phone calls."

"He means that literally." Geraghty grinned. "There are only two telephones on Bau."

Before long Nawadra returned from his desk.

"The Vunivalu will see you on Friday. Can you get to Bau Landing at nine o'clock? Someone will meet you there. Take two kilos of *waka* for *sevusevu*."

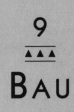

9

BAU

My rental car divided the lakes of mist that lay on the roads and fields of the delta. It had rained in the night; the countryside between Nausori and Bau was steaming in the first warmth of the sun. At regular intervals I passed Indian farmhouses with schoolchildren outside waving, waiting for their bus. The damp air carried the smells of spicy breakfasts, oxen, and opening flowers.

I reached Bau Landing with half an hour to spare. The tide was out. (There are actually two landings, an old and a new. From the old one you can see the island, but the mud appears at low water; the new landing, navigable at all times, is nearby, beside a channel in the mangroves.) At the new wharf three Fijians were loading a black pig from a boat into a pick-up truck. They had the creature by the ears; it screamed and fixed its handlers with small, intelligent, accusing eyes. When they left I sat in the car with the doors open and continued reading the account of a missionary who was here in 1841:

> We had great difficulty in getting to the canoe, the tide being out, the wind strong, and much rain making it unpleasant wading through the mud: we were almost broiled by the vertical rays of

the sun. Our canoe soon reached Bau; when we went to the house
of Tanoa [Cakobau's father], to whom all Fiji pays respect.

This morning's clouds had promised a retreat at first, but now
they seemed to be gathering for a second attack. Soon after nine I
heard the insect buzz of an outboard motor; it grew louder; other
insects paused as if to listen; a small punt came in view. The
boatman introduced himself as Jo. He was slim and tall, in his
forties, wearing a yellow plastic sailing jacket and sou'wester. He
said something in Fijian and nodded at my Datsun; I caught the
name Tevita—it seemed he expected Nawadra to be coming too.
Was I supposed to be bringing Tevita with me? Surely not.

"*Sega*," I said in my rudimentary Fijian. "*Tevita mai Suva.*"

Jo smiled and motioned me into the boat, patting the thwart
where he wanted me to sit.

"English little," he said, pointing to his mouth.

"*Vosa vaka-Viti lailai*," I answered—our command of each other's
language was evidently similar.

The punt rapidly cleared the mangrove channel and started across
the half mile of open water to Bau. Once out of the trees the sea
was choppy, the wind brisk. Forewarned of the formality of Bau,
I was dressed in jacket, tie, and a grey *sulu* Derek had lent me
before he left. Spray began to soak my tweed, and the thwart
beneath me, wet and cold, added to a general feeling of nakedness
below the waist. Seen like this, from a boat whose gunwale was
not a foot above the waterline, the sea looked formidable, capricious.
Jo popped open a striped umbrella and insisted I take it; I spread
it behind me against the wind, and tried not to reflect on how much
I must have resembled a Victorian lady enduring a wet regatta.

Bau was a silhouette above the glistening waves, tufted with
palms, low and flat on one side, rising steeply at the other, then
dropping to the shore—the shape of a boot, or perhaps a boar's
head on a platter.

Na-Ulu-ni-Vuaka, "The Head of the Pig," was in fact one of the
island's ancient names in the days before the present Bauans moved
there from the neighbouring mainland. It was also called Korolevu,
which could mean "Big Town" but probably derived from the

primary meaning of *koro* as an eminence or mound, especially one that rises from a swamp. According to legend, two related groups had lived there: the Levuka, in a village on the hill; and the Butoni, on the flat part in a village called the Pig's Head. In the mid-eighteenth century both groups were expelled by their overlords, the Bauans, who then settled on the island and renamed it Bau. The original islanders are said to have angered the Roko Tui, or sacred chief, of Bau by withholding a great fish they caught. As vassals, they should have given so fine a catch in tribute, but instead they ate it themselves. For this the Levuka were scattered to Lakeba and Ovalau, and the Butoni, compared by one early writer to the Gypsies or Jews, became wanderers among many islands, including Rabi.

Such an incident may have given the Bauans the excuse they wanted, but the main reason for their move to Bau Island was likely a strategic one. In those days Bau was a small buffer state between the much larger chiefdoms of Rewa and Verata. The Bauans' position on the mainland was insecure; often they were pawns in the struggles of their neighbours. But within a few years of the move, Vunivalu Banuve (c. 1770–1803) dramatically raised the status of Bau through marriages with Rewa and skillful interventions in wars where his forces could tip the balance of power. He also began to transform the island itself, filling in areas of swamp and shallow water, and surrounding the new works with a stone seawall indented by the docks that sheltered Bau's true defence—the wooden walls of her canoe fleet.

Banuve died of the "long disease" brought by the first Europeans, but his son Naulivou made brilliant use of Charley Savage and other beachcombers. By 1810 Verata was virtually destroyed. Bau and Rewa were then the most powerful states in Fiji, and their respective rulers renowned as the two "Hot Stones"—because their cannibal ovens were seldom cool.

◆

Jo brought the boat under the lee of the hill and skirted around the southern shore of the island. We passed a group of imposing buildings, some modern, some traditional in style, arranged around a

well-mown lawn—the chiefly compound of the Vunivalu, Ratu Sir
George Cakobau, great-grandson of Ratu Seru Cakobau, the famous
Tui Viti. In 1841 Seru's father, Tanoa, was living in this very spot:

> His house surpasses, in magnitude and grandeur, anything I have
> seen in these seas. It is one hundred and thirty feet long, and
> forty-two feet wide, with massive columns in the centre, and
> strong, curious workmanship in every part.

Jo sailed about a hundred yards beyond the buildings, tilted the
outboard, and ran the punt up into one of the stone docks. Many
of the megalithic slabs are leaning now, like tombstones in an abandoned churchyard, but they are not beyond repair. In this land of
wooden architecture the boldness and permanence of masonry are
most impressive; the stonework gives you an intimation of Bau as
the "royal city" that early visitors often called it.

Jo's home is a wooden house much like Aseri's. A thick layer of
fine mats covers the floor, and in one corner there is a raised sleeping
platform draped with a mosquito net. The rest of the room is bare
except for a cluster of Western furniture—a coffee table, sofa, and
two armchairs—pushed up against the wall as if waiting for the
movers. His wife and children came in from an adjacent building.
None spoke much English. They shook my hand and bade me
welcome in Fijian; then they went over to the pile of furniture and
arranged it for use. I was ushered into a chair, but the others sat
around me on the floor. I felt like a character in an old photograph—
an explorer, perhaps, sitting at his folding table somewhere deep
in Africa. Jo's wife brought in some doughnuts and tea, for me
alone. A religious picture on the wall, with the Orwellian message
JESUS CHRIST, AT EVERY GATHERING THE UNSEEN GUEST, AT EVERY
CONVERSATION THE SILENT LISTENER, reminded me to ask for someone to say grace.

As soon as the European tea ceremony was concluded, the Fijians
took out a *tanoa* and invited me to sit on the mats with them. A
stocky young man who spoke perfect English joined the group.

"I am Jemesa, or James if you like. They are going to make a small *sevusevu* of welcome for you. Have you had Fijian grog before?"

I realized now that I should have brought some ground kava to present, but I was expecting to see Cakobau and had brought only a large bundle of *waka* roots, neatly trussed like a bouquet by the market seller, which would be impossible to divide. I explained the problem to Jemesa.

"Don't worry. I'm afraid the Vunivalu may not be able to see any visitors today. A great lady who is related to him has just died and there will be a funeral tomorrow. Jo will tell him you are here, and if he cannot receive you himself I expect he may tell us to show you around." Jemesa handed me yesterday's *Fiji Times*. The lady was an *adi* (the female equivalent of *ratu*) who had been, among other things, Fiji's first woman member of Parliament.

The rain returned—a staccato drumming of large drops on the roof. The curtains blew like pennants in the windows. Jo closed the shutters, filling the house with a snug half-light. There was a formal round of *yaqona*, with Jemesa acting as my spokesman; then cigarettes were lit, and the match flames illuminated, one by one, the dark faces around the *tanoa*.

"I remember the Grand Pacific all right," Jemesa said after someone had asked where I was staying. "I haven't been back in five years. Last time I drank beer there they didn't like what I said to the barman—four big men threw me in the street. That's how I lost this"—he showed a missing tooth—"but I got in a punch or two before they got me out. Short temper runs in our family. My father is a chief in Namosi. When he fought on the Solomons during the war an American commander insulted him, called him a nigger or something like that, so my father knocked him flat. It was the end of his time in the army, but he never regretted it."

There was plenty of laughter at this; when it had died down Jo quietly said, "*Talo yaqona,*" and another round was served. We began to talk about Bau itself. These twenty acres hold three distinct peoples living in separate villages—Bau proper, Lasakau, and Soso—though the boundaries between them are not obvious from the air. Jo's village is Lasakau, home of the Vunivalu's fishermen, who were brought here from Beqa in the eighteenth century to replace the banished Levuka.

Together with craftsmen brought from Kadavu (to Soso), the Lasakauans quarried the great flat stones for the docks and seawalls, and hauled them forty or fifty miles by canoe from the northeast coast of Viti Levu. The stones were found in easily split strata exposed at low tide, and the method of transporting them was most ingenious. When the tide was out the Lasakauans loosened the slabs with levers and passed ropes beneath them. The ropes were then attached to large double canoes. When the sea rose the canoes lifted the stones from the bottom, suspending them in the water. Several hundred slabs were thus raised and slowly punted along the coast to Bau. The largest megalith is almost twelve feet long by five feet wide, with a weight of at least three tons.

Masonry was not the only contribution made by the Lasakau people to the edifice of Bau. In the early 1830s the Vunivalu Tanoa became increasingly unpopular for his tyranny and an appetite for human flesh excessive even by the standards of the day. It was said that whenever he set down his *yaqona* cup with a chiefly wish for *vuaka balavu* ("long pig") a prisoner would be killed and roasted. If no prisoners were on hand, a low-ranking citizen would do. In 1832, while away from Bau on a journey, Tanoa was ousted by a coup d'état and forced into exile. The Lasakauans, however, remained secretly loyal, and five years later they co-operated with Tanoa's son Ratu Seru in a daring counter-coup. One night they fortified Lasakau village with a war fence and set fire to the crowded houses on the rest of the island. Tanoa was reinstated as Vunivalu; there were bloody reprisals. The Lasakau fishermen were raised almost to the status of a Varangian guard, and the real executive power now lay with the Warlord's precocious heir, Ratu Seru Cakobau.

Tradition has it that the name Cakobau, "Destroyer of Bau" or "Evil to Bau," was taken by Ratu Seru after these events, but scholars have recently challenged this hoary assumption. It seems there was an earlier Cakobau, and the supposed etymology is in any case dubious. Be that as it may, Ratu Seru outshone any previous holder of the name and it is now the surname of his direct descendants.

(One great-grandson, Ratu Etuate (or "Ted") Cakobau, was, unlike most Fijians, fond of a joke at the expense of his anthropophagous ancestors. While commanding a counter-insurgency unit in Malaya, he was asked one night at the officers' mess about his family background. "Fijian by extraction and Scottish by absorption," Ratu Ted replied, explaining that his forebears had once dined on shipwrecked Scots.)

◆

The rain and the *yaqona* flowed all morning. At noon I was again invited to sit in the armchair. Jo's wife brought in a tray and set before me an enormous lunch: fish soup; barracuda fillets; a kind of seviche made with clams, lemon juice, and hot red chilies; three pork chops; and a pile of steamed yams—traditional Fijian foods of high prestige. They were also delicious, especially the intriguing seviche, but after breakfast, doughnuts, and several pints of kava, I wasn't able to do the meal justice. Since fishing is the speciality of the Lasakau, I decided to eat the seafood and leave part of the yams and pork.

While I feasted the others continued drinking; when the *tanoa* was dry they retired to the adjoining house for their lunch. Before leaving, Jo pulled back the mosquito net and straightened the pillows on the bed.

"You can rest here for an hour or so," Jemesa said. "Make yourself at home."

The rain was lighter now, the metal roof quiet except for occasional drips falling from the trees. A cool, moist draught, heavy with the smell of sea, land, and cooking fires, filtered through the room, removing the cigarette smoke and earthy fragrance of *yaqona*. For a while I heard the clatter of dishes and murmured conversation from next door; then a stillness covered the island: Bau was in siesta. The breeze and the rhythmic crash of the waves slowly receded from the conscious mind, becoming not sounds so much as the fabric of silence itself; I began to doze.

When I woke I couldn't for a moment remember where I was.

At first I thought I must be in Ratu Lemeki's house at Nadrau; then the sea fell more loudly in my ears and I knew that couldn't be right. This was Bau; or Mbau; or Ambow (as Lockerby wrote it)—the name has a weight beyond its single syllable, like "Gaul" or "Rome." Bau—it seemed mysterious—and the mystery was deepened by the fact that I had spent half a day on the island and seen little of it but this house. Surely this seldom happens in England or North America—to be eating and sleeping in a stranger's house in a place of which one knows nothing, has seen nothing? Bau; Mbau; Ambow—perhaps the name seemed so charged because the past was occupying the space as yet unfilled by the present.

I opened the net and gazed across the darkened room at the mats, the *tanoa*, the huddle of Western furniture against the wall. What better symbols of the Fijians' cultural dexterity, their ability to compartmentalize, to walk with foreigners nor lose the native touch? And, thinking of Kipling, was Fiji not the embodiment of all that he and his kind had hoped for: a tidy monument to the finer side of British imperialism? "The Saxon . . . never means anything serious till he talks about justice and right." Ah, if only it were true. How many such Saxons were there at Levuka in the 1860s and '70s? Thurston was one, Gordon perhaps another—somehow a few idealists had managed to guide events in the formative years of the colony. But there had been a convergence of pragmatic considerations too, or the Colonial Office would not have stood for the policy: it was cheaper to let the natives administer themselves; and the Fijians were too tough a bunch to dispossess with the usual liberalistic guile. One has only to cast one's eyes a little farther up the map (and down Gordon's *curriculum vitae*) to Ocean Island for a rather different view. From there the benign treatment of the Fijians seems an aberration, and the inherently exploitive nature of colonialism gives itself away.

The British built in Fiji a little showcase colony to give substance to their dreams of mission—dreams, it must be said, that were sincerely held by many individuals but more rarely upheld by the colonial system. Colonies, despite the cant, were not run as a philanthropic exercise. It was British government policy that colonial possessions had to generate the wealth to support their rule. Someone had to pay. And if the natives were spared, other sources of labour and capital had to be found. The survival of Fijian society was paid for by the sweat of the Indians, who made it possible for the Colonial Sugar Refining Company (such an honest name) to turn an honest profit. Later, the phosphate riches of the Banabans directly or indirectly underwrote many British operations in the western Pacific.

Perfidious Albion—how the British quote that gibe with amused condescension, yet how often they have merited it. In Fiji the Saxons didn't mow down tribesmen with machine guns, nor blow Indians from the mouths of cannon, and they did not methodically hunt the natives to extinction as they did in Tasmania and Newfoundland. They did not do such things here and it is easy, if one is British, to be proud of the fact. But they did them elsewhere.

◆

Jo and Jemesa returned soon after two o'clock.

"The Vunivalu apologizes for not being able to receive you himself. He has to go to Suva later this afternoon for the funeral arrangements. There wouldn't be time for you to make *sevusevu* to him in person."

Indeed there wouldn't: in Fiji you can't simply call on someone like the Vunivalu and say hello. Things must be done in the customary way—if we had met there would have been an hour or two of formalities around the *tanoa*.

"But he told us to show you around," Jemesa added. "He said we can show you anything you want to see."

I was not exactly sure what there might be to see on Bau, so I followed their suggestions. We began by climbing the hill, where the ancient village of Korolevu once stood. The path was very muddy, but the mud was caused less by the rain than by building activity on the summit. We climbed through the dripping shade of trees that doubtless saw the coming of the Bauans more than two centuries ago, and emerged to find a wasteland of sand and clay in which stood a half-finished bunker-like construction of poured concrete. Nearby there were cement mixers, piles of gravel, and a tall crane dangling its hook above the work like a mechanical fisher-king.

This controversial work is part of a million-and-a-half-dollar project to level the top of the hill, use the resulting fill to reclaim more land, and at the same time erect a mausoleum in honour of Cakobau on the centenary of his death. The hill of Bau has been a Christian cemetery since the island's conversion in 1854; the old graves have been opened and cleared away, and the bones they contained are now housed in an ossuary at the base of the monument.

Land reclamation has ample historical precedent on Bau, but there are many in Fiji who question the need to disturb an old graveyard, and important archaeological remains, to build a local Lenin's Tomb.

Seen today from the top of the hill, Bau is a quiet small town of about three hundred people living in neat wooden bungalows. The houses are well spaced among palms, flowering shrubs, and giant *baka* trees, which spread above them like English oaks. In its heyday the island held ten times its present population. It was a tripartite city—Bau, Lasakau, and Soso—of narrow streets between rows of beautifully made houses with steep gable roofs. From among the human dwellings, the thatched spires of at least twenty *bure kalou* rose fifty and sixty feet into the sky.

"I went over to the imperial city of Bau . . ." wrote a visitor in 1847:

Here we saw the élite. . . . The houses are far superior to anything else I have seen in the South Sea Islands. The large double canoe of the king will carry from two to three hundred men; and they are just now preparing to start on some warlike expedition. Their spirit-houses are finely ornamented. . . . Bau is the lion of Fiji; and dark are the deeds of which it is guilty.

Directly below the hill, at the edge of the triangular *rara*, is the Cakobau Memorial Church, the oldest and finest extant mission church in Fiji. Its stone walls are a yard thick, pierced with Gothic-arched doors and windows. Since the last hurricane the roof has been replaced and the ceiling refinished inside with polished planking. Before the altar stands a curious oval boulder about three feet high with a dimple in the top. This is now the baptismal font, but until Cakobau's conversion it was the braining stone of the Bauan war god, Cagawalu. It is said that a thousand skulls had been dashed against it before Cagawalu deferred to Jesus, and the stone changed its business from putting pagans out of the world to bringing Christians in.

The stone seemed to have been cracked and crudely repaired with cement.

"The builders who came here to restore the church did that," said Jemesa. "They found this big stone among the hurricane damage and didn't know what it was. They thought they had better get rid of it but it was too heavy for them—so they broke it up with a pneumatic drill and threw the pieces out. Luckily an old man saw what had happened and made them put it back together."

An ironic fate for the stone once known as the "Skull Crusher"; but, apart from this mishap, stone and church represent in a way the career of Cakobau. He built his power during the 1840s on the old gods, and for many years they served him well. With an eye on the future, perhaps, he allowed nearby Viwa to accept conversion to Christianity—but he himself remained loudly scornful of it. "Wonderful is the new religion, is it not?" Cakobau said to a recently converted Viwa chief. "But will it prevent our having men to eat? Not it!" And he told a pestering missionary, "When you have grown *dalo* on yon bare rock, then will I become a Christian, and not before."

When his father, Tanoa, died in 1852 Cakobau himself assisted at the customary strangling of the principal wives (a thing the women are said to have clamoured for), and at his installation as Vunivalu in 1853 eighteen prisoners were roasted for the feast. But by that time Cakobau was having cause to doubt the efficacy of Cagawalu.

The wars with Rewa (1843–1855) had gone well for Bau until 1850, but badly thereafter. Cakobau's puppet Rewan king; a semi-

Westernized fop who called himself Mr. Phillips, died of dysentery. The fighting chief Qaraniqio swept down from the hills; the Bauans were driven out of Rewa and their governor was eaten. Many subject towns rebelled.

The Vunivalu also had financial worries. In 1849 the American consul John Brown Williams accidentally set fire to his own house on Nukulau Island during some boisterous Fourth of July celebrations. Fijian onlookers valiantly rescued some of the consul's property from the flames and made off with it. Under Fijian custom, anything rescued from a burning house belonged to its salvager. Williams thought differently. He held Cakobau—as putative Tui Viti—liable for the losses, which he expansively estimated at $5001.38. (A consummate land swindler, Williams had bought the whole of Nukulau Island for thirty dollars.)

The consul subsequently added other Americans' claims to his own and inflated the original figures with compound interest to arrive at a sum of more than $40,000. He threatened Cakobau with deportation aboard the next American warship to call at Bau if the "debt" remained unpaid.

Cakobau had also run up some debts of his own for weapons, foreign goods, and two schooners. He tried to pay for the boats by levying a *bêche-de-mer* tax on Bauan tributaries. The tax was a failure— an interesting failure because it showed the extent that custom influenced Fijian politics. Sea slugs were not a traditional tribute item: they had little *mana*, and no prestige. Even though Cakobau set an example, fishing with his own hands, the tax was widely ignored by subjects who might gladly have contributed yams, *yaqona*, or pigs.

The Vunivalu's insolvency did not endear him to the traders of Levuka, particularly since he was sometimes highhanded with his creditors. "Why did you come here?" Cakobau reportedly said to one who turned up at Bau. "I did not send for you. However, white men make good eating: they are like ripe bananas."

Consul Williams had little trouble organizing a boycott of Bau, and he added insult to injury by writing in an open letter to the Sydney papers:

Bau ought to be destroyed, and the people swept from the face of the earth. Then, and not until then, will commerce move uninterrupted in this archipelago, where the merchants can carry on so lucrative a business. . . . A ship of war could lay off Bau, knock down and destroy that town, while one is smoking a cigar.

The letter was brought to Cakobau's attention by King George Tupou of Tonga, who pointed out that Bau's adherence to cannibalism played into the hands of unscrupulous whites looking for an excuse to commit genocide: "I wish, Cakobau, you would *lotu* [convert] . . . it will be well for you, Cakobau, to think wisely in these days." (As it turned out, the Vunivalu long outlived the consul, who died in 1860 "after eating gorgeously of green turtle.")

By 1854 Cakobau was in despair. His island was under blockade, his garrison on the nearby Kaba peninsula had mutinied, and he himself was ill and listless. Early in March a fire swept through Bau; among the buildings destroyed was the temple of the war god, Cagawalu. Three weeks later Cagawalu's priests prophesied victory over the Kaba rebels, but the loyal forces were repulsed. Cakobau decided that if the recent campaigns were a contest between old and new gods, then the old had lost. On Sunday, April 30, he publicly converted, adding the name Epenisa (Ebenezer) to his others. From that day on, pork replaced man on the bill of fare at Bauan feasts. (One imagines that many remarked, like Launcelot in the *Merchant of Venice*, "This making of Christians will raise the price of hogs.")

At first the new religion was not much help. In fact it alienated those allies who had seen Cakobau as the champion of the ancient ways. But, as the Vunivalu proved many times in his life, he was a resolute man; he stuck by his decisions. Ridiculed at first for what many observers—native and foreign—saw as a cheap political move, Cakobau took his new faith seriously and strove to impose it on his subjects. Thousands *lotu*ed with their chief; thousands more awaited the final outcome of the war.

Early in 1855 Qaraniqio of Rewa died; the conflict, which had begun as a family feud, was ended swiftly by negotiation. In April, Tongan troops defeated Kaba. The *lotu* had triumphed, and Cakobau, true to the new code, did not dash heads against the stone.

◆

From the church it is a walk of a hundred yards or so across the *rara* to the former abode of Cagawalu.

In Calvert's *Mission History* (1858) there is an engraving of the temple as it was before the fire: a two-tiered rectangular platform, faced with vertical stone slabs like those of the docks and ascended by a stone staircase. Built on top of this was an imposing thatched structure considered in its day the finest piece of architecture in Fiji. Its walls appear to have been of woven wattle with a diagonal pattern worked into them, while the roof, three or four times higher than the walls, rose from heavy eaves in a graceful concave curve— as on Oriental buildings—so that the pitch, shallow at first, became almost vertical by the time it reached the exterior ridge-pole. The pole was bound to the crest of the thatch, and indeed wholly encased, with ornate *magimagi* ropework, and it overhung the gables by about eight feet at either side, thus giving the roof an outline like the Greek letter π. From the ends of the ridge-pole heavy clusters of egg cowries hung down like ivory grapes.

I had been expecting to find at most a ruined mound surrounded by fallen stones; but the stepped platform—about fifty by seventy feet at the base and ten feet high—is not only whole but surmounted by a fine modern Fijian building with woven leaf walls and a roof of fluted aluminium in a tasteful charcoal grey. This new roof lacks the curvature of the old, but it approximates the original proportions and is styled with a cornice at the rim and two *balabala* poles protruding at the gable ends.

Jemesa led the way up the stairs and tried the doors. They seemed to be locked, but he pushed a little harder and they opened inwards as the lock disengaged. His boldness surprised me; then I remembered that Jemesa is a son-in-law of the Lasakau chief, who is second in rank to the Vunivalu.

"This is the old meeting house. It was the only one till they built the new one over there for the Queen's visit." Jemesa pointed across the *rara* to a long, low, modern building of Scandinavian appearance in the shadow of some big trees against the hill. The old meeting house, like all Fijian buildings, is constructed similarly to a pole barn—the walls and roof are built as an exterior shell over the massive frame. This system keeps the structural timbers free from any dampness or insects that might linger in the thatch, and the aesthetic effect of the robust wooden columns standing out from the walls is most satisfying. In this building the great tree trunks that stand in the middle of each gable wall and rise to support the ridge-pole are about two feet thick, as beautifully smoothed and polished as the masts of a tall ship.

I wondered how old they were. The thought crossed my mind that at the base of each might be sitting the skeletons of men buried in the post holes to ensure the building a long and stable life. But the *lotu* came soon after the destruction of the old temple by fire, and even wood of this quality could not last more than a century in Bau's climate. No dead men hold these posts; but I am willing to bet that down in the fill of the platform skeletal guardians from earlier periods still sit out the afterlife.

The worship of the Bauan war god apparently began soon after the migration to the island. Like the Aztec Huitzilopochtli, Cagawalu became the apotheosis of the rising state's bid for power. No doubt his cult expanded greatly after the young Tanoa (on Naulivou's orders) killed the Roko Tui Bau—the sacred chief—and seized the paramount chieftainship for the Warlord, or Vunivalu.

The Fijians did not make idols or images of their ancient gods, but it is known that they envisioned Cagawalu as a giant, sixty feet tall, with a colossal forehead "eight spans high," which is what his name literally means. A temple usually had a long strip of fine white *masi* cloth hanging from the ridge-pole to the floor; this was believed to be the path followed by the god when he descended to possess and inspire his priests. Captain Erskine, who visited Bau in 1849, made a detailed inspection of the war god's temple:

A cloth screen covered the sanctuary. . . . [Inside] lay a few neck-pillows, and an elephant's tusk, which had been presented many years ago to Tanoa . . . and by him dedicated to the god. As whales' teeth are much valued, and constitute, in fact, a species of currency of indeterminate value, such a specimen of ivory was doubtless considered as beyond all price. The building stood on a raised platform, and was surrounded by a few trees of graceful foliage, under one of which lay the large wooden *lali*, or sacred drum, beaten at festivals and sacrifices; and overshadowed by another was the place where the bodies of victims are dedicated to the *kalou*, or evil spirit, previous to their being handed over to those who are to cook them for the banquet. The lower branches of this tree had evidently been lately cut away to the height of eight or ten feet from the ground; and we were told that this had been done after the reduction of Rewa, a few months before, when a mound of no fewer than eighty corpses, slain in battle, was heaped up on the spot.

The ancient Fijians did not engage in regular worship—a war temple would be neglected in peacetime, or used for secular purposes, often as a council chamber. It was thus a logical transition, in Fijian practice, for Cagawalu's *bure kalou* to become the meeting house of Bau after the god fell from favour. Even in the old heathen days, the name of the building—Na-Vata-ni-Tawake, "The Platform of the Banners"—was not overtly religious. The meeting house still has its ancient name today, and at the foot of the main steps there is a flagpole.

We left by the door Jemesa had forced ("I'll get someone to shut this later") and walked around the upper terrace to another flight of stairs at the side. These stairs were very worn, many of the stones had cracked or fallen: I could easily believe those who estimate that the Na-Vata-ni-Tawake platform was built about two hundred years ago, in Banuve's reign. It is said that baskets of earth given in *soro* (symbolic submission or atonement) from all over Fiji are incorporated within it.

A large ship's anchor about eight feet high leans against the bottom terrace wall on the north side, its iron as weathered and pitted as the stone. Calvert's drawing, made in the early 1850s, shows what must be the same anchor, though he has it leaning against the stairway. The story of how it got here has been unravelled recently by Fergus Clunie.

In 1825 the Manila brig *Laurice* arrived off Bau and Viwa. She was crewed by a rascally bunch of "Manila-men"—Philippine *mestizos* notorious for violence but adept in the Oriental art of curing *bêche-de-mer*. The men mutinied and took over the ship. They knifed the officers, and presented the vessel to Naulivou in return for being allowed to settle at Bau as beachcombers. But though the Vunivalu got the ship, her weapons and stores fell into the hands of rivals later involved in the coup of 1832. These might have attempted their rebellion against Naulivou himself, had not the wily old statesman deliberately burned down Bau in order to get rid of the dangerous foreign goods. (Arson, it seems, was an old political trick on densely populated Bau. Other timely fires—perhaps even that of 1854—may not have been accidents.)

The *Laurice* lay anchored off Bau in shallow water, where she began to receive visits from Lasakau fishermen searching for iron. Like a car stranded in a tough neighbourhood, she was gradually stripped, until Naulivou had her hauled on shore and broken up. In 1827 a white sailor persuaded the Bauans to raise the anchors from the seabed. He was hoping to sell them to a passing ship, but there is no record that he did so. One has since disappeared; the other is almost certainly the anchor that still leans against the Bauan temple platform.

There is strong circumstantial evidence that the unruly faction at Bau was involved in the *Laurice* mutiny from the start. Naulivou, Tanoa, and Cakobau all tried to protect foreign vessels in their domain, but the Bauan rebels, in power from 1832 to 1837, made several attempts on ships, succeeding spectacularly with the seizure of *L'Aimable Josephine* in 1834. (The Viwa chief who led that attack took the name Varani—Fijian for "France"—to celebrate his deed.) It isn't known exactly when the *bure kalou* of Cagawalu was rebuilt after Naulivou's use of the torch as equalizer; but a white visitor in 1834 identified the temple's two main posts as the masts of the Manila brig.

Seeing this anchor here, a trophy from the old days, made the era of Bau's ferocity more palpable. Until now I had found it hard to imagine that bloody events had ever taken place on this tiny, tranquil island—just as it is difficult, when visiting the Tower of London, to get an intimation of the death and torture there. It's the same even in Mexico: one looks at what is left of Huitzilo-pochtli's great and terrible pyramid, and it now seems simply an architectural curiosity sinking beneath the traffic of Mexico City.

The Aztecs and Bauans, I think, had much in common. Both erupted from insignificant islands to dominate far larger and older peoples; both were driven by gods with insatiable hunger for enemy dead. Even the shape of the platform at Bau is reminiscent of a Mesoamerican *teocalli*—add a few more tiers and you would have a step-pyramid. A culture's tallest buildings always reveal its deep-est obsessions: in Egypt, the ruler's immortality; in Bau and Mexico, the religion of war. And we of the modern world? Why, office towers and revolving restaurants—the cult of Mammon: Alpha a car; Omega a watch.

◆

The Lasakauans were conscientious guides. They showed me, as they promised, virtually everything: lesser megalithic platforms of vanished temples and ancient chiefly houses; the brackish pond that was formerly Bau's only water supply; and the new meeting house, large enough to receive hundreds of visitors, like the great longhouse that the ancient Bauans had built near the same spot to accom-modate the Butoni and Levuka on their tributary visits. That had been the most spacious building in pre-contact Fiji, and was called Na-Ulu-ni-Vuaka ("The Pig's Head") after the early village; when-ever the Butoni came to stay in it they were given a pig's head to eat, ritually divided into portions appropriate for the different clans: the ambassadors got the ears.

The tour of Bau, seemingly so impromptu, had begun to acquire some indefinable structure. I felt I was being steered very subtly through a predetermined course, and at the same time given the impression that the choices were mine. It was the quintessence of Fijian manners to guide a stranger through the elusive yet ineluct-able requisites of *vaka Viti*, the "Fijian way," without letting him catch a hint of the cultural ignoramus he surely was.

The rain was falling in earnest; Jo suggested we go back to his house for rain jackets before proceeding to the Vunivalu's compound. Without any prior inkling, I learned now that the visit was to have an unexpected climax. Ratu Sir George Cakobau, though unable to see me, had instructed Jo and Jemesa to show me his *bure*—his traditional ceremonial house used for formal events and receptions.

Jo handed me a yellow sailing jacket.

"Put this on for the rain," Jemesa said. "You can take your tie and coat off now, if you find it more comfortable."

I asked him if I shouldn't keep my tie on since we were going to the Vunivalu's buildings.

"That's all right; you can relax a bit now. He knows you have shown proper respect—he doesn't let many people see his house."

The Vunivalu's compound occupies a *tabua*-shaped wedge of flat land (reclaimed in ancient times and enlarged more recently) bounded on one side by water and on the other by the steep face of the hill. The base of the tooth abuts the village of Lasakau but is separated from it by an unusually long canoe dock that reaches towards the hill, and probably doubled as a moat. The chiefly compound was thus accessible only by sea or through Lasakau; it could be defended against any external or internal foe who might gain control of the rest of the island—a precaution adopted, I would guess, after Tanoa's restoration by the Cakobau-Lasakau coup of 1837.

The new house, in which the Vunivalu lives, stands at the far end, near the point of the wedge, the cliff looming above it on the right, the sea behind, and the Viti Levu mainland beyond. A large tree grows beside it, but the lawn, like any Fijian *rara*, is otherwise bare. The architecture is a curious blend of ancient and modern, local and international. A tall slate-coloured aluminium roof in the classic Fijian shape surmounts a Scandinavian bungalow with plateglass windows.

In the middle distance, on the left, the great *bure* we had come to see dominated the lawn. But first Jemesa led me to a long shed-like building near the dock, the Vunivalu's storehouse for gifts and tribute. It was dark inside—the window shutters were closed against the rain—but when the eyes became adjusted one could make out an enormous inventory of Fijian traditional wealth. There were bolts of *masi* cloth, coils of coconut-fibre rope, stacks of *masima* salt blocks, drums of kerosene (*neo*-traditional, that), and, most interesting of all, a trunk of sandalwood—rare in Fiji since the predations of the early whites. I bent to where the wood had been cut and inhaled its aroma, almost like cinnamon but less pungent. Large pieces are carved into ceremonial bowls and dishes, while the sawdust and chippings are refined and mixed with coconut oil to make a body lotion used since ancient times.

This tribute is presented on ceremonial occasions to the Vunivalu as Paramount Chief of Fiji; in due time most of it is redistributed by him in reciprocal gifts to his subjects. The contents of the storehouse are a kind of social capital, a statement of prestige, and an expression of the network of loyalties binding the Fijians to their chief, and him to them. To be shown this was an essential part of the tour: these goods represented much of what this island was about. The ancient docks and temple platforms; the meal of pork, fish, and yams; the bowl of *yaqona*; these ceremonial goods: all this was Bau. I recalled Captain Erskine's account of his visit here in 1849:

> We arrived at last at the residence of Thakombau [Cakobau] himself, and here we were received with much ceremony. An entrance having been cleared for us through bundles of native cloth, immense coils of cordage, and other articles, the produce of the late Butoni tribute, the chief himself—the most powerful, perhaps, of any in the Pacific, and certainly the most energetic in character—was seen seated in the attitude of respect to receive us. He rose . . . unfolding, as he did so, an immense train of white native cloth, eight or ten yards long, from his waist.

The rain eased when we left the storehouse and the day seemed bright to eyes grown used to the gloom. We walked towards the *bure*. It is the largest Fijian building I have seen—about twenty-five by fifty feet in plan—and stands on a high *yavu*, or terrace, around which grows a well-trimmed hedge. Flights of steps ascend to doors in the front and side walls. Conch horns, symbols of royalty, are mounted on posts that flank the steps. The *bure* walls are made of leaves, the tall roof entirely of thatch, and the black *balabala* ridge-poles that protrude from the gable ends have clusters of white shells at their tips.

Jo opened the side door; Jemesa and I followed him in. One felt immediately the dark warmth of the *bure*—a venerable cosiness like that of a panelled Tudor hall or log-walled hunting lodge. The windows had glass, not shutters, but they weren't large, and the light that came in from under the heavy eaves was subdued. The house smelled of wood, straw, and wax polish.

The interior slowly revealed itself as the building's woody twilight receded up into the steeply pitched cathedral ceiling. The timbers are even finer and more massive than those of the meeting house; from the top of every pillar hangs a whale's tooth. The walls and roof are lined with pandanus mats whose light straw colour, interwoven with black geometrical patterns, sets off to advantage the sepia hardwood frame. But the chief glory of this building is its *magimagi* work—the bold yet elaborate sinnet lashings that bind the timbers together. It is done with ropes of three colours—black, white, and chestnut—combined in stripes, bands, chequers, and chevrons. The work seems equal, if not superior, to the finest ancient examples illustrated by early travellers. Wherever important beams and posts are joined, the bindings encase the timbers for a distance of several feet and are embellished with large white egg cowries. The work at the meeting of the end crossbeam, kingpost, stringer, and three struts forms a rope figure whose aesthetic virtuosity is matched only by its obvious strength.

"No nails anywhere," Jemesa said. "The whole thing is done by notching and binding. There is only one man in Fiji who can do work this good."

"I hope he's training some apprentices," I said.

The attic runs the full length of the building, but half the ground floor is separated into a private area by a mahogany partition fitted with bookshelves. These are stocked with law books, some novels, Fijiana, and a set of Britannicas. On one wall hangs Calvert's engraving of Na-Vata-ni-Tawake; and among the photographs of royalty and family members there are several studio portraits of Ratu

Seru Cakobau, great-grandfather of the present Vunivalu. The largest picture shows him in later life: a calm and penetrating gaze from a face surrounded by the bushy white cloud of his hair and beard. "It was impossible not to admire the appearance of the chief," wrote Erskine:

> of large, almost gigantic, size, his limbs were beautifully formed and proportioned; his countenance . . . agreeable and intelligent; while his immense head of hair, covered and concealed with gauze, smoke-dried and slightly tinged with brown, gave him altogether the appearance of an eastern sultan. No garments confined his magnificent chest and neck, or concealed the natural colour of the skin, a clear but decided black; and in spite of this paucity of attire—the evident wealth which surrounded him showing that it was a matter of choice and not of necessity—he looked "every inch a king."

There came a sudden peal of thunder; lightning lit up the *bure* as brightly as my camera flash. The thatch overhead began to roar like the clapping of a distant crowd. Rain came down in sheets so thick that nothing could be seen outside but the spray from the huge drops atomizing themselves on the ground. We peered out at the weather and waited. After fifteen minutes the rain eased, but as it did so there came a stealthy *drip, drop, drip*: a small puddle had formed in the middle of the hardwood floor.

I had noticed, when passing the chiefly compound by boat, that the thatch of the *bure* was getting threadbare on the seaward side. Could not some of the money being spent on the mausoleum project be diverted for repairing the canoe docks and this finest of Fijian buildings?

More than one writer has used the metaphor of a leaky roof to characterize Fijian society under the assault of the modern world. Collapse of the anomalous edifice has been prophesied with regularity for at least a hundred years—usually by outside experts with an ideological motive for tinkering with it. But so far the predicted disasters have failed to occur. Impending ruin has most often turned out to be change; and change has not yet proved ruinous.

Bau, once the terror of the archipelago, is now the shrine of Fijian identity. If the shrine appears slightly neglected, it is worth remembering that the ancient Fijians often neglected the houses of their gods whenever they felt secure. Those gods were not idols but ideas; and the health of the spirit was not the same as the condition of the spirit house.

We left the *bure* during a lull in the storm. I glanced back towards the Vunivalu's modern house. Cakobau was there, an old man with white hair, sitting crosslegged behind the plate-glass window, looking out.

Chronology

1500 B.C.	Occupation at rockshelter on Yanuca Island, near Sigatoka.
1200–200 B.C.	Makers of Lapita pottery active at several sites in southwestern Viti Levu.
200 B.C.–A.D. 1300	Steady population growth; ancient Fijians spread throughout archipelago and eventually colonize interior of major islands.
A.D. 1300–1600	Legends and genealogies suggest invasions from Polynesia, especially Tonga, during this period.
1643	Tasman sights several islands of the Fiji group.
1760(?)	The Bauans occupy the islet of Bau, after expelling its previous inhabitants.
1770(?)	Banuve succeeds Nailatikau as Vunivalu, or Warlord, of Bau.
1774	Cook lands briefly on the outlying island of Vatoa, southeastern Lau.
1789	Bligh and other *Bounty* crewmembers sail through Fiji group in an open boat.
1791	Crewmembers of the *Pandora* hospitably received by Fijians at Onoilau.

1800(?)	Wreck of the *Argo*. Significant contact between Fiji and the outside world begins. Plague of European origin ravages parts of Fiji; among its victims is Banuve of Bau, succeeded by his son, Naulivou.
1802(?)	Rescue of *Argo* survivor Oliver Slater. Sandalwood era begins. A second plague sweeps the islands.
1808	Wreck of the *Eliza*. Charley Savage arrives at Bau.
1808–09	William Lockerby active in Fiji.
1812(?)	Birth of Ratu Seru Cakobau of Bau. (1817, the traditionally accepted date, now seems doubtful; see Scarr, 1970, p. 98.)
1813	Death of Charley Savage. End of the sandalwood era.
1822–24	David Whippy arrives in Fiji and settles at Levuka. European settlement begins.
1829	Death of Naulivou, succeeded as Vunivalu of Bau by his brother, Tanoa Visawaqa.
1832	Coup d'état at Bau; Tanoa exiled.
1835	Methodist missionaries Cargill and Cross establish themselves at Lakeba, Lau.
1837	Tanoa restored at Bau in bloody counter-coup largely engineered by his son, Ratu Seru Cakobau.
1840	United States Exploring Expedition charts Fiji waters.
1843	Beginning of Bau-Rewa wars.
1844	Europeans expelled from Levuka by order of Cakobau.
1846	John Brown Williams establishes United States consulate in Fiji.
1848	Tongan prince, Enele Ma'afu, arrives in Fiji.
1849	White settlers return to Levuka. American consulate accidentally burnt down during Fourth of July celebrations. Williams holds Cakobau responsible for losses.
1852	Death of Tanoa Visawaqa.
1853	Ratu Seru Cakobau installed as Vunivalu of Bau.

1854	Cakobau converts to Christianity.
1855	End of Bau-Rewa wars.
1858	Cakobau offers Fiji to Britain.
1860	Death of Consul John Brown Williams. Substantial U.S. claims against Cakobau are still unsettled.
1862	Britain declines first offer of cession.
1865	Under European advice, Cakobau, Ma'afu, and other high chiefs form the Confederacy of the Independent Chiefs of Fiji.
1867	Confederacy splits. Ma'afu organizes the *Tovata*, or Confederation of North and East Fiji; Cakobau crowned King of Bau by Levuka whites. Death of Thomas Baker.
1868	Polynesia Company granted land at Suva and elsewhere by Cakobau in exchange for settling the foreign debt.
1871	Cakobau proclaimed King of Fiji; a new government is formed at Levuka.
1874	Collapse of the Cakobau government. Cakobau, Ma'afu, and other high chiefs cede Fiji to Britain.
1875	Measles epidemic kills an estimated 40,000 Fijians—approximately one quarter of the native population. Sir Arthur Gordon arrives as Governor.
1879	First indentured plantation labourers arrive from India.
1882	Capital moved from Levuka to Suva.
1883	Death of Cakobau.
1888	Sir John Bates Thurston becomes Governor. Birth of Ratu Sukuna.
1900	Albert Ellis discovers phosphate on Banaba, or Ocean Island.
1913	Ratu Sukuna goes to Oxford.
1916	Indian indentured labour recruiting ends; last contracts are cancelled in 1920.
1917–18	Fijian troops serve in support roles during World War I.

1920, 1921	Indian sugar workers and small growers strike against the Colonial Sugar Refining Company.
1940	Establishment of Native Land Trust Board. Ratu Sukuna appointed Commissioner.
1941	Japanese bomb Ocean Island, one day after Pearl Harbor.
1941–45	Fijian troops distinguish themselves in Pacific campaigns against the Japanese.
1945	Banabans re-settled on Rabi, Fiji.
1956	Ratu Sukuna installed as first Speaker of the Legislative Council.
1958	Death of Ratu Sukuna.
1966	First general elections. The predominantly Fijian-supported Alliance Party wins.
1970	Fiji gains independence from Britain. Ratu Sir Kamisese Mara, leader of the Alliance Party, becomes Prime Minister.
1972	Alliance Party wins general elections.
1977	Election result disputed by Alliance and Federation parties. Governor-General Ratu Sir George Cakobau appoints caretaker Alliance government. Alliance wins majority in elections held later in the year.
1982	Alliance Party narrowly wins election after an acrimonious campaign.

Glossary

adi	Lady. Noblewoman's title equivalent to the masculine *ratu*.
baka	Native banyan tree of genus *Ficus*.
balabala	Tree fern of genus *Cyathea*. The rot-resistant fibrous trunk is often used for ornamental posts and ridge-poles.
bangabanga	Banaban word for underground cave containing water.
bati	Tooth or edge; warrior; the border of a chiefdom and the borderers living there.
bete	Priest of a Fijian god or spirit.
bia	Beer (from English).
bilo	Cup or dish made from coconut shell, used especially for drinking kava.
bula	Life; health. To live, flourish. Shortened form of greeting *Ni sa bula*, "Good day," "Health to you."
buli	Native official in charge of a *tikina*, or district, in the Fijian Administration created by the British. Cowrie shell (a chiefly prerogative).
bulu	The afterworld.
bulumakau	Cattle or beef (from English "bull and a cow").

bure	House or building of ceremonial function. (Used loosely in Fiji English for any structure of traditional Fijian build.)
bure kalou	God house or spirit house: ancient Fijian temple.
colo	Hinterland, interior, or hill country. Person from highlands, especially the unconquered peoples of inland Viti Levu in the late 19th century.
dalo	The taro plant, *Colocasia esculenta*.
datuvu	A coward; a young man whose club was unstained with human blood.
dina	True, genuine, worthy.
drua	Twin-hulled sailing canoe, the largest class of ancient Fijian craft.
galala	Independent Fijian farmer exempted from customary services and obligations.
gauna	Time, season, age. Millenarian era preached by Apolosi R. Nawai.
i tokatoka	Extended family, usually a localized agnatic kin group.
ivi	Native chestnut tree, *Inocarpus fagiferus*. The fruit is eaten, and the branches are used for house rafters.
jungli (jangali)	Hindi word for forest people or savages, applied pejoratively to Fijians by Fiji Indians.
kabani	Company, as in *Viti Kabani*, the Fiji Company. (From English.)
kai	Inhabitant or native of a place, formerly applied only to males, but now may include both sexes. Thus *kai Viti*, Fijian; *kai valagi*, outlander, European.
kaka	Native parrot of genus *Prosopeia*.
kalou	Spirit, ghost, or Fijian god. Nowadays *Kalou* is also used for the Christian God.
kana	Meal, food; to eat.
kava	See *yaqona*.
koli	Dog.
koro	Mound, village, town.
koroi	Title given when a fighter killed for the first time.

kovana	Governor (from English).
lailai	Small, little, lesser.
lala	Tribute due a chief, usually in the form of labour obligations.
lali	Fijian wooden drum or gong.
lei	In Fijian, an interjection of yearning, as in "*Isa lei!*" "Alas!" In Hawaiian, a garland of flowers worn about the neck.
levu	Big, great, large.
lila balavu	Long illness; wasting sickness.
lokamu	Jail (from English "Lock 'em up").
lotu	Church, religion; especially Wesleyan Christianity. To convert to Christianity.
lovo	Fijian pit oven.
Luve-ni-Wai	Literally, "Children of the Water," an ancient secret religious society for adolescent boys and girls.
maca	Empty, dry; exclamation when a bowl of *yaqona* has been drunk.
magimagi	Sinnet; coconut-fibre rope or cord.
mai	Preposition meaning "in," but in a place that does not include the speaker. Invitation to approach or enter a house.
mana	Supernatural power; a sign or omen; ritual exclamation during a ceremony.
maneaba	Banaban or Gilbertese community meeting house.
manulevu	Hawk or falcon, especially the swamp harrier, *Circus approximans*.
marae	Polynesian word for a sacred terrace or temple platform, often faced with stone.
marama	A lady. Equivalent to the masculine *turaga*.
masi	The paper mulberry tree, *Broussonetia papyrifera*, and the barkcloth made from it.
masima	Sea salt, especially when wrapped in a cylindrical basket.
mata	Eye, face, source, or front.
matanitu	A federation or alliance of chiefdoms; a kingdom or government.

mata ni vanua	Herald, spokesman, or ambassador.
mataqali	Kin group usually comprising several *i tokatoka*; loosely translatable as "clan."
meke	Fijian dance and song, often epic in form.
moce	Sleep. "Goodnight" or "Goodbye."
na	Fijian article, often but not always equivalent to English "the." Some names are commonly written with the article attached as a prefix, for example Nakauvadra, Nadrau.
naga	Ancient religious cult of western Viti Levu, and stone enclosures associated with it.
ni	Preposition, often but not always equivalent to English "of."
ni sa bula	Greeting: "Health to you," "Good day."
ovisa	Officer (from English).
rara	Village green or central square.
ratu	Lord; nobleman's title. See also *adi*.
roko	Ancient hereditary title combined in some parts of Fiji with *tui*. The style *Roko Tui* was also given to the appointed heads of provinces in the Fijian Administration created by the British.
roro-buaka	Banaban word for "warrior" or young man of fighting age.
sauturaga	Executive chief, subordinate in most Fijian chiefdoms to the *tui*, or sacred chief.
sega	No.
sevusevu	Small presentation or ceremonial gift, often of *yaqona*.
siga	Day or sun.
soro	Peace offering, atonement, ritual surrender. When one chiefdom capitulated to another, a basket of earth was given as a symbol of submission.
sulu	A loincloth, or clothing in general; nowadays used especially for the Fijian kilt.
tabu	Holy, forbidden, reserved to a chief or god. Hence *Siga Tabu*, Sunday.
tabua	Prepared tooth of the sperm whale, used for important ceremonial presentations and exchanges.

talasiga	Scorched or barren land; especially the dry savannah of upland western Viti Levu.
talatala	Messenger, missionary; especially a Wesleyan minister.
talo	To pour a liquid. Command given when *yaqona* is ready to be served.
tanoa	Large wooden bowl for the mixing of *yaqona*. A *tanoa* is carved from a single piece of wood, and may have four, six, or more legs.
taukei	Native; landowner; Fijian. *Taukei* expresses both belonging to, and ownership of, a place, in a communal sense.
tavako	Tobacco (from English).
tavuki	To overturn, capsize. Earthquake. Reversal of world order associated with millenarian belief.
tevoro	Devil, demon, evil spirit. (Possibly from English "devil.")
tui	King; sovereign; paramount chief.
Tuka	Millenarian religious cult that flourished in western and highland Viti Levu in the late 19th and early 20th centuries. *Tuka* signifies something ancestral and immortal.
tulou	Word of apology or excuse, uttered especially when reaching over or passing behind someone.
turaga	Chief or master; also used nowadays much as the English words "gentleman" and "sir."
uma-n anti	Ancient Banaban spirit house or temple.
vaka	In the manner of; to be like. May act as a prefix or conjunction to form adverbs and adjectives. See following entries.
vakaturaga	Chiefly, chieflike, ceremonial.
vakavanua	Customs of the land; according to local tradition.
vaka-Viti	In the manner of Fiji; according to Fijian tradition. Adjective Fijian, as in *Vosa vaka-Viti*, the Fijian language.
valagi (vavalagi)	Foreign country; foreigner, especially European. See also *vulagi*, below.
vale	House, dwelling.

vanua	Land, region, place. Paramount chiefdom or confederation of chiefdoms. See *yavusa*, below.
vasu	A nephew or niece, especially a man's sister's son, who enjoys special rights and privileges in his uncle's village. He may, in theory, take or use anything belonging to his uncle. A *vasu levu*, or *vasu* of high chiefly rank, may exercise such rights throughout his uncle's (and mother's) chiefdom.
veli	The little folk: a kind of elf, gnome, or sprite often associated with water and streams. *Veli* may grant supernatural powers to men, such as the ability to "firewalk."
vesi	A native tree, *Intsia bijuga*, with very hard black or reddish wood prized for making artifacts and canoe parts.
vilavilairevo	The ceremony of walking on white-hot stones, commonly called "firewalking."
vinaka	Good; goodness. "Thank you."
vinaka vaka levu	"Thank you very much."
Viti	Fiji. In the eastern extremities of the group the pronunciation approaches the Tongan *Fisi*, from which the English version is derived.
vosa	Language, speech. To speak or talk.
vuaka	Pig or pork.
vuaka balavu	Long pig. Metaphor for human flesh.
vulagi	Stranger, guest, visitor.
vunivalu	War chief, warlord, military leader. In some chiefdoms, notably Bau, the *vunivalu* is also the paramount chief.
vusi	Domestic cat (from English "pussy").
wa	Vine, creeper. Cord or rope of sinnet. *Wa tabu*, "sacred or forbidden cord," is the name given to that which extends from the *tanoa* towards the chief in a kava ceremony.
wai	Water, liquid; stream or river.
waka	Root, especially dried whole root of the *yaqona* plant.
yaqona	Kava, *Piper methysticum*, a mildly narcotic plant; the ceremonial and social drink prepared from its roots.

yavu   House mound or site: a platform of earth generally one to three feet in height, faced with stones.

yavusa   Loosely translatable as "tribe." Large kin group usually comprising several *mataqali* descended from a common ancestor (*vu*). There are usually several *yavusa* in a *vanua*, or chiefdom.

yavutu   Place of origin or ancestral village site.

yasi   Sandalwood, *Santalum yasi*.

Source Notes

6   "*Taukei* (owners) is": *Fiji Handbook*, 1980, p. 24.

7   For a discussion of the rather different Fijian "spirit maṣks," see Clunie and Ligairi, 1983.

9–10   For the *Kaunitoni* myth, see France, 1966.

9   "The Fijian is very proud": Williams, 1858, pp. 120–121.

14   For Fijian music and dance, see Thompson, 1971.

14   "They are deadly weapons": Williams, 1858, p. 57.

17   "When we arrived": quoted in Ali, 1980, p. 6.

20   For the Lapita pottery of Fiji, see Mead et al., 1975.

29   "It is cool and empty": Maugham, 1949, p. 122.

36   "There was a total eclipse": Thomson, 1908, p. 26.

37   "The great sickness": quoted in Thomson, 1908, pp. 244–245.

37   "Lived among the savages": quoted in Gravelle, 1979, p. 31.

39   "A coward or *datuvu*": Clunie, 1977, p. 33.

40   "Where is the courageous?": quoted in Williams, 1858, p. 209.

41   "Would safely convey": Williams, 1858, p. 76.

41   "The most precise": Thomson, 1908, p. 294.

51–52   For a discussion of the *tabua*, see Nayacakalou, 1978, p. 112.

53   "[The Tuleita] passed right through": Brewster, 1922, p. 287.

56   "Women, indeed, are regarded": Williams, 1858, p. 168.

60–62   For a summary of Fijian social structure, landholding, political organization, and housing, see Bigay et al., 1981, pp. 52–87.

64   "What is the use of lying": Brewster, 1922, p. 29.

67   "Mbau [Bau] . . . is at once": Williams, 1858, p. 257.

69–70   I have adapted the text of this ceremony from Roth, 1973, p. 119.

79   For descriptions of the *naga*, see Joske, 1889, and Fison, 1884.

81–82   For the Tuka, see Brewster, 1922, and Burridge, 1969, pp. 49–53.

86   "Oh! dead is Mr. Baker": quoted in Brewster, 1922, p. 26.

87   "For I alone am the only": quoted in Macnaught, 1978, pp. 173, 184.

88   "I am the enemy": quoted in Macnaught, 1978, p. 185.

88   "I am alive": quoted in Macnaught, 1978, p. 186.

89   "Only two things": quoted in Macnaught, 1978, pp. 186, 187.

89   "The secret year is 1944": quoted in Macnaught, 1978, p. 192.

100   "The preparation for the firewalking": Bigay et al., 1981, p. 137.

101   For the Tui Qalita legend, see Bigay et al., 1981, p. 135.

107–108   "Had the Government": quoted in Scarr, 1980, p. 152.

109   "to reflect on the countries": quoted in Scarr, 1980, p. 174.

110   "the great octopus": quoted in Scarr, 1980, p. 101.

110   "Went to bed tired out": quoted in Scarr, 1980, p. 96.

121   "the first of all lands": quoted in Silverman, 1971, p. 25.

126   "During the year 1900": quoted in Binder, 1977, p. 9 (abridged).

127–128   "lay tramlines or do any work": quoted in Binder, 1977, p. 35.

128 "the said Company the sole": quoted in Binder, 1977, p. 38.

139 For a critique of Arthur Grimble's career, see Macdonald, 1978.

140 "a writer of magnificent fiction": Macdonald, 1978, p. 212.

141 "left with a depressing sense": quoted in Macdonald, 1978, p. 221.

141 "The colonial possessions": Grimble, 1952, p. 1.

142 "To the people of Baukonikai": quoted in full in Binder, 1977, pp. 154–155.

143 "We were willing to die": quoted in Silverman, 1971, pp. 127–128.

147 "It is essential that the B.P.C.": quoted in Binder, 1977, p. 96.

148 "4. It seems to me that": quoted in Binder, 1977, p. 110.

149 "So you Banabans": quoted in Silverman, 1971, p. 171.

153 "The damages shall not be": quoted in Binder, 1977, p. 166.

154 "Where is my land?": quoted in Silverman, 1971, p. 172 (abridged).

159 "I then took some long grass": Lockerby, 1982, p. 63.

159 "May 18th [1809]": Lockerby, 1982, p. 64.

159 "During that period": Lockerby, 1982, p. 20.

163 "met with no better disposed": quoted in Derrick, 1953, p. 49.

163 "did nothing to civilize": quoted in Derrick, 1953, p. 52.

165 "I shall be chief of Bau": quoted in Derrick, 1950, p. 150.

165 "motor garage style": quoted in Scarr, 1980, p. 94.

169 "All went well until": Derrick, 1950, pp. 163–164.

170 "We do not require": quoted in Narsey, 1979, p. 73.

171 "Fiji is a dark land": quoted in Derrick, 1950, p. 206.

171 "What are they but niggers": quoted in Scarr, 1973, p. 193.

171–172 "We Fijians understand revenge": quoted in Derrick, 1950, p. 212.

172 For Harry's life, see Taylor, 1983.

173 "earnestly desired by the French": quoted in Legge, 1966, p. 89.

173 "very objectionable": quoted in Legge, 1966, p. 86.

174 "loafing about the beach": quoted in Legge, 1966, p. 88.

174 "paid the debt": quoted in Legge, 1966, p. 88.

177 "Justice to the Fijian nation": quoted in Gravelle, 1979, p. 134.

178 "unconstitutional ministers": quoted in Scarr, 1978, p. 102.

178 "Should Her Majesty's Government": quoted in Derrick, 1950, p. 244.

178 "If matters remain": quoted in Derrick, 1950, p. 248.

179 "Unto Her Majesty": *Fiji Times*, 14th October 1874.

180 "Religious pilgrims are flocking": *Fiji Sun*, 7th September 1983.

186 "If I could get the natives": quoted in Heath, 1974, p. 86.

190 "The King desires": quoted in Derrick, 1950, p. 249.

194 "clubbed and ate their way": quoted in Lal, 1983, p. 5.

198–199 "We had great difficulty": quoted in Waterhouse, 1866, p. 85.

201 "His house surpasses": quoted in Waterhouse, 1866, p. 85.

202 For the early history of Bau, see Garvey, 1959, and Tippett, 1959.

203 For more on the name Cakobau, see Clunie, 1984b, pp. 99–100.

207 "I went over to the imperial city": quoted in Waterhouse, 1866, p. 153.

208 "Wonderful is the new religion": quoted in Waterhouse, 1866, p. 77.

208 "When you have grown *dalo*": quoted in Waterhouse, 1866, p. 77.

209 "Why did you come": quoted in Waterhouse, 1866, p. 151.

210 "Bau ought to be destroyed": quoted in Waterhouse, 1866, pp. 245–46.

210 "I wish, Cakobau": quoted in Waterhouse, 1866, p. 244.

210 "after eating gorgeously": quoted in Taylor, 1983, p. 90.

212–213 "A cloth screen": Erskine, 1853, p. 192.

214 For the Manila brig, see Clunie, 1984a.

217 "We arrived at last": Erskine, 1853, p. 186.

219 "It was impossible": Erskine, 1853, p. 186.

Bibliography

Ali, Ahmed
1980   *Plantation to Politics: Studies on Fiji Indians*. Suva: University
        of the South Pacific.
Arens, W.
1979   *The Man-Eating Myth: Anthropology and Anthropophagy*. New
        York: Oxford University Press.
Belshaw, Cyril S.
1964   *Under the Ivi Tree: Society and Economic Growth in Rural Fiji*.
        Berkeley: University of California Press.
Bigay, John, et al.
1981   *Beqa, Island of Firewalkers*. Suva: Institute of Pacific Studies,
        USP.
Binder, Pearl
1977   *Treasure Islands: The Trials of the Ocean Islanders*. London: Blond
        & Briggs.
Birks, Lawrence
1973   *Archaeological Excavations at Sigatoka Dune Site, Fiji*. Suva: Fiji
        Museum (Bulletin No. 1).
Brewster, A. B.
1922   *The Hill Tribes of Fiji*. Reprint. New York: Johnson, 1967.
Brown, Stanley

1973   *Men from Under the Sky: The Arrival of Westerners in Fiji*. Rutland, Vermont: Charles E. Tuttle.

Burns, Sir Alan

1963   *Fiji*. London: H.M. Stationery Office.

Burridge, Kenelm

1969   *New Heaven New Earth: A Study of Millenarian Activities*. Toronto: Copp Clark.

Calvert, James

1858   *Fiji and the Fijians, Vol. II: Mission History*. Reprint. Suva: Fiji Museum, 1983.

Capell, A.

1968   *A New Fijian Dictionary*. Suva: Government of Fiji.

Carter, John, ed.

1980   *Fiji Handbook and Travel Guide*. Sydney: Pacific Publications.

Clunie, Fergus

1977   *Fijian Weapons & Warfare*. Suva: Fiji Museum (Bulletin No. 2).

1984a   "The Manila Brig." *Domodomo* II: 42–86. Suva: Fiji Museum Quarterly.

1984b   "A Cakobau Myth?" *Domodomo* II: 99–100. Suva: Fiji Museum Quarterly

Clunie, Fergus, and Walesi Ligairi

1983   "Traditional Fijian Spirit Masks and Spirit Masquers." *Domodomo* I: 46–71. Suva: Fiji Museum Quarterly.

Crocombe, Ron, and Ahmed Ali, eds.

1982   *Politics in Melanesia*. Suva: Institute of Pacific Studies, USP.

Davidson, J. W., and Deryck Scarr, eds.

1970   *Pacific Islands Portraits*. Canberra: Australian National University Press.

Deane, W.

1921   *Fijian Society*. Reprint. New York: AMS Press, 1977.

Derrick, R. A.

1950   *A History of Fiji*. Suva: Government Press (revised edition).

1953   "The Early Days of Levuka." *Transactions and Proceedings of the Fiji Society* (Suva) II: 2: 49–58 (paper read June 9, 1941).

Erskine, John E.

1853   *Journal of a Cruise among the Islands of the Western Pacific.* Reprint. London: Dawsons, 1967.

Finney, Ben R.

1985   "Anomalous Westerlies, El Niño, and the Colonization of Polynesia." *American Anthropologist* Vol. 87, 1: 9–26.

Fison, Lorimer

1884   "The Nanga, or Sacred Stone Enclosure, of Wainimala, Fiji." *Journal of the Anthropological Institute of Great Britain and Ireland* XIV: 14–31

France, Peter

1966   "The Kaunitoni Migration: Notes on the Genesis of a Fijian Tradition." *Journal of Pacific History* I: 107–113.

1969   *The Charter of the Land: Custom and Colonization in Fiji.* New York: Oxford University Press.

Garrett, John

1982   *To Live Among the Stars: Christian Origins in Oceania.* Suva: Institute of Pacific Studies, USP.

Garvey, Sir Ronald

1959   "The Chiefly Island of Bau." *Transactions and Proceedings of the Fiji Society* (Suva) VI, 3: 157–167 (paper read October 21, 1957).

1983   *Gentleman Pauper.* Bognor Regis, U.K.: New Horizon.

Geraghty, Paul

1978   "Fijian Dialect Diversity and Foreigner Talk: the Evidence of Pre-Missionary Manuscripts" in Schütz, ed. 1978: 51–67.

1983   *The History of the Fijian Languages.* Honolulu: University of Hawaii Press.

Gillion, K. L.

1977   *The Fiji Indians: Challenge to European Dominance 1920–1946.* Canberra: Australian National University Press.

Gordon-Cumming, C. F.

1881   *At Home in Fiji.* Edinburgh: Blackwood & Sons.

Gravelle, Kim

1979   *Fiji's Times: A History of Fiji.* Suva: Fiji Times and Herald.

Grimble, Sir Arthur

1952   *A Pattern of Islands.* London: John Murray (Penguin, 1981).

1957   *Return to the Islands.* London: John Murray.

Gunson, Neil, ed.

1978   *The Changing Pacific: Essays in Honour of H. E. Maude*. Oxford: Oxford University Press.

Harris, Marvin
1977   *Cannibals and Kings*. New York: Random House (Vintage, 1978).

Heath, Ian
1974   "Toward a Reassessment of Gordon in Fiji." *Journal of Pacific History* IX: 81–92.

Heyerdahl, Thor
1968   *Sea Routes to Polynesia*. London: Allen & Unwin (Futura, 1974).

Howard, Michael C., Nii-K. Plange, Simione Durutalo, Ron Witton
1983   *The Political Economy of the South Pacific: An Introduction*. Townsville, Queensland: James Cook University.

Joske (Brewster), Adolph B.
1889   "The Nanga of Viti-Levu." *Internationales Archiv für Ethnographie* (Leiden) Band II, Heft VI: 254–271.

Knox-Mawer, June
1965   *A Gift of Islands: Living in Fiji*. London: John Murray.

Lal, Brij V.
1983   "The 1982 Fiji National Election and Its Aftermath." University of the South Pacific Sociological Society *Newsletter* (Suva) 5:3–17.

Lal, Brij, and Simione Durutalo
1982   "The 1982 Fiji General Election." School of Social and Economic Development *Review* (Suva) III, 9: 17–21.

Langdon, Robert
1979   *Tahiti: Island of Love*. Sydney: Pacific Publications (fifth edition).

Lasaqa, Isireli
1984   *The Fijian People: Before and After Independence 1959–1977*. New York, Canberra: Australian National University Press.

Legge, Christopher
1966   "William Diaper: A Biographical Sketch." *Journal of Pacific History* I: 79–90.

Legge, J. D.
1958   *Britain in Fiji 1858–1880*. London: Macmillan.

Lester, R. H.

1953   "Magico-Religious Secret Societies of Viti Levu, Fiji." *Transactions and Proceedings of the Fiji Society* (Suva) II, 2:117–134 (paper read October 20, 1941).

Lockerby, William

1982   (1810?) *The Journal of William Lockerby*. Suva: Fiji Times and Herald (originally published by the Hakluyt Society, London, 1925).

Luke, Sir Harry

1962   *Islands of the South Pacific*. London: Harrap & Co.

Macdonald, Barrie

1978   "Grimble of the Gilbert Islands: Myth and Man" in Scarr, ed. 1978: 211–229.

Macnaught, Timothy J.

1978   "Apolosi R. Nawai: The Man from Ra" in Scarr, ed. 1978: 173–192.

1982   *The Fijian Colonial Experience: A Study of the Neotraditional Order under British Colonial Rule prior to World War II*. Canberra: Australian National University Press.

Maugham, W. Somerset

1949   *A Writer's Notebook*. London: Heinemann.

Mead, S. M., Lawrence Birks, Helen Birks, Elizabeth Shaw

1975   *The Lapita Pottery Style of Fiji and Its Associations*. Wellington: The Polynesian Society (Memoir No. 38).

Milne, R. S.

1981   *Politics in Ethnically Bipolar States: Guyana, Malaysia, Fiji*. Vancouver, London: University of British Columbia Press.

Milner, G. B.

1972   *Fijian Grammar*. Suva: Government Press (third edition).

Moorehead, Alan

1966   *The Fatal Impact: An Account of the Invasion of the South Pacific 1767–1840*. London: Hamish Hamilton.

Narsey, Wadan Lal

1979   "Monopoly Capital, White Racism and Superprofits in Fiji: A Case Study of CSR." *Journal of Pacific Studies* (Suva) V: 66–146.

Nation, John

1978   *Customs of Respect: The Traditional Basis of Fijian Communal Politics*. Canberra: Australian National University Press.

Nayacakalou, R. R.

1975   *Leadership in Fiji*. Oxford: Oxford University Press.

1978   *Tradition and Change in the Fijian Village*. Suva: South Pacific Social Sciences Association.

Norton, Robert

1977   *Race and Politics in Fiji*. New York: St. Martin's Press (University of Queensland Press).

Oliver, Douglas L.

1961   *The Pacific Islands*. New York: Doubleday (revised edition).

Prasad, Shiu

1974   *Indian Indentured Workers in Fiji*. Suva: South Pacific Social Sciences Association.

Premdas, Ralph R.

1980   "Constitutional Challenge: the Rise of Fijian Nationalism." *Pacific Perspective* (Suva) IX, 2: 30–44.

Roth, G. K.

1951   "Native Administration in Fiji during the Past 75 Years: A Successful Experiment in Indirect Rule." Royal Anthropological Institute of Great Britain and Northern Ireland, *Occasional Paper No. 10* (London).

1973   *Fijian Way of Life*. Oxford; New York: Oxford University Press (second edition).

Sahlins, Marshall D.

1962   *Moala: Culture and Nature on a Fijian Island*. Ann Arbor: University of Michigan Press.

1972   *Stone Age Economics*. Chicago: Aldine.

1985   *Islands of History*. Chicago: University of Chicago Press.

Scarr, Deryck

1967   *Fragments of Empire: A History of the Western Pacific High Commission 1877–1914*. Canberra: Australian National University Press.

1970   "Cakobau and Ma'afu: Contenders for Pre-eminence in Fiji" in Davidson and Scarr, eds. 1970: 95–126.

1973   *The Majesty of Colour: A Life of Sir John Bates Thurston, Vol. I: I, The Very Bayonet*. Canberra: Australian National University Press.

1978   "John Bates Thurston: Grand Panjandrum of the Pacific" in Scarr, ed. 1978: 95–114.

1978   (ed.) *More Pacific Islands Portraits*. Canberra: Australian National University Press.

1980a   *The Majesty of Colour: A Life of Sir John Bates Thurston, Vol. II: Viceroy of the Pacific*. Canberra: Australian National University.

1980b   *Ratu Sukuna: Soldier, Statesman, Man of Two Worlds*. London: Macmillan.

1983   *Fiji: The Three-Legged Stool, Selected Writings of Ratu Sir Lala Sukuna*. London: Macmillan.

1984   *Fiji: A Short History*. Sydney, London: Allen & Unwin.

Schütz, Albert J.

1972   *The Languages of Fiji*. Oxford: Oxford University Press.

1978a   (ed.) *Fijian Language Studies: Borrowing and Pidginization*. Suva: Fiji Museum (Bulletin No. 4).

1978b   *Suva: A History and Guide*. Sydney: Pacific Publications.

Schütz, Albert J., and Rusiate T. Komaitai

1971   *Spoken Fijian*. Honolulu: University of Hawaii Press.

Seemann, Berthold

162   *Viti: An Account of a Government Mission to the Vitian or Fijian Islands 1860–1861*. Reprint. London: Dawsons, 1973.

Silverman, Martin G.

1971   *Disconcerting Issue: Meaning and Struggle in a Resettled Pacific Community*. Chicago: University of Chicago Press.

Stanley, David

1982   *South Pacific Handbook*. Chico, California: Moon Publications.

Taylor, Peter

1983   "The Celebrated Harry." *Domodomo* I: 82–101. Suva: Fiji Museum Quarterly.

Thompson, Chris

1971   "Fijian Music and Dance." *Transactions and Proceedings of the Fiji Society* (Suva) XI: 14–21 (paper read May 27, 1966).

Thomson, Basil

1908   *The Fijians: A Study of the Decay of Custom*. Reprint. London: Dawsons, 1968.

Tippett, A. R.

1958   "The Nature and Social Function of Fijian War." *Transactions and Proceedings of the Fiji Society* V, 4: 137–155 (paper read September 13, 1954).

1959   "The Survival of an Ancient Custom Relative to the Pig's Head, Bau, Fiji." *Transactions and Proceedings of the Fiji Society* (Suva) VI, 1: 30–39.

Vickers, J. Roderick, and C. E. Eyman

1980   *The 1979 Nadrau Archaeology Project, Viti Levu, Fiji.* Manuscript on file with the Fiji Museum, Suva.

Wallis, Mary

1851   *Life in Feejee, or, Five Years Among the Cannibals.* Reprint. Suva: Fiji Museum, 1983.

Waterhouse, Joseph

1866   *The King and People of Fiji.* Reprint. New York: AMS Press, 1978.

Watters, R. F.

1969   *Koro: Economic and Social Change in Fiji.* Oxford: Oxford University Press

Wilkes, C.

1845   *Narrative of the United States Exploring Expedition: Vol III (Fiji).* Philadelphia: Lea & Blanchard.

Williams, Thomas

1858   *Fiji and the Fijians, Vol. I: The Islands and Their Inhabitants.* Reprint. Suva: Fiji Museum, 1982.

Index